W9-AYE-749

Burma

'Shelby Tucker paints a colourful picture of the cultural and indeed psychological diversity of Burma's many different races. He then traces the unifying impact of colonisation, eventually torn apart by the seismic events of the Japanese invasion and British reconquest. Following the killing of Aung San and the British departure, the author analyses the downward spiral of Burman misrule, its mistreatment of minorities and co-operation with the international traffic in drugs. Written with fluency and verve, the book has to be regarded as a standard work and is indispensable for the understanding of the travails of modern Burma.'
JOHN McENERY, author of *Epilogue in Burma*

'Burma is a country blessed with rich natural resources and cultural diversity, but cursed with many problems and few solutions. Tucker's last foray into Burma was on foot with Kachin insurgents as his guides. This time he ventures into more well-trodden territory, Burma's past, and, in endeavouring to unravel its complexities, offers a fresh and hard-hitting appraisal of Burma's troubles, past and present.'
PATRICIA HERBERT, former Curator, Burma Collections, British Library

'The beginning begs one to follow the author into Burma, and the last chapter, which reviews existing interpretations and solutions not laid out in such a clear way before, picks up threads that seem promising and establishes a launching pad for new thinking. This is a must-read for anyone wishing to catch up on Burma's past, to learn what scholars recommend as ways out of the present and directions to follow to look to the future.'
PROFESSOR JOSEF SILVERSTEIN

Comments on Shelby Tucker's previous book, *Among Insurgents: Walking Through Burma*

Colin Thubron's choice as his 'favourite reading of 2000': 'astonishing . . . expert knowledge of an almost unknown region' – *Sunday Telegraph*, Books of the Year

'His thrilling book, 10 years in the writing, includes . . . an analysis of the half-century-long civil war . . . and a look at Burma's contribution to the international narcotics trade.' – Sara Wheeler, *Daily Telegraph*, Books of the Year

'Packed with insights into tribal identity and the opium trade' – Anthony Sattin, *Sunday Times*, Books of the Year

'[C]ontains lucid, scholarly chapters on the . . . knotted political manoeuvres of the last half-century . . . makes you want to stand up and applaud' – Margaret Gee, *Daily Telegraph*

'[O]utstandingly well-written . . . the most unusual and distinguished travel book I have read for years.' – Robert Carver, *Times Literary Supplement*

'[A] combination of [adventure] and an examination of Burmese history, the narcotics trade and contemporary politics' – Sarah Anderson, *Daily Mail*, Books of the Year

'This richly textured narrative of war and tragedy, of valour and the power of nature, is a magnificent human tale. It sets the framework for a land of deep tragedy and a people of abiding courage.' – Sanjoy Hazarika, *The Express Magazine* (New Delhi)

'[A]n important and interesting read for anyone who is concerned with the situation in Myanmar towards the end of [2000], as well as a useful "notebook" for the uninformed' – Oindrila Mukherjee, *The Statesman* (Calcutta)

'Painstaking research into the history, language, culture and politics of the people imparts a degree of academic rigour to the primary travel narrative' – Max Martin, *The Pelican Record*

'[E]ssential reading for anyone interested in the rich past and uncertain future of this astonishingly beautiful and tormented place' – Denise Heywood, *Traveller*

'[H]aunting and encyclopaedic' – Trevor Mostyn, *The Tablet*

Burma
The Curse of Independence

Shelby Tucker

Pluto Press

LONDON • STERLING, VIRGINIA

First published 2001 by Pluto Press
345 Archway Road, London N6 5AA
and 22883 Quicksilver Drive,
Sterling, VA 20166–2012, USA

www.plutobooks.com

Sole distribution in Thailand, Laos, Cambodia and Burma by
White Lotus Co. Ltd
GPO Box 1141, Bangkok, 10501, Thailand
tel (662) 3324915, 741 6288–9
fax (662) 741 6607, 741 6287, 311 4575
e-mail ande@loxinfo.co.th

British Library Cataloguing in Publication Data
A catalogue record for this book is available from
the British Library

ISBN 0 7453 1546 1 hardback
ISBN 0 7453 1541 0 paperback

Library of Congress Cataloging in Publication Data
Tucker, Shelby.
Burma : the curse of independence / Shelby Tucker.
p. cm.
Includes bibliographical references and index.
ISBN 0–7453–1546–1 — ISBN 0–7453–1541–0 (pbk.)
1. Burma—History—1948– I. Title.
DS530.4 .T8 2001
959.105—dc21
2001002154

10   09   08   07   06   05   04   03   02   01
10   9   8   7   6   5   4   3   2   1

Designed and produced for Pluto Press by
Chase Publishing Services, Fortescue, Sidmouth, EX10 9QG
Typeset from disk by Stanford DTP Services, Northampton
Printed in the European Union by TJ International, England

In memory of

Major Hugh Paul Seagrim, GC, DSO

and

Lance-Corporal N'Lam Awng

who gave their lives for others

Contents

Maps and Illustrations

Illustrations 1 and 2 are reproduced courtesy of *The Illustrated London News* Picture Library. Illustrations 3–20 by Shelby Tucker.

. . . seventy of the royal blood, men, women, and children, were murdered . . . and buried within the palace, in a long trench dug for the purpose. The eldest prince . . . died shrieking for mercy at the hands of his own slaves, whom he had often tortured. . . . The weakly and gentle-mannered Maingtun murmured a prayer that the hideous sin of murder might be pardoned to its instigator and perpetrators, and then resigned his neck to the club . . . The princesses were subjected to nameless horrors, and the treatment of the children recalled the days when ravaging hordes marched through the land with babes spitted on their pike staffs for standards. The poor old regent of Pegu . . . had his nostrils and gullet crammed with gunpowder, and was thus blown up. . . . All the three days bands of music were playing throughout the palace, and dancers posturing to divert attention from what was going on, and to drown the cries of the victims. The custom of putting to death all dangerous rivals on the accession of a new king was without doubt almost a recognised thing in Burma whenever there was a new sovereign. Many Burmans defend it warmly, on the plea that it secured the peace of the country.

Shway Yoe,
The Burman (1882)

. . . at a few minutes to six, McGuire informed me that Kyaw Nyein wanted to see me on a matter of great importance and would arrive at GH in about ten minutes' time with some other Ministers. My heart sank, and I was left wondering what further catastrophe had occurred. I was awaiting the Delegation in my study when at about 18.18 hours my ADC reported that the whole Cabinet had arrived and were awaiting me at my office. I proceeded as quickly as possible to the office, assured now that something frightful must have happened, and there I met Thakin Nu dressed in his best clothes with a gaungbaung on his head. Nu then told me that it had been discovered that Sunday 20th July when the majority of the new Cabinet were sworn in was a most inauspicious day. The Cabinet therefore tendered their resignations individually and in writing. I was then asked to re-swear the Cabinet in immediately as Friday 1st August between 18.20 and 18.25 hours was most auspicious. The time was then about 18.21 hours and the chap that held the key of the office containing the form of oaths and the regalia could not be found. Tin Tut reminded me that the oaths were in Government of Burma Act 1935 and that book luckily I had with me. The Cabinet stood up and with their right hands lifted repeated after me the oath of allegiance. I then discovered that the oath of secrecy was not included in the Act, so while the remainder of the Cabinet stood strictly to attention with right hands lifted, Tin Tut hastily scribbled out an oath of secrecy which was duly repeated after me. The ceremony was over by about 18.27 hours and I then called for drinks which were enjoyed by all . . . It is incidents like these that make us love the country and the people so much.

Sir Hubert Rance, Governor of Burma,
Telegram to the Earl of Listowel, 2 August 1947

Burma needs to appraise itself quite as much as outsiders need to understand Burma.

John Frank Cady, 1957

When the Army shoots, it shoots to kill.

General Ne Win, addressing demonstrators, 23 July 1988

Acknowledgements

Burma had no Herodotus, Thucydides, Xenophon, Livy or Tacitus. Until Arthur Purves Phayre published his history in 1873, the meagre records of its past consisted of court chronicles, stone inscriptions and *saga*. Moreover, no one person can be expected to master all of this long, complex story, most of which remains to be explored. Nor is the student's task helped by the military's policy since 1962 of allowing access to Burma's archives exclusively to sycophants. I stress, therefore, that responsibility for all mistakes in this study, all facts, the manner of presenting facts, and all deductions, evaluations and opinions expressed, is mine alone.

I have many people to thank, great and small, some of whom cannot be named. They include the late Colonel Seng Hpung and General Sai Lek, and Major-General Zau Mai, General Kyi Myint and Major N Chyaw Tang, who first guided me in the thickets of Burma; U Nyunt Aung, Anna Joan Allott, Colonel Ian Scott, Colonel Ray Scott and Patrick Molloy for certain facts not in the public domain or unknown to me save through them; U Kin Oung, Dr Kyin Ho, Colonel Hugh Toye and Anthony Stonor for facts concerning Aung San's assassination and U Saw's trial; U Thaung for allowing me to draw on his impressive knowledge of the military's exploitation of Burma's industrial, commercial and mineral wealth; Anne Nimmo for allowing me to inspect materials in the collection of her late husband, Bill Nimmo; Professor Josef Silverstein, Dr Robert Taylor, Dr David Steinberg, Martin Smith, Andrew Selth, Bertil Lintner and Mary Callahan for their patient assistance in defining their views regarding Burma's future prospects; Edward Stell for his painstaking and scrupulous proof-reading of the typescript; and, most especially, Patricia Herbert and John McEnery who, with erudition, tact and well-reasoned arguments, persuaded me to make certain changes to the text, and Ruth Willats for the quality and professionalism of her editing.

Acronyms and Abbreviations

ABSDF   All Burma Students Democratic Front
ABSU   All Burma Students Union
ABTUC   All Burma Trades Union Council
ABYL   All Burma Youth League
AFO   Anti-Fascist Organization
AFPFL   Anti-Facist People's Freedom League
ASEAN   Association of Southeast Asian Nations
BBC   British Broadcasting Corporation
BCP   Burma Communist Party (same as CPB)
BDA   Burma Defence Army
BEDC   Burma Economic Development Corporation
BIA   Burma Independence Army
BNA   Burma National Army
BRP   Burma Revolutionary Party
BSPP   Burma Socialist Programme Party
CAS(B)   Civil Affairs Service (Burma)
CAT   Civil Air Transport
CIA   Central Intelligence Agency
CID   Criminal Investigation Department
CNF   Chin National Front
CPB   Communist Party of Burma
CRPP   Committee Representing the People's Parliament
DAB   Democratic Alliance of Burma
DEA   Drug Enforcement Administration
DDSI   Directorate of Defence Services Intelligence
DKBA   Democratic Karen Buddhist Army
DSI   Defence Services Institute
FACE   Frontier Areas Commission of Enquiry
GCBA   General Council of Burmese Associations
GHQ   General Headquarters
HMG   His Majesty's Government
HQ   headquarters
HRC   Human Rights Commission
IBG   Interim Burmese Government
ILO   International Labour Organization

IMF	International Monetary Fund
INA	Indian National Army
KAF	Kawthoolei Armed Forces
KIA	Kachin Independence Army
KIO	Kachin Independence Organization
KMT	Kuomintang
KNDO	Karen National Defence Organization
KNLA	Karen National Liberation Army
KNPP	Karenni National Progressive Party
KNU	Karen National Union
KRF	Kokang Revolutionary (or Resistance) Force
KYO	Karen Youth Organization
LNO	Lahu National Organization
LRP	long-range penetration
MOGE	Myanmar Oil and Gas Enterprise
MNDO	Mon National Defence Organization
MTA	Möng Tai Army
NCGUB	National Coalition Government for the Union of Burma
NDF	National Democratic Front
NEC	(CPB) North-East Command
NGO	non-governmental organization
NKL	Northern Kachin Levies
NLD	National League for Democracy
NMSP	New Mon State Party
NSCN	Nationalist Socialist Council of Nagaland
NUF	National United Front
NUFA	National Unity Front of Arakan
NUP	National Unity Party
OSS	(US) Office of Strategic Services
PBF	Patriot, then Patriotic Burmese Forces
PLA	People's Liberation Army
PNO	Pao National Organization
PRC	People's Republic of China
PRP	People's Revolutionary Party
PSLP/A	Palaung State Liberation Party/Army
PVO	People's Volunteer Organization
RC	Revolutionary Council
RUSU	Rangoon University Students' Union
SEAC	South East Asia Command
SLORC	State Law and Order Restoration Committee
SNA	Shan National Army

SNUF	Shan National United Front
SOE	Special Operations Executive
SPDC	State Peace and Development Council
SSA	Shan State Army
SSIA	Shan State Independence Army
SSPP	Shan State Progress Party
SUA	Shan United Army
SURA	Shan United Revolutionary Army
TRC	Tai (or Tai-land) Revolutionary Council
UMEHC	Union of Myanmar Economic Holdings Company Limited
UMP	Union Military Police
UNGA	UN General Assembly
USPC	United Shan Patriotic Council
UWSP/A	United Wa State Party/Army
WNA	Wa National Army
WNC	Wa National Council
WNO	Wa National Organization
YMBA	Young Men's Buddhist Association

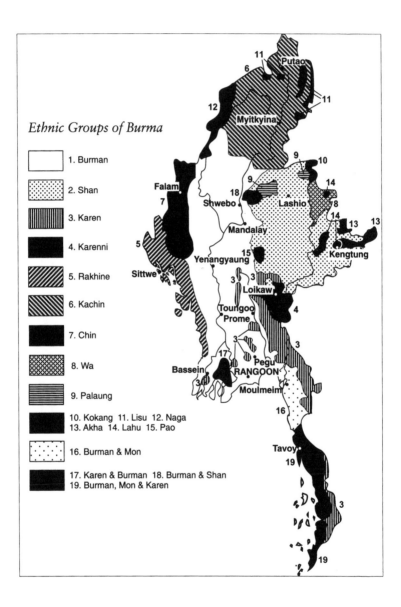

Ethnic Groups of Burma

1. Burman
2. Shan
3. Karen
4. Karenni
5. Rakhine
6. Kachin
7. Chin
8. Wa
9. Palaung
10. Kokang 11. Lisu 12. Naga
13. Akha 14. Lahu 15. Pao
16. Burman & Mon
17. Karen & Burman 18. Burman & Shan
19. Burman, Mon & Karen

Putao
Myitkyina
Falam
Shwebo
Lashio
Mandalay
Kengtung
Yenangyaung
Sittwe
Loikaw
Toungoo
Prome
Bassein
Pegu
RANGOON
Moulmeim
Tavoy

Ethnic Groups

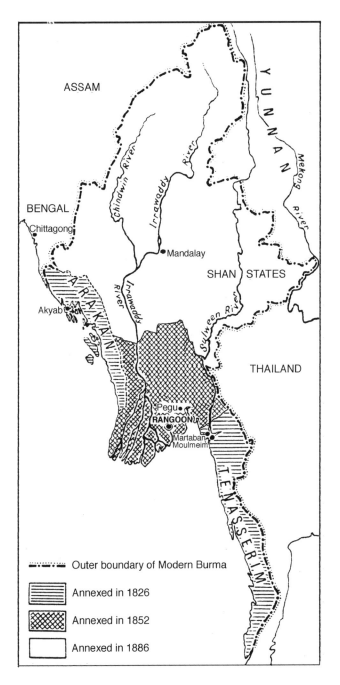

ASSAM

BENGAL

Chittagong

Chindwin River

Irrawaddy River

YUNNAN

Mekong River

Akyab

ARAKAN

Mandalay

Irrawaddy River

SHAN STATES

Salween River

THAILAND

Pegu

RANGOON

Martaban

Moulmein

TENASSERIM

┄┄┄ Outer boundary of Modern Burma

Annexed in 1826

Annexed in 1852

Annexed in 1886

British Conquest

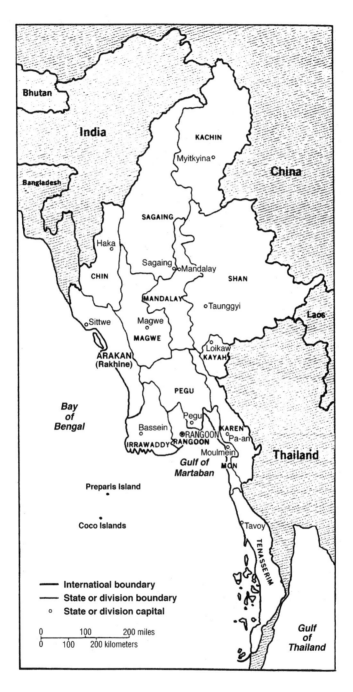

Post-colonial States and Divisions

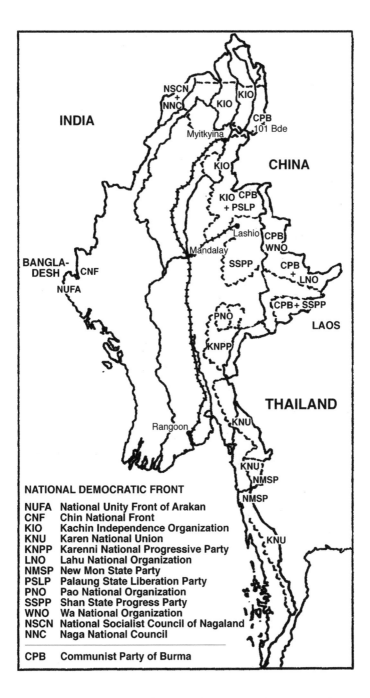

INDIA

CHINA

BANGLA-
DESH

LAOS

THAILAND

NSCN
+
NNC

KIO

KIO

CPB
101 Bde

Myitkyina

KIO

KIO CPB
+ PSLP

Lashio CPB
WNO

Mandalay

SSPP

CPB
+
LNO

CPB+ SSPP

PNO

KNPP

CNF

NUFA

Rangoon

KNU

KNU
NMSP

NMSP

KNU

NATIONAL DEMOCRATIC FRONT

NUFA	National Unity Front of Arakan
CNF	Chin National Front
KIO	Kachin Independence Organization
KNU	Karen National Union
KNPP	Karenni National Progressive Party
LNO	Lahu National Organization
NMSP	New Mon State Party
PSLP	Palaung State Liberation Party
PNO	Pao National Organization
SSPP	Shan State Progress Party
WNO	Wa National Organization
NSCN	National Socialist Council of Nagaland
NNC	Naga National Council
CPB	Communist Party of Burma

Operational Areas of Principal Insurgent Groups, 1989

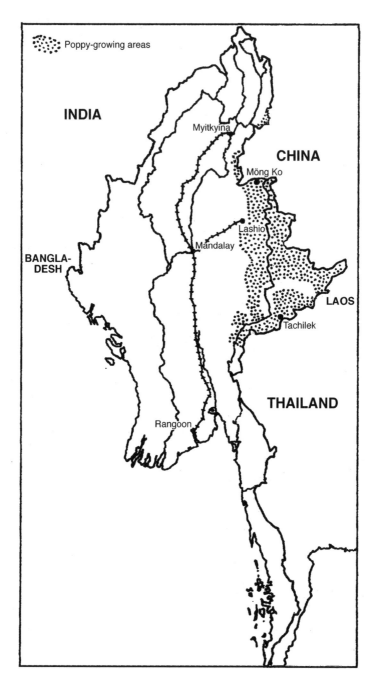

Areas of Opium Poppy Cultivation

1
The Burmese Void

BURMA FOR MOST Europeans and Americans is either a void or a sequence of random pictures contrasting Good and Evil—Aung San in uniform, wise, stoical and dignified; his brave and heroic daughter, Aung San Suu Kyi, in various poses but always wearing flowers in her hair and often addressing a crowd; ranked masses of students chanting in unison; soldiers firing assault rifles at unarmed demonstrators who scatter, screaming. We might know that Burma is inhabited by a variety of people and races. We hear about the Burmans, the majority ethnic community that has imparted their name to the country, *Bama*, but very little about the others. Exactly who are they? What do they believe? Where do they live? What is their relationship with each other—and with the Burmans? These minorities do not figure among the media images that inform our picture. There is a single heroine who represents 'democracy' and a unified body of villains, the generals who oppose her, representing autocracy and oppression. However, if we question our received picture, we immediately encounter words and names of daunting strangeness—Sinyetha Parti, Khin Nyunt, Alaungpaya, Ba Thein Tin, Bo Mya, *ka kwe yei*, Kyauksè, Myawaddy, Pyinmana and Myitkyina. There is no way of avoiding this particular difficulty. But the author believes that Burma can be rendered more accessible by providing a few basic principles for understanding Burma in the round before the general reader ventures further into this complex subject. That is the purpose of this book.

Some Europeans and Americans, of course, know a great deal about Burma, as their diligent and scrupulous scholarship impressively attests. *Burma: The Curse of Independence* does not pretend to compete with their work. It hopes to complement and build on it. Readers determined upon further investigation will find brief descriptions of some of their books in the Annotated Bibliography, but I will here mention eight in ascending order of difficulty.

Daniel George Edward Hall's *Burma*[1] is a short, very general but comprehensive history starting with the conjectural foundation of Tagaung around 850 BC and concluding with Ne Win's 'Caretaker

[1] Hall, 1960.

1

Government' of 1958–60. Hall taught for many years in the history faculty of the University of Rangoon and thereafter was Professor of the History of South-East Asia at London University.

Maurice Collis's *Last and First in Burma*,[2] Hugh Tinker's *Union of Burma: A Study of the First Years of Independence*[3] and Frank Siegfried Vernon Donnison's *Burma*[4] are concerned mainly with Britain's part in Burma's history and assessing how much of the legacy of British political institutions has survived the change to self-rule (very little, on present assessment).

Collis joined the Indian Civil Service in 1912 and served as deputy commissioner, magistrate and excise commissioner at various posts in Burma for the next 22 years, including Myaungmya, Moulmein, Sandoway, Akyab, Sagaing, Rangoon and Mergui. Particularly interesting is his examination of the complex relations between Governor Dorman Smith and Aung San.

Tinker famously compiled what is referred to often as the 'official history',[5] a representative collection of documents reflecting the actions of the British government between 1944 and 1948. His *Union of Burma* narrates the main political developments during the succeeding decade.

Donnison served as chief secretary under the last three British governors, and his study is especially valuable in separating fable from fact in the emotionally charged developments leading to the transfer of power. He writes, as he states in his preface, 'with the somewhat Victorian, and now unfashionable, conviction that law and order are a prerequisite to happiness, since without them there can be no security of person or property, and little freedom of speech or movement'. Donnison provides a useful counterpoise to those who blame the British or Ne Win for everything that is awful in Burma.

Josef Silverstein is the doyen of Burma scholars living today. He has been engaged with Burma for nearly half a century, has edited five books and is the author of two books and more than 50 scholarly articles and editorial essays about Burma. His *Burmese Politics: The Dilemma of National Unity*[6] was the first to identify the difficulties of governing Burma's many ethnic communities as one nation as the central issue of Burma's troubles. His *Burma: Military*

---

[2] Collis, 1956.
[3] Tinker, 1959.
[4] Donnison, 1970.
[5] Tinker (ed.), 1984, two volumes.
[6] Silverstein, 1980.

Rule and the Politics of Stagnation[7] attempts a causal analysis (as distinct from a mere chronicle of events) correlating the decay of *Burman* social, religious and economic institutions under British rule with the problems of governing Burma now.

Hall, Collis, Tinker, Donnison and Silverstein all write lucidly and their books are easy to read, even for readers new to the subject. At the difficult end of my list are Bertil Lintner's *Burma in Revolt: Opium and Insurgency Since 1948*[8] and Martin Smith's *Burma: Insurgency and the Politics of Ethnicity*.[9] As their titles suggest, these books concentrate on Burma's history since 1948 with all its shifting alliances and complexities.

Lintner is a journalist who, at great personal risk, visited the Nagas, Kachins and communists in their base areas (as distinct from interviewing their representatives in neighbouring countries). His studies of the communist insurgency (which harboured him for five months, three of which were spent at Party headquarters) and the narcotics component of the Burmese Civil War are impressively original contributions. Of contemporary scholars, he alone stresses the symbiotic relationship between the drugs trade and Burma's war as a central factor in sustaining the war.

Smith has fortified extensive search of materials in the India Office Library, the Public Records Office and elsewhere with the verbal accounts of many of the protagonists. Burma, whose archives are open only to those sympathetic or able to conceal their antipathy to the regime, proffers many temptations and opportunities to simplify complex issues. Smith collates the available evidence and where it lends itself to no conclusion leaves the issue open. That, I believe, is his strong point. His aim appears to have been to produce a reference work as well as a narrative. He is more comprehensive than Lintner, and, for that very reason, more difficult. These two scholars do not always agree, but that, surely, attests to their individual integrity. Our sources are too few and unsubstantiated and our perspective much too recent to allow a single canonical view on these complex issues.

My own appreciation of Burma began by delineating the picture's main outline before venturing further.

[7] Silverstein, 1977.

[8] Lintner, 1994. A second, paperback edition published by Silkworm Books (Chiangmai) and incorporating some new material appeared in 1999.

[9] Smith, 1991. A second edition, incorporating some new material, appeared in 1999.

In January 1989, Mats Larsson, a young Swede met some weeks previously on a train crossing Siberia, and I left Dali dressed as Dai tribals in pointed, broad-brimmed straw hats, jackets of coarse blue cotton with 'Mao' collars, and surgical masks (very common in much polluted China). We were bound for the Burmese border, 270 miles to the southwest, and were disguised thus because travel in this part of Yunnan was then forbidden to foreigners. Intelligence developed in Dali identified 13 checkpoints where traffic would be stopped and inspected for fugitives or arms. Our only chance of getting past them, we reasoned, would be by hitchhiking lifts with petrol tankers. These offered less capacity for concealing contraband than buses, taxis, private vehicles or box-body lorries, and the drivers, who traversed the route repeatedly in a back-and-forth shuttle between refineries and storage depots, would be known to the guards. A pleasant word or two with the driver, a quick glance beyond him, and what would they descry? Two Dai tribals asleep under their sombreros. Nothing to get excited about, and, at one checkpoint after the next, we hoped, they would wave us on. We spoke very few words of Chinese and, of course, had no interpreter with us. Never mind. Rolled up in our shirt sleeves were some scraps of paper inscribed with messages in Chinese to serve as needed—'We want to go to Yongping/Baoshan/Longling/Mangshi/Wanding/Ruili', 'How far is the border?', 'We don't want to go to Burma by the way that everyone else goes', 'We must avoid immigration control/customs', 'Do you know anyone who would be willing to act as our guide?', 'On no account must the police/border guards learn of our presence'.

All went according to plan until a policeman detected us at the Nu Jiang bridge. The risk of wearing a disguise, of course, is that you cannot pretend it was all a terrible mistake when you are caught. 'Is this not the way to Kunming? Oh, I'm so sorry. Obviously, I took the wrong turn.' No one will believe you. We affected indignation. We produced our passports and brandished our Chinese visas. Our only hope lay in awakening a doubt in the guards who had arrested us, a tiny glimmer of *self*-doubt as to whether they were exceeding their authority. How else had we got past the previous controls if we were not legal? They left us to march the driver off to some hideous interrogation ordeal in an ugly building nearby, and we exploited the moment to shred the incriminating inscriptions and conceal the scraps beneath the seat in the cabin. A young officer accompanied the guards when they returned. Prison loomed immediate and real, a Chinese prison where inmates rotted out their days 12 to a cell with a hole in the cement floor for a hygienic facility. We resumed bluffing. Happily, it was in the sweet, Yunnanese nature of this idealistic young officer to default to the option that caused the least distress. Better to radio-transmit a message to headquarters in Wanding and pass this responsibility to them. But he did not want to lose face with his men. They watched and waited for his decision, and we cooperated in pretending that his English was better than it was. He allowed us to proceed.

Early in the evening of the second day after leaving Dali, we reached the ridge above the border town of Wanding. Beyond the lights in the valley below us was a vast expanse of unbroken darkness. It was our first glimpse of the Burmese void. We knew we could attempt crossing into Burma a few miles west of Wanding by following the course of a river called the Longchuan. Or we could strike out for a Shan village with an unknown name about 20 miles east of Wanding. We decided on the second option, got down from our transport, attempted reaching the international bridge at the heart of the town, ran into soldiers, doubled back, then found an east-bound path. We walked on, using the stars as a rough navigational guide.

At about 0400 hours a column of Shans bearing firewood to sell in Wanding marched past us in silence and, a little while later, we were startled by a powerful beam of light surveying the forest around us. We dropped to the ground, remained still and wordless for what seemed a very long time, then crawled on. Dawn renewed our directional bearings. We ceased crawling and marched hurriedly on, reckoning that scarcely more than an hour remained before HQ Wanding identified us as the Nu Jiang bridge foreigners and gave chase. An hour later we heard behind us the single-cylinder piston thumps of their motorized tricycles. We crossed to the south bank of a river called the Nam Ko and found cover in a wood. We were bathing in a thermal pond there when the tricycles passed out of range of our hearing. The thermal pond was in Burma, but we did not know this at the time.

Later that morning soldiers intercepted us. They were all very young, some no more than 12. They wore schoolboy caps pinned with plastic red stars and were armed with Kalashnikovs. We thought they were Chinese border guards. In fact, they belonged to the People's Army of the Communist Party of Burma. They took us into custody and escorted us by a ridge route around the Burma Army encamped in a valley below to their Northern Bureau headquarters at Möng Ko—the Shan village of hitherto unknown name.

Möng Ko lies a little to the northwest of the epicentre of what is popularly called the Golden Triangle (see map, p. xx), and, when we were there (January), patches in the forested wall of the adjacent mountains were ablaze with white, pink-red, and purple poppies. There are heroin refineries in Möng Ko now, but as far as we could tell there were none then. Möng Ko is very near the fault lines dividing the valley-dwelling Shans and the hill-dwelling Kachins, Palaungs, Kokangs and Was. All these people were at war with the Burmans and fighting under the colours of the CPB's polyethnic People's Army and various monoethnic armies, such as the Kachin Independence Army (KIA), Shan State Army (SSA), Wa National Army (WNA) and Palaung State Liberation Army (PSLA). Supporting both the CPB and the ethnic armies was a unit of the All Burma Students Democratic Front (ABSDF) comprising Burman students outraged by the ruthless repression of their manifestations the previous summer—'Democracy Summer', as they called it. They had fled to the borders to undergo training to fight the regime in Rangoon. Hence Möng Ko served as a rallying point for insurgents: CPB, KIA, SSA, WNA, PSLA and ABSDF commanders convened there to coordinate their aims and tactics.[10] This small, somnolent, ostensibly irrelevant village nestling among poppy and cannas that we stumbled upon quite by chance in our dilettante adventure, in short, offered as good a classroom as anywhere in the world for learning the basics of Burma's troubles. The instructors included

[10] In 1989 the National Democratic Front (NDF), a military alliance of the main ethnic insurgent groups opposed to Rangoon, comprised the Chin National Front (CNF), Kachin Independence Organization (KIO), Karen National Union (KNU), Karenni National Progressive Party (KNPP), Lahu National Organization (LNO), New Mon State Party (NMSP), National Unity Front of Arakan (NUFA), Palaung State Liberation Party (PSLP), Pao National Organization (PNO), Shan State Progress Party (SSPP) and Wa National Organization (WNO). The military wings of these insurgencies were known as the Kachin Independence Army (KIA), Shan State Army (SSA), etc. The Democratic Alliance of Burma (DAB), a political alliance of parties opposed to the junta, then comprised all the members of the NDF except the KNPP and ten other groups, including the ABSDF. The CPB belonged to neither the NDF nor the DAB, but supported some of their members and other groups opposing the junta with arms. The picture was further complicated by a number of warlord groups, such as Khun Sa's and Moh Heng's Möng Tai Army (MTA), which professed political aims but were chiefly interested in narcotics.

some of the most important players in the war: General Aung Gyi, the Burman who was the titular head of the CPB's Northern Bureau; General Kyi Myint, an ex-Chinese red guard whose real name was Zhang Zhi Ming, Aung Gyi's nominal subordinate, but effectively the real head of the Northern Bureau and commander of the CPB's 202 2 Brigade; General Sai Lek, the quarter-Indian, quarter-Chinese, half-Shan commander-in-chief of the SSA and chairman of its civilian arm, the Shan State Progress Party (SSPP); Colonel Seng Hpung, commander of the KIA's 4 Brigade and a member of the executive council as well as the deputy foreign secretary of the Kachin Independence Organization (KIO); and Colonel Kol Liang, commander of the CPB's 202 1 Brigade. We were guests of a special kind. 'What do you want from us?' I asked them. 'The Rangoon government suppresses the truth,' replied Seng Hpung. 'No stranger is allowed here. We are their hidden colonies. They pretend we are bandits, opium barons, "narco-terrorists". We want you to tell the truth.'

Armed guards were ever at hand, but we were free to do more or less as we pleased. Kyi Myint put us up at his house and provided interpreters, and while we promoted our ambitions for crossing Burma and waited for a decision from our hosts, we discussed Burma's troubles. There gradually emerged a coherent story of inherent instability having to do with Burma's geography, ethnic heterogeneity and political history, and poppy and personal corruption.

2
Geography and Ethnicity

BURMA LIES BETWEEN longitudes 92° and 102° east of Greenwich and latitudes 10° and 28° north, and its area, 230,800 square miles, more or less equals that of Spain. Three main rivers cross it from north to south. The Irrawaddy, with its two upper tributaries rising in the ramparts dividing Tibet from Burma, is about 1500 miles long and runs through the heart of the country. It swells in the rainy season and subsides in the dry, while its current, like its width, varies correspondingly from 5–6 to 1½ knots. It is navigable for about 800 miles, from Bhamo (with difficulty at the end of the dry season) to the Andaman Sea, and has always been and remains Burma's main artery of commerce and communication. One of the enduring sights of the country is a paddle-steamer with pointed stack driving a flotilla of roofed barges crowded with passengers and goods, often glimpsed through toddy palms fringing the river.

The Chindwin drains the ranges bounding the Hukawng Valley, then cuts a gap through them and flows on until it joins the Irrawaddy near the temple sites at Pagan. It is navigable for about 400 miles to vessels whose draught does not exceed 2' 6".

The Salween rises in central Tibet and runs at furious speed over cataracts and through deep gorges for most of its long route to the sea, entering Burma at the northeast corner of Shan State and providing an imposing natural barrier behind which hill peoples such as the Kokangs, Was, Akhas, Lahus, Karens and Mons have sheltered almost entirely free of external interference for most of Burma's recorded history. Navigable only for the last 90 miles before it reaches the Gulf of Martaban, it has little commercial but great political and military significance.

In addition to these rivers, there is the Sittang, much shorter and slower than its sisters, charting a course to the sea between the Irrawaddy and the Salween, draining the Karen Hills to its east and the Pegu Yoma to its west but dangerous to shipping, especially in its lower reaches. It has little commercial or political significance but imposes a formidable barrier for large, mechanized armies, as both the British and Japanese learned in 1942 and 1945.

Into these rivers feed thousands of others. During the monsoon, which lasts from May to October inclusive and coincides with the melting of the snow in the north, every watercourse in Burma is bloated. Even the *chaung*, waterless gullies in the dry season, are raging torrents, and the valleys degenerate into marshes. This too has tended to the isolation of Burma's hill minorities, for no commander, whatever the size and power of his forces, would commit them to expeditions extending into the monsoon.

The direction of the rivers defines the grain of the country, which in turn has determined the routes of successive waves of immigration. Who preceded whom in this sequence of population drifts is a subject of hot debate, with exponents of different theories commonly pressing partisan claims,[1] but the view adopted by most scholars, chiefly on philological grounds, as to the *pattern* of movement still holds perhaps, despite a recent attempt at discrediting it.[2] According to this view, the migrants belonged to three discrete language groups—the Mon-Khmers, who include the Mons, Was, Palaungs and Padaungs; the Tibeto-Burmans, who include the Burmans and Rakhines, Chins and Kachins; and the T'ai-Chinese, who include the Karens and the Shans.[3] All came from China. Probably we shall never know from exactly where in China or what pressures or prospects drove them south, but south they came, following the line of least resistance along ridges and river valleys.

The Mon-Khmers tracked the Mekong as far as Cambodia before they looped westward to Burma, where pressures from other migrants scattered them.[4]

The Tibeto-Burmans branched when they reached the high mountains forming the watershed between the Salween and the Brahmaputra. Some continued west as far as the passes that led towards Assam and crossed them, or spread south along the valley of the Chindwin and the ridges of the Chin Hills. These included the Chins, the Jinghpaw and Rawang Kachins and, perhaps, the Rakhines (Arakanese). Some continued south, first along the Nu Jiang (Salween), then along the Nmai Hka, and finally along the

---

[1] See, e.g., Lintner, 1994: 46, citing Rong Syamananda (1977) *A History of Thailand* (Bangkok: Chulalongkorn University), p. 8; Dun, 1980: 2–3; Enriquez, 1933: 23.

[2] See Leach, 1954: 230–1.

[3] Lowis, 1919: 1–4; Donnison, 1970: 33–4; Enriquez, 1933: 23.

[4] Enriquez, 1933: 23.

Irrawaddy. These included the Burmans, the Atsi, Lashi and Maru Kachins, and the Lisus.[5]

The evidence suggests that the two peoples mainly comprising the T'ai-Chinese separated long before leaving China. The Karens appear to have descended the Mekong and entered Burma a little north of Karenni.[6] The T'ais travelled in every direction. Some trekked across the Kachin Hills and on to Assam. Some descended the Salween and Mekong. Some tracked the Taiping. And some forded the Shweli and continued south along the Irrawaddy.[7]

Harvey gives us a vividly imagined picture of these early migrants: 'tribe after tribe of hungry yellow men with the dust of the world's end upon their feet, seeking food and warmth in tiny homesteads along the fertile river banks, seeking that place in the sun which has been the dream of the northern races in so many ages'.[8]

So far there is general agreement. It is when we try to fit a chronology to these layered populations that opinions diverge.

Indonesians may have been the first inhabitants of Burma, and they may have been cannibals;[9] but, if so, little or no trace of them survives. Or the first inhabitants might have been the Karens;[10] or, perhaps, the Pyus, the remains of whose capital at Old Prome have been excavated,[11] and two other peoples to whom tradition awards the names Kanran and Thet (who *may* have been Chins and Rakhines). Of these, all but the Karens have disappeared, though it is believed that their blood was absorbed by the peoples who displaced them. The Pyu language 'still existed in the thirteenth century; up to that time the Arakanese, and the Chinese until the tenth century, knew the people of Burma as the Pyu'.[12] Lowis believes that the Mon-Khmers were the first immigrants, 'for no

[5] Lowis, 1919: 6–7; Enriquez, 1933: 24; Davies, 1909: 362–3.
[6] Lowis, 1919: 16; Coèdes, 1966: 22; Census Report, 1911, vol. ix, part I, p. 254; Enriquez, 1933: 25.
[7] Lowis, 1919: 17; Lintner, 1994: 46; Scott and Hardiman, 1900–1, part I, vol. I: 187 ff.
[8] Harvey, 1967: 4.
[9] Hall, 1960: 7.
[10] 'The AI LAOS who came down with the first great Tai migration southward in the 6th Century B.C. found the country east of the Salween river already in possession of the Karens. It is therefore evident that the southward migration of the Karens took place before that date.' Dun, 1980: 3. For a recent discussion of various theories of the origin of the Karens and the dates of their arrival in Burma, see Falla, 1991: 13–17. See also Harvey, 1967: 3.
[11] Hall, 1960: 8. For a detailed discussion of the Pyu, see Stargardt, 1990.
[12] Harvey, 1967: 11.

other reason than that [their] traces seem the most diffuse and faint',[13] and this view appears to have won general acceptance.[14] Their scattered clans came to occupy the whole of the coast from Victoria Point to Cape Negrais as far north as Henzada, as well as the *ledwin* (rice country around Kyauksè), but they probably did not unite politically until some time after traders from India introduced the art of writing in about AD 300.[15] But Donnison, without assigning reasons or citing authority, believes that the Pyus were Proto-Burmans and that, hence, Tibeto-Burmans were the first inhabitants of Burma.[16] Harvey, who tests rival, language-based theories against epigraphical and other evidence, suggests that the order of Burma's multiple-layered populations is 'purely conjectural'.[17]

Burma's demography has been further complicated by cultural assimilation and cross-breeding. As these diverse peoples swept over the land, as their power and influence ebbed and flowed, they exchanged language, modes of dress, customs, beliefs, ideas and blood. The Mons and Burmans absorbed the Pyus, then mixed with and influenced each other; and, similarly, Burmans and Shans, Shans and Chinese, Burmans and Chinese, Kachins and Shans, Palaungs and Shans, Rakhines and Indians. Nor can we now say with any confidence what originally was whose contribution, who borrowed what from whom. However mixed, these various peoples nevertheless *consider themselves* to be discrete races and cultures.

The terms 'Burman' and 'Burmese' were once used interchangeably, but, as Josef Silverstein notes, 'Most scholars since World War II use them as follows: Burman is an ethnic term identifying a particular group in Burma. Burmese is a political term including all the inhabitants of the country—Burmans, Mons, Karens, Shans, Kachins, Chins, and so on.'[18]

[13] Lowis, 1919: 2.
[14] Enriquez, 1933: 23.
[15] Those supporting the view that the various peoples inhabiting Burma today migrated there from elsewhere include Lowis, 1919: 1–17; Harvey, 1967: 3 ff; Donnison, 1970: 33–5. Falla sheds doubt on the theory as regards the Karen, without, however, addressing Dun's point. He also claims (379–80, endnote 1 of chapter 2) that Leach rejected the theory as regards the Kachins, but this is incorrect. See Leach, 1954: 230–1.
[16] Donnison, 1970: 3. *Accord* Hall, 1960: 10.
[17] Harvey, 1967: 1 ff.
[18] Silverstein, 1977: 4.

The heart of the country, where are most of its population, industry and cities, is the hot, flat, fertile, open, tropical valleys of the Chindwin, Irrawaddy and Sittang that fan out at their southern limits and join to form a continuous coastal plain. This is *Bama*, the land of the Burmans, what was in the colonial era called 'Burma Proper'.

The Burmans[19] arrived between AD 850 and 1050.[20] T'ai pressure, it is surmised, forced them to leave Yunnan. As we shall see, some irony attaches to their comparatively late appearance in what they call their Suvannabhumi (Pali), or 'Golden Land'. Nor were they as advanced as the Mons. In the course of their trek south, they had lost any knowledge they once might have had of writing and arts such as pottery and faïence work—but they brought with them skills of wet-rice cultivation, hill terracing, use of water buffaloes and wheel carts, horse breeding and, most important of all, organized warfare. They seized the *ledwin* from the Mons, then expanded west into Minbu and north into Shwebo, Tabayin and Myedu. They established settlements up the Chindwin and along the Chin Hills as far as Akyab. And at some point, they began building the great temple city of Pagan.

Their greatest king was Anawrahta (1044–77), remembered chiefly for his conquests. He subjected northern Arakan and desecrated the Mahamuni image at Dinnyawadi in Akyab District to prevent the Rakhines from invoking its magical formulas and trees in their defence. He pushed east as far as the foothills of the Shan Plateau, built a line of fortified garrisons there and required the Shan *saohpas* (princes) to acknowledge his suzerainty. But his most important conquest was in the south. The story goes that he wanted to break the hold on his people of a perniciously dangerous band of Mahayana priests who pretended to powers that freed men from the law of *karma* but apprehended that, without a copy of the *Tripitaka* (lit., three baskets), the pure Theravada Buddhist canon, he would not succeed; that a great sage from the south named Shin Arahan advised him to request a copy from the Mon king, who had 30 sets of the *Tripitaka*; and that the Mon king rejected his request with insults. This was Anawrahta's *casus belli* for conquering the Mons.

Martial prowess spawns myths, and Burmans are apt to believe that an inherent superiority of culture and intelligence anoints them

---

[19] As distinct from Donnison's 'Proto-Burmans'.
[20] Hall, 1960: 11.

to rule over other peoples inhabiting Burma. This *Herrenvolk* notion is apparent in many of the attitudes struck by their military and political leaders. But we have already seen that the skills which the Burmans introduced to Burma were from Yunnan, and much else of what they ascribe to Burman genius is in fact Indian, Pyu, Mon or Shan. Irrawaddy is a Sanskrit name (Iravati = 'giver of refreshment'); Mogaung is a Shan name (Möng Kawng = 'Drum Town'). Early epigraphy and sculpture in Burma show animism; then animism infused with Brahmanism; then, after Asoka conquered Kalinga in south India (261 BC), animist Brahmanism commingled with Buddhism. The legend of a Pyu chief depicts him as a triocular Shiva. Excavation at Pegu unearths phallic emblems. Buddha appears as an incarnation of Vishnu. Assuming the first Burman immigrants had any religion at all, it would have been the ancestor veneration of the Han Chinese or the Mahayana variety of Buddhism of their Tibetan or Yunnanese forebears. It is from the Mons that the Burmans received the pure Theravada creed. Their writing derives from south India, again, transmitted via the Mons. After defeating the Mons, we are told, Anawrahta returned to Pagan with '30,000 monks, scholars, artists, craftsmen and other hostages', who 'uplifted . . . the hitherto rustic Burmans socially and culturally'.[21]

An unbroken horseshoe of hills bounds modern Burma on the east, north and west, insulating it almost entirely from the outside world. Along the Chinese border, the hilltops are scarred by patches of cultivation called *taungya*;[22] along the Indian border they are blanketed by green climax jungle. The hills amount to nearly half of the country's land surface but support a much smaller proportion of its population[23]—Burma's hill peoples, who are, naming only the

---

[21] Lintner, 1994: 42; drawn from Silverstein, 1980: 14, and Harvey, 1967: 28–9.

[22] O'Brien, 1987: 238.

[23] Burma's population numbers are both hypothetical and vexed politically. The last complete census was in 1931, and it was flawed, in that Burmese-speaking Buddhists living in Burma Proper, regardless of ethnicity, were tallied as Burmans. There was a count in 1941, but the Japanese invaded before it could be classified and analysed, resulting in a bald statement of totals by administrative district, and civil upheaval has prevented a complete census since then. There was an almost complete count of urban areas in 1953 and a count of about 15 per cent of rural districts in 1954, together amounting to a count of about a quarter of the population. However, only a fifth of this count, a twentieth of Burma's total population, was classified and analysed. Modern estimates are based on growth rates and classifications derived from the above.

larger groups as they occur cartologically from the Tenasserim in the southeast to Arakan in the southwest, the Karens, Mons, Karennis, Paos, Shans, Akhas, Lahus, Was, Kokangs, Palaungs, Kachins, Nagas and Chins. Beyond the line of hills in the southwest are another minority, the Rakhines.

The Mons (*Burm.*, Talaing) inhabit the Tenghy, Thanintari and Dawna Ranges, where they mingle with the Karens, and the coastal strip between the Tenasserim and the Sittang, where they are all but indistinguishable from the Burmans,[24] but, until the rise of Anawrahta, they were the dominant power in Burma, with their capital at Thaton, Pegu, Martaban or Donwun.[25] Arab geographers recorded that their king possessed 50,000 elephants and that the kingdom produced cotton, velvet and aloes wood.[26] The Mons reasserted their dominance in 1385, again in 1551, and were not defeated finally until 1774.[27] They are related to the Khmers of modern Cambodia, whose monuments at Ankor Wat exhibit marked Mon attributes.[28] The most important monuments at Anawrahta's capital city and Burma's most formidable ancient site, Pagan, are Mon.[29]

The Census Report of 1911 states that Karens entered Burma 'peacefully, quietly, unobtrusively . . . avoiding all contact with the tribes they passed . . . preferring the hardship and obstacles of hills, jungles and uninhabited regions to the dangers of conflict with fellow beings'.[30] Early Western visitors noted this reclusiveness, as well as their 'cringing ways' and their desire 'to live . . . on inaccessible heights . . . for the sake of their independence'.[31] But Christian missionaries and colonial servants, both civil and military, extolled the sweetness of their nature, and their courage, integrity and loyalty. Today the Karens are the most numerous of Burma's minorities and are concentrated in the Tenasserim Yoma (where they mingle with the Mons), the Pegu Yoma of Toungoo and Salween Districts (where they are the majority population), the Arakan Yoma, and around Bassein, Myaungmya, Insein and Henzada (where they

---

[24] Donnison, 1970: 33.
[25] Ibid.
[26] Hall, 1960: 11.
[27] Enriquez, 1933: 30.
[28] Hall, 1960: 17.
[29] Ibid.
[30] Quoted in Enriquez, 1933: 25.
[31] Mouhot, 1864: 110. Quoted in Falla, 1991: 18.

mingle with the Burmans). They are the Palestinians of Burma, enslaved first by the Mons, then the Burmans, who arrived after them.[32] An early book about them calls them 'the loyal Karens',[33] with good reason. Of all the minorities of Burma, they were the most loyal to the British, who, as we shall see, used them, then turned them over to the Burmans.

Just over a million of the 1.37 million Karens in Burma recorded in the 1931 Census were Sgaw and Pwo, or 'White Karens'.[34] The Sgaw are found chiefly in the Irrawaddy delta, the Pwo along the coast. Another branch, anthropologically distinguished by dress and mutually unintelligible languages from the Sgaw and Pwo, are Karennis, or 'Red Karens', who inhabit the southern spurs of the Shan plateau east of Loikaw. Three *myosas*[35] ruled the state of Western Karenni and another *myosa* ruled Eastern Karenni or Kantarawaddi[36] in 1869 when Major E.B. Sladen, a British political agent attached to the Burman court, sought to intervene in a quarrel between them in the interest of the Crown. In 1875, the British forced an agreement on the Burman king guaranteeing the independence of Western Karenni, and the British respected this independence after annexing the king's dominions.[37] When, however, the *myosa* of Kantarawaddi in 1888 invaded a British protectorate in the Shan States,[38] the British deposed him and obliged his successor to accept a *sanad*; and thereafter the Crown's relations with the three other *myosas* were formalized in a similar way. While conceding an obligation to pay annual tribute and to act upon British political advice, Western Karenni nevertheless remained in theory an independent state. These legal warrants of more than a century ago today are the basis of the Karennis' claim to independence.

Still another branch of the Karens are the Taungthus (*Burm.*, farmers) or, as they call themselves, Paos (a corruption of the Karen

[32] San Crombie Po, 1928: 1; Silverstein, 1980: 69; Morrison, 1947: 16; Dun, 1980: 65.
[33] Smeaton, 1887.
[34] Lintner, 1994: 45; Enriquez, 1933: 76.
[35] A Burmese title meaning 'town-eater' conferring tax collection powers in exchange for payment of tribute to the Burman king.
[36] Woodman, 1962: 205 ff.
[37] The agreement, made in 1875, stated: 'It is hereby agreed between the British and the Burmese Governments that the State of Western Karenni shall remain separate and independent, and that no sovereignty or government authority of any description shall be claimed or exercised over that State.' Reproduced in Frontier Areas Committee of Enquiry, *Report*, 1947: 11.

Pwo, whose language resembles their own), who are found chiefly around Taunggyi, Loikaw and Paan, on the plateaux around Loilem and Yawnghwe, and at Toungoo, Pegu, Thaton and Kawkareik.

The T'ais defeated the Chinese imperial army in the eighth century and established the kingdom of Nanchao,[39] which ruled a large part of southern China and exerted considerable influence beyond. It has been suggested that, perhaps as early as the first century BC, under pressure from the Han Chinese and Mongols, small bands of T'ais began moving into what is now Laos, Thailand and the Shan highlands of Burma.[40] At any rate, by the late twelfth century, significant numbers of them had settled in India, Burma, Laos and Thailand.[41] In 1229 they founded the Ahom kingdom in what is now Assam, having left behind pockets of T'ais in the Irrawaddy, Hkamti Long and Hukawng valleys in the course of their trek west. In 1253 those living south of Yunnan succumbed to the Tartar horde of Kublai Khan. In 1287 the Tartars overwhelmed Pagan,[42] and, for the next two and a half centuries, the T'ais—or Shans as we shall call them henceforth—asserted political ascendancy over the Burmans. It was a Shan king, Thadominbya (1364–68), who established the capital at Ava, but his descendants and the other Shans penetrating Upper Burma soon became indistinguishable from Burmans.[43] From this moment on when history speaks of the Burmans gaining ascendancy over their rivals, it is referring to the ascendancy of Burmanized Shans, or kings with

[38] Mawkmai.
[39] Alt., Nanzhao, from Chinese *nan* (south) + *chao* or *zhao* (prince), being the southernmost limit of Chinese cultural influence. See Harvey, 1967: 312. Dun, 1980: 64, suggests that *sao* of the Shans and *saw* of the Karens are forms of *chao*.
[40] Lintner, 1994: 46, citing Syamananda (see *ante*, note 1), p. 8. For a detailed (but controversial and somewhat conjectural) account of T'ai migrations from Yunnan, see Saimong Mangrai, 1965: 15 ff.
[41] T'ai, Dai, Thai, Shan, Siamese, Hkamti and Kampti are different names for the same people. In Nanchao times they were called T'ai; hence Tali-fu or Dali, their capital. Now in Yunnan Province they are known as Dai, in Thailand as Thai, and to the Jinghpaws, Lashis, Atsis, Achangs and other northern Burmese hill tribes as Sam—hence Assam.
[42] But see Aung-Thwin, 1998: esp. 63–92, which challenges previous views that the Tartar attack was a catastrophe disrupting the continuity of Burman power.
[43] In the oldest surviving records of a Burman kingdom the kings have Nanchao titles. 'It was this 11th century kingdom, originally an offshoot of Nanchao, which developed as the [Burman] Kingdom of Pagan.' Leach, 1954: 240.

mixed Burman–Shan pedigrees, over other Shans.[44] Shan levies, moreover, served in Burman armies. Nevertheless, war between them continued. The Shans invaded the Burmans again in 1507 and wrought such destruction that the Burmans abandoned Ava and established a new capital at Toungoo. Then, in 1555, the Burmans struck back, reconquered Ava, invaded the Shan principalities to the north and east[45] and established the Theravada doctrine there.[46] The *saohpas* were not reduced to abject submission, however. The suzerainty asserted over them was more akin to the Austro-Hungarian model than to that of the Tartars. Their rule in their own dominions was not disturbed, and they continued to participate in the life of the Burman court, kings of Ava often taking Shan princesses as their queens, much as German principalities provided consorts for most of the royal houses of Europe. Thibaw Min (1878–85), the last king of Burma, was half Shan.

The Was inhabit the barren hills between the Mekong and the Salween above the Shan state of Kentung. It is difficult now to appreciate the impression they made on the young British officers leading the columns sent to subjugate them; indeed, on anyone who ventured into their highlands. They were head-hunters. The Chinese graded them into four classes in ascending order: those who decapitated indiscriminately, those who decapitated only people who offended against morals, those who bought in the severed heads (European heads cost more than local heads; most prized of all were Sikh heads with their magnificent beards and moustaches), and, the most civilized, those who collected only the heads of buffalo and other large game.[47] Their villages were adorned with these propitiatory skulls, mounted on columns.[48] They consulted the occult with

[44] Aung-Thwin, 1998: 2–3, 121–43, contends that the Shan dynasty notion appeared first in Sir Arthur Phayre's history of Burma, the first to be published in English, and has been perpetuated in subsequent histories, but is untenable.

[45] Saimong Mangrai, 1965: 49 ff.

[46] Ibid: 51, maintains that Bayinnaung ended the practice of interring a *saohpa*'s favourite elephant, horse and slaves with him when he died. He cites the *Hmannan Chronicles* for this claim. Various Shan princes maintained dynastic records or chronicles of uncertain historical value. The *Hmannan Yazawin* (Glass Palace chronicles) have not been translated into English, save for a very small portion on the Pagan period. Email from Patricia Herbert, 29 August 2000.

[47] Saimong Mangrai, 1965: 270–1.

[48] They hunted 'especially before sowing time so as to ensure the presence of a new ghost to look after the fields'. Harvey, 1967: 344.

chickens' shanks and wing bones, then stuck the bones in pairs to the roofs of their houses to deter malevolent spirits. They drank copiously of alcohol and ate dogs, believed that raw opium made them powerful and prevented fevers, and their body filth was 'only limited by the point beyond which extraneous matter refuses to adhere to human flesh'. Tidy minds in Simla and London countenanced restraint, doubting that any advantage could accrue to Britain by absorbing these savages into Burma,[49] nor would they be easy to conquer or administer. Their valleys were malarial.[50] But others took the view that leaving them alone would not of itself prevent trouble from them.[51] Moreover, their ghoulish hills were rumoured to be full of minerals.[52] 'Britain's main concern was to prevent China from extending her influence in the Irrawaddy,' suggests Woodman,[53] and there were French ambitions to consider. The optimists won the day, and the Wa states were annexed to Burma.

The Wa chiefs, who were not consulted, protested at this entirely novel assertion of alien authority over them:

> We beg that you will not come into our States. Please return by the route you came. Ours is a wild country, and the people devour rats and squirrels raw. Our people and yours have nothing in common and we are not your enemies. Please settle the dispute at Loi Long at that place alone, and [do] not bring it over to our country. Please do not come beyond the Nam Peg. Ngek Lek is a barren place and we beg that you may not come through it. The expedition would alarm the women and children.[54]

Their protest was ignored, and route marches into their hills were still continuing until the very eve of the Japanese invasion.[55] When the Frontier Areas Committee of Enquiry (FACE), set up in 1947 in contemplation of independence, inquired of a Wa representative what

[49] Woodman, 1962: 300.

[50] See Harvey, 1957: 129.

[51] Letter from Mr Warry, a political officer attached to the British Consular Service in Yunnan, *Letters from India*, vol. 64, 1891. Quoted in Woodman, 1962: 322.

[52] 'The Wa are unattractive but may have gold', wrote a chief secretary to the Government of India in 1893. Quoted in Woodman, 1962: 323.

[53] Ibid.

[54] Letter from the *sawbwa* of Ngek Lek to Sir George Scott, who led an expedition into the Wa states in 1897. Quoted ibid.: 450.

[55] Smith, 1991: 41.

future administration his people wanted, he replied, 'We have not thought about that because we are wild people.' When asked as to what constitutional reforms they sought, he answered, 'None, only more opium.'[56] '[I]t was neither their Shan neighbours, nor the British colonial ruler, nor even governments in Rangoon since independence, that finally brought an end to . . . [the Was'] independence, but the insurgent Communist Party of Burma . . . , which first "invaded" the state in the late 1960s', notes Martin Smith.[57]

The Kokangs inhabit the northeastern corner of the Shan State, and, as with so many other Burmese minorities, their Burmese nationality is a whim of political history. They are Han Chinese whose natural ties, in so far as these transcend local attachments, are with China, not Burma, and, until very recent times, they were ruled by *hengs* of the House of Yang, who trace their aristocratic line to a soldier who served the Ming dynasty in the stormy twilight years of its power.[58] The *heng* formerly paid annual tribute to the Shan *saohpa* of Hsenwi but professed allegiance to Peking.[59] A convention between Great Britain and China on 1 March 1894 gave Kokang to China.[60] However, with the Peking Convention of 1897, China ceded it to Britain as a reparation for having ceded two other districts to France in alleged breach of the 1894 convention.[61] Britain was content to continue the *heng*'s authority over the district through the *sanad* system applied to the Shan *saohpas* and Karenni *myosas*. 'Kokang and British cooperation consisted mainly in keeping peace on the border, establishing boundary posts, demarcating the China/Burma frontier, and adjudicating frontier trading and border problems such as civil and criminal cases.'[62] It is here worth noting that there are other pockets of ethnic Chinese elsewhere in what is now the Shan State, at Mending, Zhenkhan and Gengma.

The Palaungs[63] were formerly present in Myitkyina and Bhamo Districts. They shifted south in very recent times, probably under pressure from the Kachins, and are now most strongly represented in

[56] Ibid.: 84 and note 104, citing Tinker (ed.), 1984, vol. II: 883.
[57] Smith, 1991: 27, from a 10 January 1987 interview with Maha San, WNO president.
[58] Yang Li, 1997: 6.
[59] Ibid.: 14.
[60] Woodman, 1962: 295.
[61] Ibid.: 324–31.
[62] Yang Li, 1997, 30–1.
[63] A Burmese name; the Palaungs call themselves Rumai. See Enriquez, 1933: 38.

the former Shan state of Taungpeng and east of Taungpeng along the Salween, though scattered pockets of them are found on the hills banking the Shweli river and elsewhere in Shan State. Although related to the Was,[64] they are known for their gentleness. Their chief produce is tea.

The Kachins inhabit the more precipitous mountains of the far north of Burma and what the KIO today calls the 'Kachin Substate'— North Hsenwi and other parts of Shan State as far south as Kengtung. Their villages rarely comprise more than ten houses. They were the last of the 'indigenous races' to migrate south into Burma, a migration that was still in progress when the British annexed Upper Burma in 1886. Their different tribes speak mutually unintelligible languages, but Jinghpaw, the language of the largest tribe, is widely used as a lingua franca; very few of them speak Shan or Burmese. Their idea of political organization allowed them to accept or reject the leadership of their *duwas* (hereditary chieftains) as it suited them,[65] amounting in effect to anarchy. Shans and Burmans treated them as vassals but never subjected them to effective control. They were perceived as savages who emerged from their tangled glooms only to raid their neighbours for plunder, or to exact tribute with threats of abducting women or devastating crops, or to prey upon one another[66]—useful only as mercenaries.[67] The British 'pacification' of the Kachins consisted of investing their valley towns, establishing stockades and fortified posts along lines of communication, and dispatching incendiary columns against recalcitrant villages to discourage future resistance.[68] North of the Mali Hka–Nmai Hka confluence it achieved little more than the construction of a dirt road linking Myitkyina with Putao. Only by respecting their traditions, customs and local leaders did the British eventually win a measure of respect from the Kachins (there are perhaps lessons here for the regime in Rangoon today), and, by the

---

[64] Lowis, 1919: 37.

[65] Leach, 1954: 8–10, 197 ff.; Enriquez, 1933: 1, 3. Leach, a social anthropologist whose 'dynamics' theories of social change enjoyed a great following a quarter of a century ago, impressed on Kachin political structures a classification into *gumsa* (hereditary rulers) and *gumlao* (popular choice rulers), but this appears merely to confirm that a chief's hold on power often depends on his competence to govern.

[66] Leach, 1954: 21.

[67] Kachin levies served in both Bayinnaung and Alaungpaya's armies. See Leach, 1954: 22, fn 8, 186.

[68] Woodman, 1962: 337.

turn of the century, Christianity began to take hold. Three American Baptist missionaries served between them 108 years,[69] and there were many others. They opened schools and hospitals and provided an orthography for Jinghpaw,[70] until then unwritten.

The Nagas occupy the parallel folds of high mountains on both sides of the Burma–India border between the valley of the Chindwin and the Brahmaputra plains, merging with the Kachins in the north and the Chins in the south. For centuries they lived in these hills, as on some atoll, undisturbed by successive waves of migrant populations who surged through the valleys around them, and this isolation continued under the British. After the British annexed Upper Burma to India, there was no border to secure and, hence, their pacification was 'not a matter of imperial moment'. Nor was there any other prospective advantage in subjugating them. Their timber was less valuable than that found elsewhere in Burma, they had no mineral wealth to exploit, and, like the Was, their appetite for human heads to propitiate the spirits that ruled their superstitions rendered them unsuitable for military service. A village of ten houses would sacrifice one human every three to five years, and most of the victims were children who were bought for that purpose.[71] Missionary activity beginning in 1860[72] eventually brought an end to these grim practices, but they continued until as late as 1983.[73]

[69] William Roberts (1879–1913), Ola Hanson (1890–1928) and George Geis (1892–1916, 1924–36). See Tegenfeldt, 1974: 365.

[70] Ola Hanson, whose first language was Swedish, was the author of the Jinghpaw dictionary, which was published in 1906 and remains the authoritative orthography of the Jinghpaw language. Bertil Lintner, who is himself Swedish, attributes Hanson's success to his use of Swedish phonetics, 'which are more consistent [than English] and better suited the Jinghpaw language' (1999: 73).

[71] Enriquez, 1933: 17. A sequence of able British district commissioners whose interest in the tribes entrusted to their care greatly exceeded the requirements of their official duties laid the foundations of the ethnography of the Naga Hills. But, as they describe different communities of Nagas at different times, the customs and rites they portray vary in detail. See Hodson, 1911; Hutton, 1921; Mills, 1922, 1926 and 1937. Compare Fürer-Haimendorf, 1939, and Lintner, 1990b: 71–104.

[72] Neill, 1964: 363.

[73] Lintner, 1990b: 83. Frontier Areas Committee of Enquiry, *Report*, 1947: 23, manifested the arbitrariness of including the Naga Hills and the Wa States in modern Burma. 'We . . . have no hesitation in recommending that representatives need not be sought from these areas for the Constituent Assembly on account of the primitive nature of their civilization and the impossibility of their finding persons who will be able to assist in the drawing up of Burma's future constitution.'

South of the Nagas are the Chins, who inhabit a chaos of jungle-matted, knife-edged ridges, running up to peaks of over 8000 feet, split by almost bottomless valleys riddled with fevers and drenched throughout the rainy season with torrential rains. Like the Was and Nagas, their conspectus was limited to their immediate environs.

> It was in vain I tried to explain by means of stones placed on the ground the distance between Fort White, Kalemyo and Myingyan and the distance at which Her Majesty resides [London]. They have never been to Tashon Ywama even, and imagine Kalemyo is the end of the world and Myingyan as a place altogether unreachable.[74]

They speak a bewildering variety of dialects, the speech of one village being at times unintelligible to those who occupy the neighbouring village, likening them in one writer's notes to the people of Babel.[75] Like the Kachins, they had no political organization other than the governance of village headmen[76] and plundered their valley neighbours for farm produce, women and 'protection' money.[77]

The Shans and Burmans left the Chins undisturbed in their wild state. However, a 'British Administration could not show the same indifference'[78] and sent a succession of punitive expeditions against them. If a village submitted, a tribute was assessed and a headman responsible for its payment appointed; if the village resisted it was destroyed. The Chins fired their own villages rather than yield them to the intruders.[79] 'The Siyins [Chins] have surrendered,' wrote the political officer most concerned with these expeditions, 'but they are not afraid of us and this is due to the fact that we only travel by paths, that we do not know the country as we should, that we never night-march, and that we move about in large columns hampered by coolies and never surprise the Chins.'[80] Eleven years of 'pacification' were needed to break the Chins' resistance and integrate them into

---

[74] Captain Rundall, a political officer, 1890. Quoted in Woodman, 1962: 397.
[75] Enriquez, 1933: xiii, 52.
[76] Crosthwaite, 1912: 287. Woodman (1962: 380) adds that they were 'grouped tribally under chiefs', but it is clear from Crosthwaite's and her accounts of the pacification campaigns that such groupings were temporary and involved no more than a few villages.
[77] Crosthwaite, 1912: 287.
[78] Ibid.
[79] Woodman, 1962: 384–5, 392.
[80] Carey and Tuck, 1983. Reproduced in Woodman, 1962: 397.

the system of indirect rule that the British applied to all their 'frontier peoples'—but, again, only by respecting their subjects' traditions, customs and local leaders did the British eventually gain willing acquiescence to their overlordship.

Finally, along the swampy coast of the Bay of Bengal and inland as far east as the Arakan Yoma, are the Arakanese or Rakhines. Their speech is an early form or dialect of Burmese, rather than a discrete language,[81] and it is generally accepted that they are of 'Tibeto-Burman' or 'proto-Burman' stock,[82] intermingled with an antecedent people of Bengali type and migrants from Bengal. Secluded by geography from the Mons, the Shans and their Burman kin, they looked to the sea. Their contacts were with the Portuguese in Dianga and Goa, the Dutch in Batavia, and especially Bengal, with whom they alternated in paying and receiving tribute. For over two centuries, from 1459 until 1666, they were masters of Chittagong. Their sailors raided the Mon kingdom of Pegu and returned laden with treasure, including a white elephant and the king's daughter.[83] Hall has likened their capital, Mrohaung, to 'an eastern Venice'.[84] Of all the communities in Burma, they are considered to be the most scholarly. At any rate, disproportionate numbers of them functioned as clerks in the colonial administration.

These diverse peoples have discrete physical attributes, as shown by the anthropometric data collected by British recruitment officers.[85] The average Rakhine is darker than the average Chin, Naga, Kachin, Palaung, Wa or Karen, who is darker than the average Burman, who is darker than the average Shan. The average Burman or Shan is taller than the average hill tribal, but his chest and legs are not so well developed. These diverse peoples speak mutually incomprehensible languages: a linguistic survey begun in 1917 disclosed 242 languages and dialects, before it was abandoned as 'a thing beyond our present capacity'.[86] Their customs, traditions and institutions differ. Their religious beliefs differ. Nearly all Burmans, Mons, Shans, Paos and Palaungs are Buddhists. Nearly all Kachins, Chins, Karennis and Nagas are Christians. While most Karens are Buddhists, almost all

[81] Hall, 1960: 57; Donnison, 1970: 35.
[82] Donnison, 1970: 33; Lewis, 1919: 10; Enriquez, 1933: 25.
[83] Hall, 1960: 57–60.
[84] Ibid.: 58.
[85] Enriquez, 1933: 6.
[86] Ibid.: xiii–xiv.

their leaders are Christians. Most Lahus, Akhas and Was are animists. Most Kokangs are animists. Some Burmans, Mons, Shans, Paos, Kokangs and Palaungs, on the other hand, are Christians, and some Kachins, Chins, Karennis and Nagas are shamanists, animists or Buddhists. Some Karens, Mons, Was and Burmans are Muslims. Most Rakhines, the majority community in Arakan, are Buddhists, but nearly all Rohingyas, the minority community in Arakan, are Muslims. Indians are Muslims, Hindus, Christians or Sikhs, and shamanist and animist practices to some extent infuse all faiths. These differences in physical attributes, language, customs, traditions, institutions and religion have given rise to different values.

At the heart of much of this diversity lies the contrast between difficult-to-manage hill jungle and flat, easily cultivable river basins. The one produces subsistence farmers, hunters, gatherers and mercenaries; the other, a surplus of wealth and its attributes, merchants, lawyers, bankers, architects, engineers, a civil service responsible for maintaining a complex trading infrastructure, and security forces to police large urban populations.

Consider the typical Kachin highlander. He lives with his wife, children and other dependants in a house that might comprise one large room and two smaller rooms. The house stands on stilts and is constructed entirely of bamboo and thatch, materials gathered from the forest. At the centre of the floor of the large room is an earth-filled square called a *dap*, or fireplace. Under the house are two or three pigs, a dozen chickens and a store of firewood gathered from the forest. Rice and yams are stored in a small bamboo and thatch barn nearby. Our Kachin's village of three to ten such houses is perched on the shoulder of a hill. Two hundred yards below is a stream that provides him with an abundant supply of fish and water for drinking, cooking and washing. He might cultivate a small private *yi* (garden or orchard), or share with his neighbours a communal *yi*, that is planted with rice, yams, chillies, a kind of spinach, orange, lemon, grapefruit, pomelo, plum and fig trees. The forest also provides him with wild bananas, wild plums, mushrooms, honey, cinnamon and other spices, boar, deer, gaur, monkeys, gibbons, grouse, peafowl and the materials he needs for making fences, bridges, clothes, spits, vessels, baskets, mats, looms, bows and arrows. The Kachin has very few possessions, but he is not poor in his own esteem, because he has enough to supply his necessities, and what he has is neither more nor less than his neighbours' possessions. His youngest son will succeed to his house, his *nhpye* (cotton shoulder bag), his *nhtu* (machete), and his gun or crossbow, while his daughters might expect to inherit from their mother a *gumhpraw palawng* (necklace crafted of silver rupee and eight-anna coins), some sticks of *tanakha* wood (for making foundation cream) and an assortment of baskets. Locks are unknown in his village, and a stranger arriving at his house when he is absent may abide there, burn his wood and consume his food free of cost.[87] Possessing all that he needs and depending upon and envying no one, our Kachin's only ambition is to be left alone to cultivate his *yi* and fish, hunt and forage in the forest. His leisure time—and there is lots of it during the rains—he spends around a *dap* discussing with other Kachins matters of common interest: their blood lines and which bard's version of their descent from their common progenitor, Wahkyet Wa, is correct;[88] who among the Marip, Lahtaw, Lahpai, N'Hkum and Maran (clans) outrank whom in seniority; whose son consanguinity bars from marrying whose daughter; what careless act offended the *nat* that visited them with the storm; how the old Sama *duwa* accepted death rather than submit to British rule; the heroic feats of this or that uncle during the 'Japan War'; how the Sama *duwa*'s son, Sinwa Nawng, foolishly trusted the Burmans after the war; whether the truce between the KIO and the Burmans will hold; whether the Malizup *duwa* should continue as chairman or hand over to a younger man. Our Kachin esteems truthfulness, personal honour, fearlessness in combat and loyalty to his tribe above all virtues. The pride of the warrior is in him. Not so long ago, be it remembered, he was raiding his lowland neighbours for plunder or ambushing other Kachins to avenge a wrong. He has a low opinion of those who know nothing of the forest, do not carry their own baskets, 'travel by paths . . . never night-march . . . move about in large columns hampered by coolies' and prosper by trading, which is women's work.

Consider now the typical Burman. Pre-colonial Burman society, suggests Josef Silverstein, reflected three institutions, the monarchy, the bureaucracy and Buddhism.[89] The monarchy was absolute but, lacking a settled rule of succession, inherently unstable, as was

---

[87] When our column marched into Hpung Gan Yang and scavenged chillies from its *yi*, no one took the slightest notice. It was expected. Tucker, 2000: 143.

[88] Ancestor myths define identity in other ethnic groups. For a Karen example, see Gravers, 1999: 46, fn 10.

[89] Silverstein, 1977: 6–11.

therefore the bureaucracy that depended on it. Buddhist natural law, *dhamma*, assigned each Burman his place in this life according to his *kamma*, or conduct in past lives, and conditioned him to accept whatever excesses the monarchy or bureaucracy imposed on him. He might invoke Buddhist precept or local custom to secure his 'rights', but no legal system guaranteed his 'rights' or afforded him redress if deprived of them. The ordinary Burman, in brief, was a mere subject. And he farmed only for sustenance and to pay his taxes, bartering any surplus for commodities that could be transported short distances by river.

Nevertheless, our Burman has the consolation of his religion. He ascribes everything to *kamma* and accounts himself blessed that he is not a Kachin, Wa or other primitive living without knowledge of means of improving his status in the next incarnation by meritorious conduct in this incarnation. Whatever his personal condition, his self-styled Golden Land epitomizes for him Civilization. Unlike the wild hills, this Golden Land has navigable rivers, tarmacadam roads, irrigation canals, art, architecture, literature, monasteries, universities and, most important of all, true religion. The great brick *zedis* and *pahtos* at Pagan, King Mindon's moated palace at Mandalay, the majestic *payas* of Shwedagon and Shwemawdaw are all Burman.[90] A society without such a cultural and technical overlay is primitive, nearer to the grosser form of incarnation of animals.

Burma thus is a portmanteau of diverse peoples joined artificially by history and politics. The Burmans claimed suzerainty over the hill tracts for centuries, but their hold on them was never secure, the hill peoples paying nominal tribute to Chinese or Siamese overlords as often as to the kings of Burma and sometimes themselves reducing the Burmans to submission. Karens and Mons, who lived in closest proximity to the Burmans, had a particularly parlous relationship with them. Let us now look at how British and Japanese conquest affected this mix.

---

[90] There is irony in this conceit. Both the Shwedagon and the Shwemawdaw were originally Mon constructions. As noted, the Mons transmitted the Theravada to the Burmans, and the finest monuments at Pagan were of Mon design. Tarmacadam roads and universities were introduced by Europeans.

3
British vs. Japanese Line-up

THE BRITISH EMPIRE was not simply the product of racial arrogance, commercial greed and superior technology directed and controlled by a kind of ruthless genius. The truth is rather more complex and much more interesting. The empire differed from time to time and from place to place.

Early in the seventeenth century, British merchants began establishing factories and trading posts in India.[1] Although they operated under a charter from the Crown, this was a formality of the licensing provisions of the Companies Acts. It is probably fair to say that the merchants themselves simply aspired to a more interesting life in a sunnier place offering a possibility of greater material reward *for themselves*. But their success, not unnaturally, excited the ambition of local rivals. This posed a danger to their survival, and they raised levies called *sepahi log*, or sepoys, from the local population for their own protection and provided them with superior weapons and a new kind of military discipline. They did not divide the local population in order to rule it—the local population was already divided by language, religion, castes, sects, the political and commercial ambitions of individual rajahs, geography and all the other hatreds, prejudices, unrenounced grievances and charged emotions that divide people everywhere. Being few in number and strangers in a remote land, they merely accepted help from whatever quarter it came. For a hundred years or so none of them would have had the vaguest notion that his modest enterprise in this remote place would contribute to the building of an empire ruled from Westminster.

By the late eighteenth or early nineteenth century, however, another ethos began to complicate this simple impulse. By now it was becoming increasingly plain to many in Britain that these nabobs, as they were called, exercised considerable power over the natives and that their power should be constrained by Westminster.

---

[1] Surat (1614); Armagaon on the Coromandel Coast (1625–26); Maderaspatam, or Madras (1639–40); Hooghly, later Calcutta (1642); Bombay (1668), ceded to the Crown in 1661 as part of the dowry of Catherine of Braganza.

Similarly British conquest of Burma arose from no premeditated plan of imperial ambition. It was an organic extension of British rule in India.

In the late eighteenth and early nineteenth centuries, the Konbaung dynasty in Burma founded by King Alaungpaya (1752–60) reached the zenith of its power. Its armies defeated the Mons, then marched on the Manipuris, Shans and Siamese,[2] then repelled the Chinese and replaced the King of Manipur with a Burman vassal. When they annexed Arakan and Assam, however, their conquests brought them into conflict with British power in India. Stragglers from the forces opposing them regrouped in British territory, there were a number of border incidents, and, when the Burmans positioned their armies along the border, the British reacted. The Burmans, blinded to the possibility of defeat by nearly 70 years of triumphs, underestimated British strength. The First Anglo-Burmese War (1824–26) ended with the Treaty of Yandabo (1826). The Burmans renounced their claims to Assam and Manipur and ceded Arakan and Tenasserim to the British.

The Burmans learned no lessons from this defeat and made no improvements in their military technology.[3] Instead, they decapitated the commanders of their beaten armies, for however loyally, however bravely they had served their king, news displeasing to his 'golden ears' was punished with death.[4]

In 1837, King Tharrawaddy (1837–46), deposed his older brother, Bagyidaw (1819–37). Tharrawaddy reputedly was a 'hot-headed and arrogant chauvinist';[5] at any rate, relations with the British soured again. British merchants were snubbed, and border irritations resumed. Tharrawaddy's successor, King Pagan (1846–53), arrested two British sea captains and falsely charged them with murder—false charges and unwarranted arrest being a standard ruse for extorting money—and, in 1852, Pagan repudiated the Treaty of Yandabo. The Second Anglo-Burmese War (1852–53) ended in the British annexation of the rest of Lower Burma[6] and the administrative addition of British Burma as a new province of India.

---

[2] Siam or Siamese derives from 'Shan', the Burmese name for the Tai, T'ai, Dai or Thai people.
[3] Silverstein, 1977: 6.
[4] Marrat, 1890: 20.
[5] Donnison, 1970: 59.
[6] Effectively, the old kingdom of Pegu.

Relations with the British improved under Pagan's successor, King Mindon (1853–78). Towards the end of Mindon's reign, however, he began granting trading rights to the French and Italians. Wanting to forestall further French influence and eager to open a land route through Bhamo to China,[7] the British were now ready to expand into Upper Burma. Mindon's successor, King Thibaw (1878–85), presented them with an opportunity when his customs officials fined the Bombay-Burmah Corporation for fraudulently withholding royalties on exported timber. The British issued an ultimatum effectively relegating Thibaw to the status of a vassal prince. He was already angry with the British for their indignation at the slaughter of more than 80 of his half-brothers and sisters,[8] an established tradition whose purpose was to eliminate possible rivals and ensure the stability of the throne.[9] Now, like Priam drawing 'onto shoulders trembling with age his long unused corslet', he repudiated the ultimatum with desperate defiance:

Those heretics, the English *kalas* barbarians, having most harshly made demands calculated to bring about the impairment of our religion, the violation of our national traditions and customs, and the degradation of our race, are making a show and preparation as if about to wage war with our State. They have been replied to in conformity with the usages of great nations, and in words which are just and regular. If, notwithstanding, these heretic *kalas* should come and in any way attempt to molest or disturb the State, His Majesty, who is watchful with the interests of our religion and our State shall not suffer, will himself march forth with his elephants, captains and lieutenants, with large forces of infantry, artillery, elephanterie, and cavalry, by land and by water, and with the might of the army will efface these heretic *kalas* and conquer and annex their country.[10]

It was the final salvo for the Burman monarchy, triggered in part by hints of French support that never materialized. The Third

[7] Woodman, 1962: 222 ff.
[8] O'Brien, 1991: 26; Thant Myint-U, 2001: 160–1.
[9] For seven instances of such massacres and a general commentary on the practice, see Harvey, 1946: 75, 80, 117, 120, 145, 201, 264 and 338.
[10] 'Correspondence relating to Burmah', presented to Parliament, 1886, C. 4614, pp. 256–7; quoted in Scott and Hardiman, 1900–1, part I, vol. I: 110, and Woodman, 1962: 236–7.

Anglo-Burmese War (November 1885) lasted just two weeks.[11] Upper Burma was annexed on 1 January 1886.

British conquest coincided with a period of great technological and cultural change everywhere. The first transcontinental railway reached the Pacific coast of America. The Suez Canal opened. Pre-colonial Burma had been a buffalo and water wheel-driven economy of peasants protected by custom and hereditary chieftains in their tenure of small plots of communal land producing rice, millet, fruit, vegetables, vegetable oils, fish, salt and cotton. There were no real cities, and the villages were almost entirely self-sufficient. Very little minted coin circulated. Almost all transactions were by barter. Trade was a limited exchange of commodities that could be transported short distances by river. Values were fixed at what was thought to be fair.[12] Government at national level might be unstable,[13] but its effect on the serenity and continuity of life in the country at large was minimal, nor did the people expect from it other than theft, war and plunder. There now appeared industrial enterprises powered by petro-carbons and electricity and a baffling new kind of impersonal, supply-and-demand commerce assisted by coinage and banks. Businessmen, soldiers, civil servants, architects, engineers and technicians of every kind arrived from all parts of Britain's empire. The building of railways, the use of steam on rivers, a modern postal system, the telegraph, the telephone opened new channels of communication. The old system of families farming to supply their own needs changed to one of producing huge surpluses for export.

The British encouraged the peoples in upper Burma to move south and cultivate the rich delta soils. At the same time, the colonial

---

[11] 'It was not a war at all—it was merely a street row. The Burmans had not prepared for war; they never believed it would come. There was the ultimatum, it was true, but the Burmans did not know anything about the ultimatum. How could great questions be discussed and settled in five days? Such a thing was never heard of . . . The Kinwoon saw that nothing could be done by arms and imagined that the difficulties could be settled by negotiation. And when the English Army came, he advised the King to surrender everything and not to fight. He thought that the King would be then put back by the English, with some limitations of his power, no doubt, but he would still be left of his palace and on the throne.' Geary, 1886: 60–1.
[12] Donnison, 1970: 69–70.
[13] Owing to the multiplicity of the king's wives and the absence of an established order of succession, power struggles in both the palace and the civil service attended every change of monarch.

authorities opened Burma to immigration of Indian labourers, merchants, and moneylenders. Both Burmese and aliens moved into the delta and established new communities. Coming as individuals they owed no allegiance to a traditional chieftain and were not subject to social pressure and surveillance of lifelong friends. Most came to depend upon Indian moneylenders for the annual capital they needed. Since land ownership was a legal right under the British, land could be sold, traded, or repossessed without consideration of the rights either of the village or of the owner's family, as had been customary under the Burman kings. Tenancy, rack-renting, and land alienation became commonplace, and people drifted from area to area with no ties to bind them. The system produced rice; it also allowed the land to fall into alien hands and created a landlord class that dealt in land speculation rather than in cultivation.[14]

Ejected from the land they had owned and tended for centuries, the deracinated peasants drifted in ever-increasing numbers to the cities, where they had neither family nor community ties.[15] The moneylenders were Chettiyars from southern India. Other Indians opened small shops. Others built small factories that grew into bigger factories. At the turn of the century, a quarter of a million Indians were arriving in Burma every year, 'and the number was rising steeply'. By 1930, nearly half of the population of Rangoon was Indian.[16] The business life of Rangoon was dominated by Indians, Mandalay by Chinese.

Maurice Collis gives us a depressing picture of the post-colonial status of the Burman:

> [N]early all the rich people in the country were foreigners and . . . the Burm[ans], from being poor in a poor country, had become the poor in a rich one . . . which meant that . . . from every psychological and human point of view they were worse off than they were before. All sorts of foreigners lorded it over them, and had little opinion of them because they were poor . . . The Burman became steadily less important industrially in his own country. In

---

[14] Silverstein, 1977: 13. For a detailed account of these developments, see Adas, 1974.
[15] Silverstein, 1977: 13.
[16] Hall, 1960: 158.

the capital, Rangoon, he was nobody. The stigma of poverty beat him down.[17]

There were other changes too. Adoniram and Ann Judson arrived in Burma in July 1813,[18] and, after the annexations, they were followed by other missionaries, who proclaimed the Good News and established schools and hospitals. The colonial authorities by and large let them get on with their tasks, for, after all, they provided at private expense a vital part of the province's infrastructure. Very few *Burmans* converted to Christianity, but, increasingly, they entrusted the education of their children to the missionaries and resorted to mission doctors for their medical care. The new schools and cures deprived the *sangha* (community of monks) of their most important functions, and, as the monks declined in importance, the harmonious relations that had existed between them and the people weakened.

Where an indigenous population is ruled by a small body of expatriate civil servants, security is more safely entrusted to foreigners and local minorities, and some of these minorities, the colonial authorities soon discovered, made better soldiers than others. 'Malaria, opium, and the enervating climate of the [Hkamti Long] plain have killed the old martial spirit of the Shans, who now love ease, and are poor material so far as soldiering is concerned', while the Karens of Bassein, Toungoo and Thaton in particular and Kachins and Chins in general are 'valuable military material', writes the chief recruiting officer for Burma in 1923.[19] Hkahku (up-river) Kachins are 'the very best type'. The mean chest size of Karen, Kachin and Chin recruits exceeds by an inch that of Burman recruits. By 1938 the Burma Army comprised 1587 Britons, 1423 Indians and Gurkhas, 3040 'other indigenous races' (Karens, Kachins and Chins) and 159 Burmans—one Burman for every 39 non-Burmans. Officers included 163 British, 36 Indians, 75 other indigenous races and four Burmans—one Burman for every 69 non-Burmans.[20] The borders were defended by the Burma Military Police, later the Burma Frontier Force, commanded by British officers (usually on secondment from the Indian Army) and manned mainly by Indians and Gurkhas. Christian proselytization was the effect rather than the instrument

[17] Collis, 1938: 286–7.
[18] Neill, 1964: 293.
[19] Enriquez, 1933: xi, 2–3, 6, 11.
[20] Trager (ed.), 1971: 9–10.

of British conquest, but most of the converts were Karens, Kachins and Chins, and they supplied most local recruits to the army and police. Baptism accordingly came to assume to the Burmans the significance of a badge of foreign allegiance.

The qualities that endeared the minorities to the British outraged the Burmans. Soldiers deployed in pacifying the Was and Nagas brought back stories of stacks of sacrificial human skulls; Kengtung, a valley town near the Was, even boasted a market for human skulls, partly supplied from executed prisoners. The British allowed that the Kachins were 'dirty, ugly and barbarian (Fytche)' and 'robbers who systematically plunder caravans whenever they get the chance (Davies)',[21] yet they used these 'barbarians' and 'robbers' to hold the more civilized parts of the country in subjection. Apart from despising the other indigenous races as their cultural, educational and religious inferiors, many Burmans also despised the Indians for their darker skins. British policy appeared to them to be cynical, exploitative and partisan.

Most of the conditions for the civil war were thus in place by the first decade of the twentieth century. Burmans were the majority community, yet foreigners made most of the important decisions affecting their lives and economy. English was replacing Burmese as the language of the educated elite. An alien religion was spreading among them, diminishing the influence of the *sangha*, and Western newspapers and books, that of the *Tripitaka*. And this inversion of the natural order, the Burmans believed, would not have been possible but for the treasonable collaboration with the British invaders of some of the despised minorities—their former subjects.

1906 saw the foundation of the Young Men's Buddhist Association. Its members had no quarrel with the British or with the Burmese minorities. Their aims were not political. The YMBA's president, U May Oung, had studied for the bar in England, and when he addressed the YMBA, he addressed it in English. The YMBA was a specifically Buddhist response to social changes of concern to Buddhists. Two years after its foundation, U May Oung assessed the effect of the changes in Burman society as follows:

By the expression 'The Modern Burman' he did not mean the native of Burma in general. . . . [H]e meant the Burman who had received the not unmixed blessing of a Western education. . . . For

[21] Enriquez, 1933: 32.

it was on them and those like them— on their training, acquire-
ments, exertions—that the future of their race would . . . depend.
On all sides they saw the ceaseless, ebb-less tide of foreign civilization and learning, steadily creeping over the land, and it
seemed to him that unless they prepared themselves to meet it,
to overcome it, and to apply it to their own needs, their national
character, their institutions, their very existence as a distinct
nationality, would be swept away, submerged, irretrievably lost.[22]

However, the YMBA's membership quickly expanded beyond the
elite circle of Western-educated Burmans who founded it, and soon
others were exploiting it for political ends. Notices forbidding the
wearing of shoes appeared at Buddhist shrines. The motive for
posting them was not reverence for the holy images. It was to foster
contempt for Britons, who might treat the notices as an attack on
their prestige.[23]

In 1918, U Ottama, a monk who had visited Japan, began
organizing *wunthanu athin* (preserving one's race societies). Their
objective was home rule.

The following year the YMBA met in Prome and transformed itself
into a nationalist umbrella organization known as the General
Council of Burmese Associations (GCBA),[24] and, the year after that,
university students camped at the foot of Burma's most revered
Buddhist shrine, the Shwedagon Pagoda, to protest at new
educational measures modelled on Oxford and Cambridge that
favoured the wealthier classes and were designed to equip them
better to serve the colonial government. This first student strike
quickly spread to schools and colleges throughout Burma Proper.

---

[22] *Journal of the Burma Research Society*, vol. xxxiii, part I, April 1950. Quoted
in Donnison, 1970: 103.

[23] Donnison, 1970: 105.

[24] The GCBA, though governed by a *Baho Sayadaw* (Board of Noble Teachers),
was a largely middle-class affair that drew its energy from lawyers,
businessmen, landowners and journalists who had been educated in the
English vernacular schools and spoke and wrote in English. See Dr Maung
Maung, 1959: 15, and 1969: 8–9; Lintner, 1989: 28. U Chit Hlaing, a wealthy
barrister from Moulmein, was its star performer. 'When he came to
conferences—often dressed in European clothes, complete with winged collar
and waist coat—golden umbrellas were opened to protect him from the
colonial sun. Women knelt along the way and spread their long hair on the
ground to make him a carpet to tread on. The people called him . . . the
Thamada, the "uncrowned king".' Dr Maung Maung, 1969: 9.

In 1930, an ex-monk pronounced himself a *thupannaka galuna raja* (illustrious mythical bird king) and began inciting rebellion with claims of magical powers. Maurice Collis describes the spell he cast over his followers:

> By tattooed charms, pills, oils, needles buried under the skin, he made men invulnerable, invisible, their bodies would rise and fly through the air, they could cause a hostile army to drop its weapons by merely sounding their enchanted gongs, and if they pointed their fingers at an aeroplane it would crash on the spot. They advanced on to our machine-guns believing these things, and they continued to believe even after they were wounded.[25]

British authority was secure in 1930, but the rebellion provoked disquiet. 'It seemed to me,' notes Collis, concerned to explain why thitherto loyal subjects of the English Crown 'praised for their gentle religion and manners' flung themselves in front of machine guns,

> that we had done two things . . . which we ought not to have done. . . . [W]e had placed English interests first, and we had treated the Burmans not as fellow creatures, but as inferior beings. The Burmese were a people of extraordinary charm. Their religion was admirable. They were manly, sportsmen like ourselves; they were artists, amateurs of music and the drama; they were wits, with a vast relish for the ridiculous; they were good-looking and their women, who had rights under their own Buddhist law which Englishwomen have only recently acquired, were beings whose conversation was infinitely diverting. But there was one thing against the Burmans. They were poor. A Burman who had . . . his own house and his own farmland, a wife and lots of children, a pony and a favourite actress, a bottle of wine and a book of verse, racing bullocks and a carved teak cart, a set of chess and a set of dice, felt himself at the summit of felicity . . . Yet he was poor, from the capitalist angle . . . [T]hese Burmans . . . were like orphans after the loss of their king; they were children compared to us, because they had fallen behind us in the modern world. But, surely, they were good and interesting material? If we had adopted them as our own, if we had determined to take the place of their king and to be to them everything which an understanding government

[25] Harvey, 1967: 73. Quoted in Donnison, 1970: 120.

should be, if we had protected them, brought them up like a father bringing up his sons to take their place in the world, and had acted as trustees for the riches which were hidden in their soil, what a great thing we should have accomplished, how proud we should have been of the modern Burmans, our creation. And the Burmans themselves would have loved us, with a passionate open devotion, which might have made us feel shy, but which would have warmed our ancient hearts. Instead of that, after a hundred years we were mowing them down with machine-guns.[26]

As most of the troops used in putting down the Saya San rebellion[27] were Indians and most of the more than 3000 casualties were Burmans, it would enter the nationalist pantheon as an event of critical importance. Kodaw Hmaing, patron of the Dobama Asiayone (We Burmans Association), which grew out of the Indo-Burman riots of 1930; Dr Ba Maw, founder of the Sinyetha (Poor Man's) Party, which fused messianic notions of Buddhism with the egalitarian concerns of Western democracy, who (with Aung San) also founded the Freedom Bloc; U Ba Pe, leader of the United General Council of Buddhist Associations Party; U Saw, founder of the Myochit (Nationalist) Party; and the student activists who were to play such a prominent part in the transition to independence, all drew on its inspiration.[28]

What passes for history today is a paradigm that imputes political change in Burma *entirely* to nationalist pressure, instancing the Saya San rebellion as an example. This is owing to the fact that, with one notable exception, the story of the nationalist movement in Burma has been the preserve of Burman nationalists such as Dr Maung Maung, U Maung Maung and U Nu and liberal and paternalistic

---

[26] Collis, 1938: 283.

[27] *Saya* is a prefix meaning teacher. Burmans do not have forenames and surnames, though their names generally comprise multiple words, e.g., Aung San. Greater use is made of titles, such as Ko for a younger young man, Maung for an older young man, U for an adult man, Ma for a young woman, Daw for an adult woman. These vary according to the relationship between the person addressed or referred to and the person addressing or referring to him. Save between very close friends and family members, it is considered rude not to prefix this title to the person's name.

[28] Ba Maw founded a private army, the Dahma Tat; U Saw founded the Galon Tat. Both men were 'prepared to seize power by force and were ready to cast themselves for the part of dictator . . . both *Tats* . . . partaking of the character of the contemporary Black Shirts in Britain'. Donnison, 1970: 117.

historians such as J.S. Furnivall, Maurice Collis, Jan Běcka, Hugh Tinker and Frank Trager. Modern political historians, Silverstein, Taylor, Steinberg, Smith and Lintner, appear to disregard the exception, Donnison, and the result is a political correctness that demonizes colonial rule and beatifies those opposed to it. But it needs to be said that local political awakening was also in part the consequence of British opinion and the relative freedom of political debate in Burma that Britain allowed. Legislation expanding Burmese participation in government fuelled nationalist agitation for yet more participation.[29]

Britain's presence in Burma was always ancillary to its interests in India, and change in India usually begat change in Burma. In 1909, a decade before U Ottama's first *wunthanu athin*, the Morley-Minto reforms granted limited participation in government to Indians and Burmese. In 1917, Westminster accepted home rule as the ultimate aim for India. Although the issue was deferred in respect of Burma,[30] in 1923, seven years before Saya San proclaimed himself the mythical bird king, Burma got its first elected assembly.[31] The countdown to independence began not in 1945, but in 1931, when Westminster effectively gave an undertaking that constitutional advance in Burma would mirror that in India.[32] Four years later, the Government of Burma Act provided for separating Burma from India and a legislature in Rangoon with reserved seats for certain minorities.

The statute came into effect on 1 April 1937. Thenceforth, Burma Proper was, like India, a dyarchy in respect of nearly all internal matters with a cabinet responsible to the governor and a parliament elected by popular franchise. While the governor retained a veto over

[29] Ibid.: 122.

[30] The Montagu-Chelmsford Committee's 'Joint Report on Constitutional Reforms' (1918) stated that 'the desire for elective institutions has not developed in Burma' and 'Burma is not India' (p. 162). It described Burmans as 'another race in another stage of political development'. See Donnison, 1970: 113. The Committee did not visit Burma, and 'Edwin Montagu . . . recorded in his diary his impression of the Burmese leaders who came to see him as "nice simple-minded people with beautiful clothes. Complete loyalty; no sign of political unrest."' Tinker, 1959: 2, 2, fn 3. '[I]t was obvious to all who knew Burma that her people lacked the political experience and education necessary for working a democratic constitution on the western model.' Hall, 1960: 149.

[31] And its own governor. The legislative council comprised 79 members elected by democratic franchise, two ex officio and 22 nominated by the governor. Ibid.: 150.

[32] McEnery, 1990: 13.

his cabinet's decisions, his Instrument of Instructions exhorted him 'to be studious so to exercise his powers as not to enable his ministers to rely on his special responsibilities in order to relieve themselves of responsibilities which are properly their own'.[33] 'Indeed,' notes Donnison, 'it cannot be too strongly emphasized that, whatever the written constitution may often seem to say, the Burmese parliament now had complete control, at least in internal matters.'[34] But no legislation or declaration of a better future, however genuine or well-intended, could redress the intrinsic insult of foreign rule, and the reforms applied only to the 70–80 per cent of the population inhabiting Burma Proper.[35] The hill people were not affected. British policy was to leave their governance to their hereditary leaders, mandating them 'to administer according to the custom of the country, and in all matters subject to the guidance of the [Crown-appointed] Superintendent . . . [and] to recognize the rights of the [hill] people and continue them in the same, and [not] oppress them or suffer them in any way to be oppressed'.[36]

Hence, the Resistance, as nationalists called their ever more strident demands for home rule, was viewed differently according to whether you were a Burman, Karen, Shan, Kachin or Chin. The Burman, whose ancestors had fought with Anawrahta and Alaungpaya, but who now were outnumbered 39 to 1 by non-

---

[33] Quoted in Donnison, 1970: 116.

[34] Ibid.

[35] The estimate of 20–30 per cent of the total population for the Frontier Areas, a figure extrapolated from the 1931 census, is conjectural. Everyone whose mother tongue was Burmese was classified as Burman. The best discussion of this hotly contentious issue is Smith, 1991: 29–39. See also Donnison, 1970: 35; Silverstein, 1977: 15.

[36] See the standard form of *sanad*, or patent of authority, used in the Shan States, reproduced in Saimong Mangrai, 1965, appendix VII: xxxi–xxxii. The other conditions are: the prince's chosen successor to be approved by the chief commissioner; payment of the tribute previously paid to the Burman king for five years and thereafter an amount fixed by the chief commissioner; all forest and mineral rights vest in the Crown; the prince to maintain public order and keep open trade routes within his domain, to maintain an agent at the headquarters of the superintendent of the Shan States who will advise on conditions in his domain; to submit disputes with other states to the superintendent's decision; to allow no raids on other states; to provide land for and assist in the building of any railway through his domain; to pay the prescribed duties on opium, spirits, fermented liquors and other articles exported from his domain into Upper or Lower Burma; to deliver to the government criminals taking refuge in his domain; and to refer to the superintendent any criminal charge against a European British subject.

Burmans in the army and the police and by perhaps 20 to 1 in senior positions in industry and commerce, whose portion of government was that of a clerk as often as not working under an Indian *babu*, perceived British rule as having deprived him of his right of pre-eminence in his own country. For most minorities, however, for the Karens and Mons in particular, self-rule effectively portended Burman rule or, at best, Burman domination. It threatened the Shan *saohpas* with the undermining of the aristocratic basis of their authority, and Christians and Muslims with the nationalization (Bur-manization) of their schools. If British rule exacerbated divisions already present in Burmese society, the Resistance intensified them.

Burma in the tense months before the Japanese invasion was thus a country divided. Most of the ethnic and religious minorities (including, most significantly, the Karens, Kachins and Chins serving in the army and police), Anglo-Burmans and expatriates (including almost all Indians and Chinese), and the capital-owning classes, civil servants and others with a vested interest in the status quo stood four-square behind the British, while most Burmans were either hostile to the Crown or, at best, lukewarm in their loyalty.

For millions of people under colonial rule in Asia the Japanese defeat of Russia in 1905 shattered the myth of congenital European superiority and invincibility and signalled a new era. In 1940, the Japanese army controlled the whole coast and much of the interior of China, and Chiang Kai-shek's armies, despite American aid, seemed powerless to resist them. It seemed only a matter of time before the Japanese would extend their conquest into the French, British and Dutch possessions to the south.

While most Burmans shared the goal of a free and independent Burma, they differed in the tactics to be used to that end. Some felt safer contesting the devil they knew within the limits allowed by the Government of Burma Act and saw in the Japanese threat an opportunity to press their demands for home rule. In this camp were communists such as Thakin Soe, Ba Hein, 'Tetpongyi' Thein Pe Myint and Aung San's brother-in-law, Than Tun, who dismissed Japan's proffered utopia of a 'Greater East Asia Co-Prosperity Sphere' as a euphemism for continued foreign rule under new masters and believed they should support Britain in its efforts to defeat 'the fascists' before entering the final phase of the 'struggle against Imperialism'. Other Burmans such as Ba Maw, Ba Sein, Tun Ok and Thakin Nu looked to the Japanese for deliverance—in the full knowledge that a military caste ruled Japan, that the Japanese army had committed unspeakable atrocities in China, that Japan was in league with a like authoritarian order in Germany and Italy, and that Berlin's and Tokyo's ultimate intention was to impose their rule on the entire world.

Aung San's position, we are told, was equivocal. Aung San, among his other offices, was the CPB's first general secretary, and when, on 8 August 1940, he secretly boarded a Chinese freighter bound for the international settlement of Kulangsu at Amoy, he *intended*, we are told, to make his way to Shanghai and link up with the Chinese Communist Party, but once in Amoy, *Kempetei* (Japanese secret police) agents contacted him (and not vice versa).[37] In any event, he proceeded to Tokyo and negotiated terms with Colonel Keiji Suzuki. Suzuki would become the head of the Minami Organ, an intelligence unit of the Japanese army whose remit was to close the Burma Road[38] by fomenting rebellion in Burma.

Aung San's recruitment to the Japanese cause was an important development. Suzuki had previously taken an unauthorized initiative at some risk to his own career in promising to support a nationalist uprising with weapons, ammunition, money and military training outside of Burma that had induced the conservative, or Ba Sein–Tun Ok, faction of the Dobama Asiayone (chapter 4) to throw in their lot with the Japanese,[39] and here was the Marxist, or Kodaw Hmaing, faction joining up as well. Aung San prepared for

[37] Tatsuro, 1981: 22–3; Lintner, 1994: 35–6. Ba Maw (1968: 120, 124) states that prearrangements for Aung San to meet Japanese agents in Amoy were made in Rangoon prior to his departure and that he went to Amoy aboard a Norwegian freighter because Japanese boats in Rangoon were under surveillance. Smith (1991: 58) also maintains that Aung San shipped out of Rangoon aboard a Norwegian freighter. According to Smith, Aung San 'said he had an open brief', while 'others, including the CPB, say he was trying to contact the [Chinese Communist Party]'. Another version of the story is 'Aung San had made no previous arrangements with the Japanese, but came across them, more or less accidentally, in Indo-China and was sent to Japan for military training.' J.S. Furnivall, introduction, Nu, 1954: xxiv.
[38] The Burma Road ('that miracle of engineering which like the pyramids owed almost everything to human muscle power'—James Lunt) was built for the purpose of supplying Anglo-American aid to the Chungking Government. It was completed in March 1940 and ran from Rangoon via Mandalay and Lashio to Kunming. It is often confused with General Stilwell's Ledo Road from Assam, which joined the Burma Road where it crossed the Burma–China border.
[39] Tatsuro, 1981: 21.

circulation among the Imperial (Japanese) Army's Supreme Command his 'Blueprint for a Free Burma' that famously envisaged bringing Burma into Japan's Co-Prosperity Sphere.[40] Suzuki reciprocated with a 'Plan for Burma's Independence', formally adopted as imperial general headquarters policy on 3 February 1941, whereby Japan pledged to recognize 'the Provisional Government of independent Burma' as soon as the 'revolutionary forces' secured the Tenasserim districts.[41]

After getting what he wanted, Aung San returned to Rangoon disguised as a Chinese seaman to raise the vanguard of what was to become the Burma Independence Army (BIA). By March, he was back in Tokyo, and military training began in April on Hainan Island, then held by the Japanese. All the levies save one, who was already in Japan, were smuggled out of Burma aboard Japanese vessels. The last batch to reach Hainan included Shu Maung (later to be named Ne Win). There is no record of the training they received, but Dr Maung Maung's description of his experience at the military academy in Mingladon four and a half years later affords us a likely picture:

> Training was tough; discipline was strict: punishments, the most common of which was face-slapping, were severe. . . . Maung Myint, a short man . . . was quick to slap faces. Most of us were taller than he, and he would have to jump to reach us. Often we would help him by stooping to offer our cheeks. He changed his tactics later and made us . . . slap each other. I wore glasses and had to take them off for this treatment. When we meet today, fellow cadets of those days, we often remember the experience . . . even with some nostalgia.[42]

Burman nationalism has beatified these young levies as the 'Thirty Comrades', but relations between them were not as harmonious as the name suggests:

> Frictions soon arose between the original group and the late-comers. According to Bo Kyaw Zaw: 'Aung San and Ne Win

---

[40] U Maung Maung (1989: 27) gives the impression that the author of the Blueprint was Suzuki, but Smith (1991: 59) suggests that it was drawn up at Suzuki's suggestion.
[41] U Maung Maung, 1989: 27.
[42] Dr Maung Maung, 1974: 39–40.

quarrelled quite often . . . Aung San was always very straightforward; Ne Win much more cunning and calculating. But Aung San's main objection to Ne Win was his immoral character. He was a gambler and a womaniser, which the strict moralist Aung San—and the rest of us as well—despised. But for the sake of unity, we kept together as much [as] we could.'[43]

Whatever their internal differences, the Comrades composed them sufficiently to present a united front to their patriotic following,[44] and on the eve of the Japanese invasion, we find them in Bangkok drinking their common blood from a silver bowl, while pledging oaths of enduring loyalty to each other and their cause.[45] The seriousness of the occasion demanded *noms de guerre*. Aung San became Bo Teza (Commander Fire); Tun Shein, Bo Yan Naing (Commander Vanquisher); Hla Pe, Bo Let Ya (Commander Reliable, lit. Right-Hand Man); Aung Than, Bo Setkya (Commander of the Flying Weapon[46]); Shu Maung, Bo Ne Win (Commander Sun's Brilliance). Tun Ok took a Japanese name.[47]

Suzuki's Plan for Burma's Independence provided for pre-invasion airdrops of Japanese-trained 'patriots' and ordnance to a force in Burma that, in the spirit of the times, was known as the Underground, which was to organize a national uprising fixed for June 1941. But the date set and the need to smuggle the patriots out of Burma in twos and threes precluded any possibility of carrying through with these promises. Nor did the Underground amount to more than half a dozen or so cells in Rangoon. Nor is it likely that the Japanese wanted a nationalist government already in place when they invaded Burma, and, in any case, whatever the original intention, the decision to attack Pearl Harbor overrode it.[48] Thus, no

---

[43] Lintner, 1994: 36. 'Thirty Comrade' Bo Kyaw Zaw was one of the leading commanders of the BIA and, later, the Burma Army. He joined the CPB in 1944 but took no role in its activities. In 1956, Ne Win accused him of leaking secrets to the CPB and dismissed him from the army. He later rejoined the CPB and was a member of its central committee and its vice-chief of general staff until 1989, when the CPB collapsed.

[44] U Maung Maung, 1989: 28.

[45] Tinker, 1959: 8; Smith, 1991: 59.

[46] According to Tinker, 1959: 8. A rival view derives the name from Setkyar Min; hence Commander King Setkyar.

[47] Ibid.: 8; Lintner, 1994: 38; conversation with Nyunt Aung, 12 September 1999.

[48] The Minami Organ's activities might alert the Americans. U Maung Maung, 1989: 29.

force of trained, armed partisans rose to join the 300 or so men[49] of the embryonic BIA[50] when they marched into the Tenasserim behind the 55th Division of Lieutenant General Iida Shojiro's 15th Imperial Japanese Army. Instead, the BIA

> recruited as they went and were joined . . . by large numbers of rogues and ne'er-do-wells. . . . As the British withdrew, thousands of miscreants were released from the gaols. These flocked to the standard of the BIA. The term BIA suggests an army. In reality it was little more than a horde of undisciplined riff-raff. Many Burmese joined the BIA or started to call themselves Thakins because it gave them power, others because they hoped thereby to protect themselves and their property, others because they were out for loot and saw an opportunity of looting under a cloak of legality.[51]

They turned on everyone suspected of British sympathies.

> After the Deputy Commissioner evacuated Myaungmya on March 1, a self-appointed committee of three young Burmans, all in their early twenties, took over the administration. Their first action was a trifle unfortunate. They released over a thousand criminals from the gaol, saying that they could neither feed them nor take responsibility for them. Almost at once Burmese criminal elements

---

[49] McEnery, 1990: 16. Lintner (1994: 38) estimates the number at 2300, and Běcka (1983: 76) claims it was 3776. Whatever the number, only the Minami Organ members and participating Thirty Comrades were trained soldiers. The rest were merely men bearing arms.

[50] They were divided into six columns commanded by Suzuki. Aung San was his chief of staff.

[51] Morrison, 1947: 68–9. Morrison's 'little more than a horde of undisciplined riff-raff' is confirmed by Dr Maung Maung, Aung San's aide from March 1942, who describes it as a 'rabble army with a minimum of military training'. See 'On the March with Aung San', in Dr Maung Maung (ed.), 1962: 59. The training that this 'army' received before the first of its 'soldiers' accompanied the Japanese to Victory Point on 31 December 1941 and the bulk of them to Moulmein on 20 January is evident also from Běcka's chronology (1983: 76): On 25 December, the decision is taken to raise troops for a volunteer Burmese Army. On 28 December, Colonel Suzuki and Minami Kikan members officially establish the BIA, consisting of Japanese officers, some of the Thirty Comrades and about 200 Thais. On 31 December, the BIA numbers 3776 men, chiefly Thais of Burmese descent.

started looting houses and property belonging to Karens, Chinese and Indians. On March 5 an advance detachment of the BIA arrived from Wakema, about twenty-five Burmans armed with *dahs*, led by a yellow-robed Buddhist monk carrying a *dah* and a double-barrelled shot-gun. The main body of the BIA arrived the following day . . .

Tension rose at once. The Burmans painted their slogans and emblems on all the government buildings, collected all the police and other arms which had been left for the protection of the town, and began to collect money for the BIA. They confiscated money from government servants, who had been given six months' pay in advance when the British left. They insisted on all notes being stamped and would not permit an individual to keep more than 200 rupees. They made a lot of money by the forced sale of paper flags bearing the peacock flag which had to be displayed outside houses. In fact the opportunities for personal gain for a member of the BIA were almost unlimited. They also started to try and recover all arms in the district and to round up ex-soldiers of the British Army. All the latter, of course, were Karens. The Karens became thoroughly frightened. The Karen quarters were searched for arms, during which the Burmans helped themselves to anything they fancied. Two Karens were bayoneted in public in front of the BIA headquarters, one allegedly for rape, one for theft, and the bodies then hacked into small pieces. Under the circumstances it was hardly surprising that Karen villagers who did have arms did not surrender them.[52]

The BIA unit sent to subjugate the Karens in Papun imprisoned then massacred the elders, looted and incinerated the villages and molested the women. The BIA unit occupying Kadaingti announced that the Japanese had licensed them to kill Christians and required the Christians to pay homage to some Buddhist monks in their party. By the end of May, there was communal war throughout Salween District.

Similarly in the Delta, where most of the plains Karens were concentrated. The BIA rabble garrisoning Myaungmya went to the Roman Catholic Mission compound and

[52] Morrison, 1947: 186–7.

proceeded to massacre 152 men, women and children in cold blood . . . Father Blasius, the Karen priest in charge, was sick in the clergy-house. The Burmans set fire to the house and burned him and the two men who were looking after him. They then burned down the church, first removing the surplices and chalice. At the orphanage another Karen priest, Father Pascal, came out on to the veranda and said there were only girls inside. The Burmans shot him in the stomach. The girls took refuge upstairs. The Burmans shot up through the ceiling [and w]hen certain [that] there were no armed men upstairs . . . went up and cut down the girls with *dahs*. Another Karen priest, Father Gaspar, was killed from behind with an axe. Four Karen lay sisters were killed. The great majority of the girls were cut down inside the mission compound, some on the road outside. The youngest victim was a baby of six months. Only about half a dozen children escaped. The remaining buildings were then razed to the ground . . . [T]hese hysterical Burmans . . . [then] went in a mass to the . . . Karen quarter . . . on the other side of the town. Here they killed another fifty-two people, all Karens, men, women and children . . . A few days later forty-seven Karen men were taken out [of gaol] and bayoneted to death.[53]

Aung San later managed a reconciliation with some Karen leaders, but the bloodletting was not forgotten, as events would prove.

Other minorities also suffered the BIA's special kind of 'patriotic' zeal:

There was [an] incident in the Shan State which was . . . nearly as damaging to the popularity of the BIA. One young officer, leading a force of one hundred men, went on a spree through the State. The forces looted and plundered. In Hsipaw, they broke into the palace of the chief, helping themselves freely to what valuable things they could find. The officer then mounted the throne and cursed the 'feudal lord' of the palace in pithy language. . . . In Lashio they shot cows in the market-place for meat.[54]

The BIA units that preceded the Japanese army into Myitkyina demanded the villagers' arms, looted them and, abducting the girls,

53 Ibid.: 188–9.
54 Dr Maung Maung, 1969: 122.

raped and killed them.[55] The support that the Shan and Kachin leaders later gave to Aung San did not erase these memories in their wider communities.

Such was the ensuing chaos that the Japanese, whose interest post-conquest was to maintain rather than undermine social order, disbanded the BIA in July 1942 and replaced it the following month with the Burma Defence Army (BDA), laced with Japanese officers and NCOs. Although the BDA's titular commander was Aung San, its uniforms were identical to those worn in the Japanese Army, the drill was Japanese, the words of command were Japanese, and the officers led with swords outstretched.

Burman nationalists today describe the BIA's excesses as 'teething problems' in the transition to a national army, and, rather than recognize that their leaders showed a spectacular lack of judgement in trusting the Minami Organ, they have enshrined Suzuki in historical memory as a Lawrence of Burma whose fierce attachment to the ideal of Burma's independence led him to collude with them against his superiors. But Suzuki's promise to recognize 'the Provisional Government of independent Burma' as soon as the 'revolutionary forces' secured the Tenasserim districts was not honoured. Instead, the Japanese established a military administration.[56] Suzuki then encouraged his nationalist followers to believe that recognition of their provisional government depended on whether they reached Rangoon before the Japanese[57]—and they did. But as soon as the Japanese arrived the military administration was extended to Rangoon. Suzuki then created the *Baho Asoya* (central government), headed by Tun Ok. Real power, however, remained with the Japanese. Nor was the independence proclaimed on 1 August 1943, when the BDA was renamed the Burma National Army (BNA) and Dr Ba Maw was declared *adipati* (great lord or prime minister) and

[55] The Kachins were also beastly to the Burmans. A correspondent (who has requested anonymity) remembers capturing a Japanese rifle in March 1942, before the BIA units reached Kachinland. 'I examined the rifle with much interest, reaching the conclusion that it was greatly inferior to our Lee Enfield. A Kachin recently arrived in Lower Burma asked me if he could test the weapon. I handed it to him. He loaded and lay down, seeking a target. It happened that a Burman, not armed or in uniform, ran across the fields at a range of about 200 yards, and before I realised what was about to happen, the Kachin fired and felled him. He handed the rifle to me, saying, "An excellent weapon, sir. Very accurate!"' Tucker, 2000: 39, fn 10.
[56] U Maung Maung, 1989: 39.
[57] Ibid.

Bogyoke (major-general) Aung San the minister of war, anything but a charade, as the young nationalists soon discovered. Independence was in fact a policy decided upon by the Japanese to rally diminishing Burman support and to encourage Indians disaffected with the British to support Subhas Chandra Bose's *Azad Hind* (free India) movement and his Indian National Army (INA).

After British forces retreated to India, most hill soldiers of the old Burma Rifles battalions faded into their jungle villages, each with his rifle, 50 rounds of ammunition, three months' pay and orders to await reconquest. Loyalty to the British was a matter of pride for them. The Burmans' behaviour, moreover, had intensified their loathing of nationalists. They would form the backbone of the real resistance, which grew in strength as the Japanese occupation continued.[58] A few gallant British officers like Hugh Seagrim[59] stayed with them. A small force of Chin Levies under British officers held out in Tiddim until detachments of 17 Division reached them.

Seven battalions of Burma hillmen, Gurkhas and Indians did reach Manipur as fighting units[60] and were there reorganized and assigned new duties. Experienced soldiers like Naw Seng and N Chyaw Tang[61] were sent back to their native hills to help their British officers raise the irregular hit-and-run Northern Kachin Levies (NKL). Chyahkyi Hting Nan[62] joined the Kachin Rangers, irregulars led by American officers. Shan Lone went to a Special Operations Executive (SOE) Force 136 unit in the hills above Sinlum Kaba. Karens like Bert Butler, Kyau Thu, Ba Chit, Aung Bwe and Torrey were sent to assist the NKL, while other Karens like Kan Choke and Ba Gyaw were dropped into the Karen Hills to join Seagrim. Hill people were also used as interpreters and guides to long-range penetration (LRP) expeditions. They all made significant contributions to expelling the Japanese.

The Kachins impeded Japanese advance beyond Myitkyina by destroying all the bridges. Ian Fellowes-Gordon, who commanded one of the NKL companies, has paid this tribute to their effort:

[58] Slim, 1956: 113.
[59] Morrison, 1947.
[60] 2nd Burma Rifles, a pre-war battalion, and six battalions of the Burma Regiment, newly mustered from Burma Frontier Force and the Burma Military Police.
[61] Tucker, 2000: 61, 78–80, 87, 90, 96–8, 102, 127, 165, 173, 206, fn 3, 243, 349.
[62] Ibid.: 164–5.

[I]n 1942 it seemed a solitary stroke of Allied good fortune that these hardy and aggressively pro-British people should have chosen to live in the extreme north of Burma. Had they . . . been domiciled in the south, leaving the top end of the country as a home for Shans and others, the Japanese would have taken the whole of it immediately. There would be no question of any road from Assam, cutting across north Burma to supply China; little chance of a successful airborne invasion of a sort the Chindits would some day be doing, not in a country which the Japanese had been permitted to consolidate.[63]

Had the Japanese positioned their air bases north of Myitkyina, they might have mastered their 'China incident' (Chiang Kai-shek's army holed up in Chungking), for the only means of supplying Chiang after the closure of the Burma Road was over 'the hump', an air route that, in the event, was beyond range of their Zeros. Chiang's forces obliged them to anchor men and arms in China that might have been deployed elsewhere. Hence, it may be argued, the Kachin resistance was indispensable to Allied victory in the wider war. One did not have to accept Stilwell's dream of a new Chinese Army under his command driving back the invaders and ultimately striking at Japan itself to understand its importance.

The Anglo-American combined chiefs of staff decided over Mountbatten's head to overwhelm by superiority of numbers 18 Japanese Division impeding the construction of the new road to China, and, in October 1943, two Chinese divisions and a tank group trained in India began their advance from Ledo into the Hukawng Valley. Supplying them was the No. 1 Air Commando of the 10th United States Army Air Force. A third Chinese division and an American LRP regiment, known to history as 'Merrill's Marauders', followed. On 27 December 1943, Mars Force took Shingbwiyang. As the main Chinese–American force, aided by Kachin Rangers and the wider Kachin community, pushed south to Maingkwan, Walawbum, Shaduzup and Kamaing, constructing the 'Ledo' road as they went, the first three of Wingate's LRP brigades, known as the Chindits, flew in to cut the Bhamo–Myitkyina road and threaten the Japanese supply dumps at Indaw and the rear of the Japanese 18 Division, then locked in battle with Mars Force. On 17 May 1944, the Marauders, aided by Kachin intelligence, took the

[63] Fellowes-Gordon, 1971: 22.

airfield at Myitkyina, and, on 3 August, combined Allied forces took Myitkyina. Meanwhile, the NKL and a battalion of Gurkhas were busy ambushing the enemy's supply convoys along the Myitkyina–Putao road, cutting his communications and denying him means of reinforcing his forward positions.

The Allies' successes on the northern front were their first victories, and they exploded the myth of Japanese invincibility.

Further successes were to follow in Arakan and at Kohima and Imphal, where the lines were clearly drawn between local tribesmen, who supported the British, and the 'Burma Traitor Army' (BNA) and 'Jifs' (Japanese Indian Forces, or INA). These local tribesmen, Slim records,

> were the gallant Nagas whose loyalty, even in the most depressing times of the invasion, had never faltered. Despite floggings, torture, execution, and the burning of their villages, they refused to aid the Japanese in any way or to betray our troops. Their active help to us was beyond value or praise. Under the leadership of devoted British political officers, some of the finest types of the Indian Civil Service, in whom they had complete confidence, they guided our columns, collected information, ambushed enemy patrols, carried our supplies, and brought in our wounded under the heaviest fire—and then, being the gentlemen they were, often refused all payment. Many a British and Indian soldier owes his life to the naked, head-hunting Naga, and no soldier of the Fourteenth Army who met them will ever think of them but with admiration and affection.[64]

The tide of war turned at the great battles of Kohima and Imphal, which began in March 1944 and lasted until November. But Burma still had to be cleared of the enemy, and it was now the Chins' moment to show their value. One of the exit routes by which the Japanese and their allies retreated led through the Chin Hills. Here the Chin Levies and their kin from the Indian side of the border, the Lushai Levies and Scouts, four Indian battalions and some V-Force detachments, crept through the rain-sodden, cloud-shrouded jungles and harried them relentlessly. The drive was on for their ancestral capitals, Falam and Haka, and, 'overjoyed at the prospect of liberating their own country . . . they took with them their families,

---

[64] Slim, 1956: 341–2.

rather like the Children of Israel trekking out of Egypt, dumping them in their own villages as they recaptured them one by one'.[65] Falam and Haka were taken on 18 and 19 October 'amid great rejoicings and reunions of the loyalist tribesmen, not a little enlivened by the free distribution of rice and stores captured from the Japanese'.[66]

By the end of November, the Levies and Scouts were at the Chindwin. Six weeks later they delivered Gangaw. They then protected the right flank of 4 Corps from ambush as it marched to the Irrawaddy. 'There is no doubt,' writes Slim,

> that the enterprise and dash of this improvised and light-hearted brigade was a very real contribution to the pursuit to the Chindwin. It had operated for six months on pack transport, supplemented by an unavoidably meagre air supply, across two hundred miles of jungle mountains, against the enemy flank and rear. Considering the paucity of its equipment and resources, it gave one of the most effective and economical examples of long-range penetration.[67]

By exploiting the enemy's existing forward positions or drawing him in to fight and starving him of supplies with broad pincer movements behind his lines, first on the northern front, then at Kohima and Imphal, then in Arakan and Upper Burma, the Allies systematically destroyed him. These were the encirclement tactics that previously the enemy had used against the Allies, but opposing the Japanese now were Karens, Kachins, Nagas, Chins and Lushais, who out-endured, outmanoeuvred and outwitted them at every turn. The Japanese were no match for these jungle-wise and fearless hill fighters; no longer the bogey supermen of the forest.

We may now resume the story of the Burman nationalist movement. While the communist followers of Thakin Soe, 'Tetpongyi' Thein Pe Myint and Ba Hein had been venomously critical of the nationalists' support of the Japanese after Germany attacked the Soviet Union, the first *firm* indication of disenchantment within the wider ranks of the nationalist movement was a signal the British received from

[65] Ibid.: 350–60.
[66] Ibid.: 364.
[67] Ibid.

Major Seagrim in November 1943, soon after he established wireless communication with India.[68] Some of the younger nationalists, advised Seagrim, were resolved upon revolt, but just how resolved is unclear. It is possible that nothing more would have been heard from them had the Japanese won at Imphal, for November 1943 was also the month in which the Assembly of the Greater East Asian Nations convened in Tokyo, described by Dr Ba Maw as 'the first visual manifestation of the new spirit in Asia, the spirit of Bandung as it was called twelve years later when it was reincarnated at the Bandung conference of the Afro-Asian nations'.[69]

As 1943 passed into 1944, however, the nationalists had more than conjectural grounds for wondering if they had backed a loser. Victory in the West was no longer assured. Zhukov's wholesale destruction of *Panzer* at the Kursk bulge and the Sicily landings were in July 1943. The Italians capitulated two months later, and the Allies landed in Normandy the following June. The revolt of the Indian masses against British rule, which had seemed so imminent in 1942 when the Raj was mocked as a toothless lion, had failed to materialize. Rather, there was a steady strengthening of Indian, British, Chinese, American, Gurkha, West African, East African, Anglo-Burman, Kachin, Naga, Chin, Lushai and Karen forces along the Indian border and elsewhere. Instead of overrunning Kohima

---

[68] Minute, SAC Meeting, 6 September 1945 (IOR: R/8/20); Tinker (ed.), 1984, vol. I, item 262: 439–40. It has been suggested that PRO HS 7/104 shows that the nationalists communicated their intention to turn against the Japanese 16 months before Seagrim's signal, but this document merely states in pertinent part: 'In July 1942, two members of the [nationalist] party came out to India professing disillusionment on the score of Japanese promises of independence for Burma. Just why they were so sure of this alleged double crossing by the enemy is not quite clear but it resulted in their being somewhat suspect on their arrival.' The two unidentified nationalists may have been communists, perhaps Thakin Soe and 'Tetpongyi' Thein Pe Myint themselves. See Nu, 1954: 21, 31. Certainly, '[n]o national leader of standing was willing to lead such a revolt . . . Aung San . . . from 1942 until late in 1944 [was] impervious to any mention of an anti-Japanese revolt.' U Maung Maung, 1989: 118, 125. See also Tatsuro, 1981: 204 ('[I]n March 1944 . . . the anti-Japanese young officers scheduled an uprising for 22nd June. . . . At this time, Aung San had not yet decided on rising up against the Japanese Army') and Ba Maw, 1968: 388, pointing out that Aung Sun opposed tempering the language of a statement issued by the *adipati*'s government on 1 February 1945 dedicating itself 'unconditionally to . . . defending [Burma's] independence against the Anglo-American enemies in the closest unity with Nippon and other East Asiatic nations'.

[69] Ba Maw, 1968: 339.

and Imphal, the three crack Japanese divisions assigned that task were all but annihilated. Nor had the Japanese destroyed Chiang, whose reinforced armies now were pouring into Burma from Yunnan with a spirit and confidence new to them, while sea and airborne American forces moved inexorably across the Pacific ever nearer to Japan itself. It is inconceivable that the nationalists were indifferent to these realities.

At a meeting in Pegu in August 1944 the leaders of the CPB, the BNA (Aung San, Ne Win and Let Ya) and the (socialist) Peoples Revolutionary Party (Ba Swe, Kyaw Nyein and Chit) agreed to suspend their ideological differences and collaborate as the Anti-Fascist Organization (AFO), soon to be renamed the Anti-Fascist People's Freedom League (AFPFL). Still, no definitive decision to revolt was communicated to the Allies until early March 1945,[70] by when the Allies were already masters of Upper Burma north of a line from Yenangyaung to Pyawbwe and gathering for the march down the rail line and the Prome roads to Rangoon. No one now believed even in the possibility of the Greater East Asia Co-Prosperity Sphere, yet, we are told, fear of prosecution for treason, which carried the death penalty, played no part in the nationalists' decision, that patriotism alone overcame their doubts:

> [W]e had no alternative . . . as true patriots of our land and as lovers of Justice. . . . [W]e [acted] with our eyes open . . . having no mistake about the possible music and carrying no spirit of bargain or opportunism whatsoever in our action. We got no promises from the Allied Forces nor did we ask for any. . . . We fight on their side . . . because we believe they are heading towards a new world of freedom and peace . . . in which our country can have and maintain her freedom in security.[71]

But the nationalists *always* had the alternative of not supporting the Japanese, and, although their reconstructions of history ignore the fact, *other* Burmans, ex-Burma Rifles men and levies raised in the Chindwin country, backed the British. Indeed, a full month *before* the nationalists discovered afresh the Allies' 'new world of freedom and peace' and committed the BNA to the Allied cause, SOE teams were already supplying them with arms. Perhaps the moment of

[70] Slim, 1956: 484.
[71] Aung San, 1946: 41–2. Quoted in Trager (ed.), 1971: 21.

decision came when Aung San received orders, also in early March, to deploy the BNA's seven battalions to assist the crumbling Japanese forces in their hour of greatest need.

On 17 March, BNA troops about to leave Rangoon for the field paraded on the maidan now known as Resistance Park. Japanese fighter planes flew over and dipped their wings, and rousing martial music rose from Japanese army bands, as the Burman soldiers passed the reviewing stand, where Prime Minister Ba Maw, Deputy Prime Minister Thakin Mya, Major-General Aung San, the Commander-in-Chief of Japanese Allied Forces in Burma, Lieutenant General Kimura Heitaro, and other senior Japanese officers took the salute. General Kimura's words are not recorded. Ba Maw declared that the BNA was going into battle 'to repay the debt of history', and Aung San's 'speech was on the lines that the time had come to go out and fight; he himself would lead; danger, hardship and perhaps death lay ahead, but they would all go forward together'.[72] The *Bogyoke*, however, delicately omitted to identify the enemy. Collis, perhaps the most devout apologist for the nationalist cause of all the British who served in Burma, notes: '[It was] a great send-off; the Japanese were jubilant that the Burm[ans] were so loyal to them. Ba Maw smiled; he was in the secret. It was one of those tricks so much to Burm[an] taste.'[73] The BNA marched north out of Rangoon and into the jungle and, on 27 March, began attacking isolated Japanese units.

Meanwhile, after crossing the Irrawaddy in January 1945, Slim's Fourteenth Army launched separate attacks, one on Mandalay, the other, masked by the attack on Mandalay, a brilliant double thrust down the Myittha valley at the heart of the Japanese army in Meiktila. After these towns fell, the race to reach Rangoon before the advent of the monsoon was on. Messervy (4 Corps) and Stopford (33 Corps) swept aside Japanese resistance at Pwebwe, Thazi, Chauk, Letse, Pyinmana and Yenangyaung, and were storming south. To the east of 4 Corps, in the Shan hills, were the Japanese 15th and 53rd Divisions and the fugitive survivals of their 15th Army, whose orders were to regroup in defensive positions south of the British advance. Messervy's immediate task was to block their escape by seizing Toungoo, where the Loikaw–Mawchi road from Taunggyi joined the

[72] McEnery, 1990: 22; Dr Maung Maung, 1974: 57.
[73] Collis, 1956: 235. However, Ba Maw (1968: 388) dismisses this colourful imputation as 'ridiculous propaganda' at odds with an 'unbroken background of statements made during all the war years'.

Rangoon road. Straddling the route south were some 12,000 Karen Levies, raised, trained or led by Tulloch, Ba Gyaw, Peacock, Saw Butler, Turrall, Kan Choke, Howell and Critchley and other officers and NCOs and over 200 other ex-Burma Rifles Karens who had dropped into the Karen Hills after the Japanese killed Seagrim in September 1944. Slim:

> Kimura was driving his men as hard as Mersservy and I were driving ours. He had ordered all his troops in the Shan Hills to get to Toungoo with sleepless speed [and] it looked as if they might beat us to it. But I still had a shot in my locker for them. . . . [T]heir way led them through the country of the Karens, a race which had remained staunchly loyal to us even in the blackest days of Japanese occupation, and had suffered accordingly. . . . It was not at all difficult to get the Karens to rise against the hated Japanese; the problem was to restrain them from rising too soon. But now the time had come, and I gave the word, 'Up the Karens!' Japanese, driving hard through the night down jungle roads for Toungoo, ran into ambush after ambush; bridges were blown ahead of them, their foraging parties massacred, their sentries stalked, their staff cars shot up. Air-strikes, directed by British officers, watching from the ground the fall of each stick of bombs, inflicted great damage. The galled Japanese fought their way slowly forward, losing men and vehicles, until about Mawchi, fifty miles east of Toungoo, they were held up for several days by road-blocks, demolitions, and ambuscades. They lost the race for Toungoo.[74]

4 Corps pushed on and was locked in battle for Pegu (113 miles south of Toungoo), when the Japanese counter-attacked in an effort to cut their communications. Again, the Karens 'clung to the Japanese coat-tails' (Slim).

Pegu was taken in fierce, hand-to-hand fighting; not, however, before the Japanese garrisoning Rangoon escaped across the Sittang in advance of an air and seaborne assault on the city. After heavy air bombing of phantom defences and the drop of a Gurkha parachute brigade at Elephant Point, an RAF pilot overflying the capital spotted a message written by Allied prisoners in large white letters on the roof of Rangoon Jail: 'JAPS GONE. EXDIGITATE.'[75] The message was

---

[74] Slim, 1956: 499–500.
[75] Ibid.: 506. Variants of the message reported by different authorities are, 'Japs gone. Exdigitate!', 'Japs gone. Extract digit!' and 'Japs gone. Extract finger!'

soon confirmed by another pilot, who landed his reconnaissance Mosquito at Mingaladon and walked into town, and, on 3 May, the advance units of a brigade of 26 Division under Major Chambers entered the city to the unrestrained cheering of the population, who turned out in the rain in their thousands to greet them.

British forces had resumed dominion over 80 per cent of Burma's population in just over four months. Still, the enemy remained scattered along the Irrawaddy (15,000, mostly on the west bank) and in the Shan uplands east of Meiktila (6000), and they had to be prevented from joining the much larger and still organized enemy forces concentrated on the Sittang's east bank opposite Nyaunglebin (25,000) and along the Martaban Gulf coast (24,000). Slim thus had interconnected problems, one tactical, the other political: how to expel the remaining Japanese with minimum further cost, and how best to deal with Aung San.

The difficulties confronting Slim were immense. 'With the vast majority of the Burmese the trouble was that they expected us to bring them an immediate return to the carefree conditions of happy Burma before the war. This, alas, we could not do at once.'[76] Retreating British and Japanese armies had destroyed blue water port facilities, brown water port facilities, airports, aircraft, railways, rolling stock, roads, bridges, power stations and water supply systems. Many areas of the country were already degenerating into dacoity. Slim's description of these difficulties conveys the impression that they, rather than any local clamour for independence, determined the crucial decisions imparted to the *Bogyoke* when the two men met in May 1945. Slim has left us a record of that meeting. As Burman nationalists tailor it to suit their cloth,[77] I reproduce it here in full:

> [T]he agents of Force 136 offered Aung San on the 21st April [1945] a safe conduct to my headquarters and my promise that, whether we came to an understanding or not, I would return him

[76] Ibid.: 514.
[77] For example, Dr Maung Maung (ed.), 1962: 83–5 omits *without indicating omissions* the references to (1) the ability of Slim's forces to expel the Japanese from Burma without the BNA's help; (2) the murder allegation against Aung San; (3) Aung San's treason; (4) Aung San's inability to supply and pay his men; (5) Aung San's recognition of HMG as the only government of Burma; (6) the involvement of many of the BNA in dacoity; and (7) the BNA's subordination to British Army command as the basis of any agreement reached between Slim and Aung San.

unharmed to his own people. He hesitated until the 15th May, but on that day it was reported to me that he and a staff officer had crossed the Irrawaddy at Allanmyo, and were asking to meet me. I sent an aircraft, which flew them to my headquarters at Meiktila the next day.

The arrival of Aung San, dressed in the near Japanese uniform of a Major-General, complete with sword, startled one or two of my staff who had not been warned of his coming. However, he behaved with the utmost courtesy, and so, I hope, did we. He was a short, well-built, active man in early middle age, neat and soldierly in appearance, with regular Burmese features in a face that could be an impassive mask or light up with intelligence and humour. I found he spoke good English, learnt in his school and university days, and he was accompanied by a staff officer who spoke it perfectly, as well he might, if it were true as I was told that his father had been a senior British official who had married a Burmese lady.

At our first interview, Aung San began to take rather a high hand. He was, he said, the representative of the Provisional Government of Burma, which had been set up by the people of Burma through the Anti-Fascist People's Freedom League. It was under this Provisional Government that he and his National Army served and from whom they took their orders. He was an Allied commander, who was prepared to co-operate with me, and he demanded the status of an Allied and not subordinate commander. I told him that I had no idea what his Anti-Fascist People's Freedom League was or represented. As far as I and the rest of the world were concerned, there was only one Government of Burma and that was His Majesty's, now acting through the Supreme Commander, South-East Asia. I pointed out that he was in no position to take the line he had. I did not need his forces; I was destroying the Japanese quite nicely without their help, and could continue to do so. I would accept his co-operation and that of his army only on the clear understanding that it implied no recognition of any provisional government. He would be a subordinate commander, who would accept my orders and see that his officers and men also obeyed them and those of any British commander under whom I placed them. He showed disappointment at this, and repeated his demand to be treated as an Allied commander.

I admired his boldness and told him so. 'But,' I said, 'apart from the fact that you, a British subject, have fought against the British Government, I have here in this headquarters people who tell me that there is a well substantiated case of civil murder, complete with witnesses, against you.[78] I have been urged to place you on trial for that. You have nothing in writing, only a verbal promise at second-hand, that I would return you to your friends. Don't you think you are taking considerable risks in coming here and adopting this attitude?'

'No,' he replied, shortly.

'Why not?'

'Because you are a *British* officer,' he answered. I had to confess that he scored heavily—and what was more I believe he meant it. At any rate he had come out on my word alone. I laughed and asked him if he felt like that about the British, why had he been so keen to get rid of us? He said it was not that he disliked the British, but he did not want British or Japanese or any other foreigners to rule his country. I told him I could well understand that attitude, but it was not for us soldiers to discuss the future government of Burma. The British Government had announced its intention to grant self-government to Burma within the British Commonwealth, and we had better limit our discussion to the best method of throwing the Japanese out of the country as the next step towards self-government.

We resumed in good temper, and I asked him to give me the strengths and present dispositions of his forces. This he was either unwilling or unable to do—I thought a bit of both. I pressed him in this, but could get nothing definite. I had the impression that he was not too sure what his forces were, where they were, or what exactly some of them were doing. I said I had had reports that there were many bands of armed Burmans roaming about, claiming to belong to his army, who were no better than dacoits preying on their own countrymen. Rather to my surprise, he agreed and said he hoped we would both of us deal severely with these men, who were no troops of his. He went on to say that, at first, he had hoped the Japanese would give real independence to Burma. When he found they would not, but were tightening the bonds on his people, he had, relying on our promises, turned to

---

[78] He murdered the headman of a village in Thaton District.

us as a better hope. 'Go on, Aung San,' I said. 'You only come to us because you see we are winning!'

'It wouldn't be much good coming to you if you weren't, would it?' he replied, simply.

I could not question the truth of this. I felt he had scored again, and I liked his honesty. In fact, I was beginning to like Aung San.

I told him that after the war we should revive the old regular Burma Army, under British officers, on the basis of the Burma Rifles battalions which still existed, and that there would then be no place for any other army—his would have to go. He at once pressed that his forces should be incorporated in the new army as units. This was obviously not altogether the solicitude of a general for his men, but the desire of a politician to retain personal power in post-war Burma. I answered that I thought it most unlikely that the Burmese Government would accept them as units, but that I saw no reason why they should not, subject to a check of their records, be enlisted as individuals on the same terms as other recruits. He persisted in pressing for incorporation as units, but I held out no hopes of this. He then asked me if I would now supply and pay his units in the field? He was obviously finding this beyond his powers, and I knew that, if we did not accept the responsibility, his men would be reduced, as many were already, to living by exactions from the people—as dacoits in fact. I said I would not consider paying or supplying his troops unless he and they were completely under my orders. In our final talk, he had begun to take a more realistic view of his position, but he still would not definitely commit himself. Before he accepted the role of a subordinate commander, he said, he must consult with his 'Government', and he asked to be returned, suggesting that he should meet me again in about a week's time. I agreed, warned him of the consequences of refusing terms which, in view of his past, were most generous, shook hands, and sent him off by air again.

I was impressed by Aung San. He was not the ambitious, unscrupulous guerrilla leader I had expected. He was certainly ambitious and meant to secure for himself a dominant position in post-war Burma, but I judged him to be a genuine patriot and a well-balanced realist—characters which are not always combined. His experience with the Japanese had put his views on the British into a truer perspective. He was ready himself to co-operate with us in the liberation and restoration of Burma and, I thought, probably to go on co-operating after that had been accomplished.

The greatest impression he made on me was one of honesty. He was not free with glib assurances and he hesitated to commit himself, but I had the idea that if he agreed to do something he would keep his word. I could do business with Aung San.[79]

The important detail in this record is Aung San 'had come out on [Slim's] word alone'. Slim was implementing instructions from Mountbatten to encourage BNA *military* cooperation without offering them any *political* commitment.[80] But if, as Slim's record of his meeting with Aung San suggests, his thoughts were already half on what would happen *after* the conclusion of hostilities, Aung San must have struck him as a godsend. The important detail to note in respect of Aung San is that he wanted to retain his army as a discrete force under his own command. He was anticipating the revival of the *tats* or private armies that had featured so prominently in pre-war Burman politics. The record is also an admission that the BNA changed sides only *after* they concluded that Japanese defeat was certain.

Despite rough handling by 33 Corps, considerable numbers of Sakurai's 28th Army stranded along the Irrawaddy managed to reach cover in the Pegu Yoma, while the remnants of the Japanese 15, 18, 53 and 56 Divisions remained east of Meiktila. On 3 July, they all made a dash to join the rest of Kimura's forces east of the Sittang. They had no armour and only a few light guns and hand weapons. In addition to the 32,000 or more troops of a reinforced 4 Corps poised along a 150-mile, north–south front to intercept them, were five battalions (2000 men) of the BNA—known now as the Patriotic Burmese Forces (PBF)[81]—who, in the ensuing Battle of the Break-Out, accounted for 600 or 700 Japanese kills.[82] Slim says of their role: 'They proved definitely useful in gaining information and in dealing drastically with small parties of Japanese.'[83] Others were less

---

[79] Slim, 1956: 516–19.
[80] Collis, 1956: 238.
[81] The original name was Patriot Burmese Forces. The choice was Slim's. It excited derision from Burmese who had supported the Allies throughout the war.
[82] These are Slim's figures, repeated in Louis Mountbatten, 'Report to the Combined Chiefs of Staff by the Supreme Allied Commander, South-East Asia, 1943–45' (1951). Also quoted in Tinker, 1959: 15, and McEnery, 1990: 25, fn 7. 'BNA leaders were later to claim to have inflicted some 16,000 casualties, including over 12,000 killed and 4,000 wounded.' Smith, 1991: 61.
[83] Slim, 1956: 520.

generous. 'They did what they did best, what they had done in 1942. They eliminated the walking wounded, sick and starving'[84] and, as in 1942, were responsible for a great deal of looting. Their contribution to the Allies' victory was nugatory beside that made by the Burmese minorities. In the race for Toungoo and the Battle of the Break-Out, the Karens alone killed at least 12,500 Japanese and partly accounted for the deaths of thousands more by directing air strikes against their positions and impeding their mobility and sapping their morale through sabotage of their installations and mining their escape routes.[85]

The Battle of the Break-Out was the last major engagement of the Burma campaign. The bombs fell on Hiroshima and Nagasaki on 6 and 9 August, and, on 14 August, Japan surrendered unconditionally.

Aung San was 25 in 1940 and 30 when the war ended, which was about the average age of his closest confederates.[86] He was one among several Burmans who aspired to power after the British departed. The pace and form of the ensuing transfer of power would be determined not by merit or the candidates' practical qualifications for holding high office, but by their rival skills at generating ever more strident nationalist rhetoric, and the truth about the BIA/BDA/BNA/PBF's role in delivering Burma from foreign rule was their first casualty.[87]

The following description of the BNA's actions on *20 March* illustrates this:

> Colonel Ba Htu of the [BNA] was the first to order his troops into battle. The Japanese in Mandalay, poised and ready to fight the oncoming Allies, were broken up in confusion by Ba Htu and his brave men, and when the XIVth army and Maj. General Rees

---

[84] Conversation with Ian Fellowes-Gordon, November 1989.
[85] Morrison, 1947: 164.
[86] Compare Smith, 1991: 59 (average age of the Thirty Comrades on 28 December 1941 was 24); Dr Maung Maung, 1974: 25 (Aung San 28 in 1943; Ne Win, Let Ya and Setkya a few years older; Bo Zeya and Yan Naing a few years younger; the BNA's battalion commanders were in their early twenties).
[87] See Chao Tzang Yawnghwe, 'The Burman Military: Holding the Country Together?', in Silverstein (ed.), 1989: 93, fn 34 ('the popular belief among politicized Burmans especially up to the 1970s, was that they drove the British out single-handedly, and fought the Japanese who subsequently invaded the country').

arrived the backbone of Japanese defensive power had already been snapped.[88]

In fact, a battalion of Gurkhas stormed Mandalay Hill, which dominates the northeastern quarter of Mandalay, taking it on 11 March after two days of close, hand-to-hand combat. Three divisions of the Fourteenth Army under Rees all but completed their encirclement of the city by 12 March, only minimal Japanese forces remaining to cover the retreat of the main garrison. Rees's other battalions 'fought their way street by street through the city, suffering heavily, especially in officers, from snipers' until 15 March, by when they completely surrounded the remaining Japanese position in Fort Dufferin, which, after heavy bombardment, the Japanese evacuated overnight on 19/20 March.[89]

Even more fantastically:

Rangoon was taken by leaders of the Anti-Fascist Organization who were in the Government of Dr. Ba Maw, with the help of Burma National Army troops remaining in the area as well as those left unmolested by the Japanese through the good offices of Bo Yan Naing and Dr. Ba Maw.[90]

And:

It is probable that Burma National Army Zone 4, commanded by Major Kyaw Zaw, took Pegu, for they were pursuing the Japanese

[88] Dr Maung Maung, 1974: 22. U Maung Maung (1989: 125–6) contradicts this absurd claim. '[T]he [BNA's] North Western Command under Major Ba Htoo was lost before it could receive withdrawal orders. Aung San had delayed his decision making [to revolt] so long that when he did send his Chief of Staff, Colonel Zeyya, with military and political instructions and funds for Ba Htoo, the Japanese would not allow Zeyya to go beyond Toungoo because Meiktila had already fallen. However, Ba Htoo was a man of determination and initiative, and on his own he revolted before the British troops drew near Mandalay. As he was barred by the original plan of revolt from contacting the British, and his troops were too few to attack the main Japanese force facing the Indian 19th Divison coming south toward Mandalay, he moved his forces to the east towards the foothills of the Shan States, positioning himself astride the eastern flank of the Rangoon–Mandalay highway and railway line.'
[89] Slim, 1956: 469–70.
[90] U Maung Maung, 1989: 152, citing a report in *New Light of Burma*, 3 May 1945, p. 1, that the 'Burma Revolutionary Army' captured Rangoon. See also Trager (ed.), 1971: 21. Other Burman nationalists base the claim on the assertion that *some* BNA troops entered the city on 1 May.

as the latter retreated east out of Rangoon, and Toungoo, similarly, was probably taken by Burma National Army Zone 5.[91]

Toungoo was taken by 5 Division of 4 Corps. 'The signals of a protesting Japanese military policeman on point duty were disregarded, and the first tank went over him. Panic reigned as our tanks roamed the streets, the enemy flying in all directions, intent only on escape. They left behind them only fifty dead, so fast did the living make for the jungle.'[92] And, as we have seen, Rangoon was evacuated under pressure of the advance of the Fourteenth Army. The departing Japanese released about 600 communist prisoners who, on regaining their liberty, began calling themselves the 'Burma Revolutionary Army', then issued a proclamation stating that they had 'occupied' Rangoon and took 'the fullest responsibility for the maintenance of law and order in the city and for the safety of the citizens' lives and homes'.[93] Nothing further was heard of the 'Burma Revolutionary Army' after Major Chambers's men marched into Rangoon, until the name surfaced as the basis of the claim that the BNA had taken the city. Pegu was captured by 4 Corps.

Most astonishing of all, though, is this claim:

Books . . . by British and American authors and historians . . . say the resistance forces made a small contribution by sending in reports and falling upon small groups of Japanese stragglers . . . We on our part say we won the war, and allied effort was of small significance.[94]

We might ask ourselves why Burman nationalists have reconstructed history in this crude way. One can accept that they might have wanted to expiate the embarrassment of their allegiance to the Japanese, but it would have been better had they simply admitted that they had erred in their judgement. They were very young. Young men make mistakes. One can accept that they believed they were acting in Burma's interest, or that they felt humiliated and demeaned by British conquest, then Japanese conquest, then British re-conquest. One can even forgive them inflated views of themselves

[91] U Maung Maung, 1989: 152. See also Dr Maung Maung, 1969: 154–6.
[92] Slim, 1956: 500. See also Perrett, 1978: 227.
[93] Dr Maung Maung, 1969: 154–5.
[94] Dr Maung Maung, 1974: 75.

or a perverse unwillingness to accept reality. But I submit that they had a cold, practical motive in promoting this fantasy of their contribution to expelling the Japanese—to magnify themselves and depreciate rivals in their bid for power.[95] Hence, 55 years on, Burma celebrates 27 March, the anniversary of the day the BNA openly revolted against the Japanese, as Resistance Day, and children are schooled to believe that the BNA expelled the Japanese, as though the Fourteenth Army and its American, Chinese, Karen, Kachin, Chin, Naga, Anglo-Burman and Burman allies had not existed. This refashioning of history has undermined both Burman and the minorities' trust in the integrity of their post-colonial masters and deepened the divide between them.

The decision first to supply arms to the BNA, then to treat it as a co-belligerent provoked sharp differences of opinion in 1945. Civil Affairs Service (Burma) and General Leese, Commander-in-Chief Land Forces South-East Asia, foresaw that such a policy would exacerbate government's difficulties once restored to power. They wanted to prosecute the nationalist leaders as traitors and ordered the arms supply stopped. But Admiral Mountbatten, Supreme Allied Commander South-East Asia, fancied it was better to treat them as allies. He reasoned that he was 'running only a trifling risk . . . would himself be administering Burma for some months after the defeat of the Japanese [and], as the head of a great and victorious army and supported by a brilliant staff . . . would be able to control the

[95] Dr Maung Maung (1969: 154) provides glimpses of the hostility or indifference to the BNA in Rangoon and Henzada after the Japanese vacated those cities. 'City elders, high officials, and political leaders had to be searched out and persuaded to stand together and talk with one voice for the national interest when the British arrived. Some agreed to come in. Many were uninterested. They did not know how the BNA itself would be treated by the British; it might prejudice their careers if they were seen in the company of the revolutionary elements. Anxious thoughts among Burmese officials tended to dwell mainly on back pay, seniority in service—which they hoped the war had not affected—and whether they might be penalized for having served under the occupation government. Some took out their morning coats from the dusty boxes, cleaned them and prepared to meet the returning British bosses in proper style. They also started to practise the handshake, the smile, the words of welcome, the excuses to offer for working in the occupation government.' Then a lieutenant commanding a BNA unit that bussed into Henzada, Maung Maung visited the principal magistrate and asked him to reopen the courts (1974: 66). But the judge 'made it obvious . . . that he was only awaiting the arrival of the British, "the legal government" as he called them'.

Burm[an] forces, disarm them at leisure, win over their leaders and prevent any of their adherents from disturbing the peace'.[96] Such confidence in 1939 would not have seemed out of place. However, the age of enlightened Europeans ruling backward colonies for the benefit of the natives had ended with the retreat from Burma and the fall of Singapore. The 'great and victorious army' Mountbatten headed was, in the main, an Indian army, and it was this mainly Indian army that had defended India and recovered Burma. Britain, technically bankrupt and exhausted, had neither resources nor appetite for further foreign adventures.

It was a difficult and expensive decision—expensive above all for the Burmese, for it released a *djin* of self-serving demagogy that destroyed the possibility of an orderly reconstruction of the devastated country and a rational and just transfer of power. After the Allies retook Rangoon, Ne Win, then the BNA's commander-in-chief, broadcast to the country, ominously, that the BNA was 'not only the hope of the country but its real life and soul'.[97]

[96] Collis, 1956: 234.
[97] Donnison, 1970: 45.

4
We Burmans

AUNG SAN WAS born on 13 February 1915, the youngest of six children of U Pha, a not very successful pleader, and Daw Su, whose uncle had been decapitated for leading a resistance group against the British. His early schooling was at a Buddhist monastery, then, after staging a hunger strike to secure his mother's consent, he was sent to the National School at Yenangyaung, where his elder brother, Ba Win, was a teacher. He won the top marks in the country in examinations set by the government and was awarded a prize and scholarship. At 16 he went up to Rangoon University to read Burmese and Pali.

Daw Aung San Suu Kyi in her biography of her father offers us two observations about him very worth noting. First, fear of criticism or ridicule did not deter him from standing up for his beliefs. She cites this example from his time as an undergraduate.

> At the end of a debate in English organized by the Students' Union during his first term, Aung San rose from the floor to support the motion which had been proposed by his elder brother, that monks should not participate in politics. This was a case of conviction rather than of family solidarity. Aung San's badly accented, clumsy English and unpolished manner of delivery made his speech practically incomprehensible, raising jeers and catcalls and causing his brother some embarrassment. However, Aung San was not to be intimidated or shouted down, he continued until he had said all he wanted to say, interweaving his inadequate English with Pali words and phrases, ignoring the insults and the rude interjections to stick to Burmese.

Second,

> Aung San, whom popular opinion has often cast in the role of a completely political animal, had a deep and abiding interest in religion. As a student at Yenangyaung, the sorrow of his father's death had filled him with a desire to become a monk. Later,

towards the beginning of his university career, he apparently conceived a great admiration for an Italian Buddhist monk, U Lawkanada, and asked his mother's permission to follow the venerable *sayadaw* ('holy teacher') in his missionary work. Permission was refused, but his preoccupation with spiritual matters did not cease. Even after he had entered the world of student politics, which was to absorb him so completely, he wrote to one of his closest friends of his 'pilgrimage in quest of Truth and Perfection' and of his conscious striving after 'sincerity in thought, word, and deed'. He also expressed his concern over the 'spiritual vacuum . . . among our youth' and the fear that 'unless we brace ourselves up to withstand the tide . . . we will soon be spiritual bankrupts par excellence'.[1]

Aung San was only five years old at the time of the student sit-in on the Bahan foothill of the Shwedagon and all of 15 when the 1920s, the decade that witnessed the first real manifestation of political discontent, ended. Encouraged by the success of the GCBA-supported sit-in, the nationalists decided to open their own national college, where one of the teachers was Maung Lun—later Thakin

---

[1] Aung San Suu Kyi, 1991: 5–8. This book, originally published as a monograph by the University of Queensland in 1984, offers a personal but balanced and intelligent assessment of the author's father, who, however, died before she was old enough to remember him. Other attempts on the same subject include Dr Maung Maung (ed.), 1962, a collection of Aung San's speeches and writings and eulogistic essays by his friends and colleagues, a book seriously flawed by selective editing, and Josef Silverstein (ed.), 1993. As Professor Silverstein points out on the opening page of his introduction, 'Thus far, no official or authoritative biography of Aung San has been written and no systematic and complete collection of his speeches, writings, and papers has been published. This is not because the necessary documents do not exist or are difficult to find; indeed, through the efforts of Col. Ba Than and his successors at the Burma Defence Services Historical Research Institute (BDSHRI) in Rangoon, much of what Aung San said and wrote has been stored in its air-conditioned archives. But, although a few scholars have used some of these papers, neither the Government nor any independent agency—such as the now-defunct Burma Research Society—has sponsored or published research on Aung San. So long as the BDSHRI remains open only to government officials seeking an occasional quotation or document to bolster a particular policy, and the government in Burma does nothing to encourage indigenous and foreign scholars to use the Institute's resources, there is little likelihood that a clear and complete picture of Aung San will emerge. Nor will his full impact upon the nationalist movement and subsequent period of independence be completely understood.'

Kodaw (Exalted Holiness) Hmaing.[2] The GCBA hoped to unite various *wunthanu* (nationalist associations) led by individual *sayadaw*, but the perennial centrifugalities of Burman politics, personal rivalry and the lure of power, tore it asunder.

To ensure that Burmans would not dominate the legislative council established under the Montagu-Chelmsford reforms, 21 of its 103 seats were reserved for Europeans, Anglo-Burmans, Karens and Indians, and 24 were in the governor's gift. The council's remit ('transferred subjects') included only 'nation-building' matters touching agriculture, forests, education, health, veterinary services, public works, excise, local government and the cooperative movement, and its decisions were subject to the governor's veto. All other matters were reserved to the governor, who also controlled the purse. Although intended as an experimental step in 'the gradual development of self-governing institutions', for many in the GCBA the council was a provocation, and whether to participate in or boycott the election to it held in November 1922 was a divisive issue. Twenty-one supporters of the dyarchy (the 'twenty-oners' or 'dymen') decided to participate (a minister's monthly salary, Rs. 5000, was a small fortune), ushering in the era of the 'politics of office seeking' or 'legislature politics',[3] in which 'lawyers, skilled in the art of rules of procedure, speech-making [and] splitting legal hairs . . . shone like stars in the political sky'.[4] Division in the laity split the clergy. Some switched allegiance to a rival leader, who, in 1925, was elected president of the GCBA. There was thus a Chit

---

[2] Kodaw is a form of address reserved for royalty or monks highly reputed for their holiness. Kodaw Hmaing (1875–1968) was not royalty; he was a devout Buddhist and the author of poetic works written as pious learned commentaries (*tika*) with a political and nationalist dimension. He wrote plays under the name, Maung Lun, and would then have been addressed as Saya Lun, and, in 1921, a novel by him appeared under the pen name, Mit-sata Maung Hmaing, a name that mocked Burmans who aped British manners by using 'Mr' (Mit-sata) as a form of address, while Hmaing was the name of a rogue and womaniser, the hero of a popular Burmese novel published in 1904. Hence, Thakin Kodaw Hmaing was a donnish cock-a-snook at British rule. The pseudonym stuck after he joined the Dobama (1934) and the publication of his *Thakin Tika* (1935), Kodaw ackowledging his serious writings. See 'Literature and Nationalism in Burma', in Aung San Suu Kyi, 1995: 148–50, and entry of Thakin Ko-daw Hmaing by Anna Joan Allott in *Encyclopedia of World Literature in the 20th Century* (New York: Frederick Ungar, 1984), vol. 4, p. 429.

[3] U Maung Maung, 1989: 4.

[4] Dr Maung Maung, 1969: 12.

Hlaing GCBA and a Soe Thein GCBA, and, by the end of the decade, an U Su GCBA as well. Parties

> grew like mushrooms after the rains: the Home Rulers, the Swarajists, the People's Party, the Progressives, the Twenty-Oners, the splinters from the Twenty-Oners, the Twenty-Oners of Mandalay. All hit the high road to the legislative council, political jobs and privilege. . . . [P]olitical activity swirled round the council, the secretariat . . . Government House, the headquarters of the party—if there was any—the homes of the politicians, the hotels where the members of the legislative council were offered their inducements to cast their votes at the proper moment in the right way. A vote, just one tiny vote, how much for a vote?[5]

This early experience in 'democracy' was to have solemn implications for the future, as we shall see.

The Venerable U Ottama, the Venerable U Wisara and others concerned to preserve their race pressed ahead with Gandhian tactics of non-cooperation. They challenged the authority of local headmen, the bedrock of colonial government, and in some areas replaced them with *wunthanu* administrations. U Wisara was arrested for sedition and died in prison after a hunger strike lasting 166 days,[6] the first martyr to his cause. The authorities then arrested and imprisoned U Ottama, a further instance of disrespect for a *sayadaw* that inflamed the entire country. Still, as the 1920s drew to a close, there was more in-fighting than out-fighting, protest rather than violence, in the nationalist cause.

This changed with the appearance in 1930 of Saya San, Glorious King of Winged Creatures, awaited by the peasants since the fall of Thibaw. 'Astrologers would announce the arrival of the time and the man; there would be whispers in the villages and excitement; the pretender would appear and declare that it was he,' avows Dr Maung Maung.[7] 'Astrologically, the end of English rule in Burma was indicated,' allows Collis.[8] Saya San, born in Shwebo, Alaungpaya's capital, teacher, preacher, politician, alchemist and practitioner of indigenous medicine, fitted the messianic mould perfectly. Planting himself under a white umbrella, the traditional Buddhist symbol for

[5] Ibid.: 13–14.
[6] Maung Maung Pye, 1952: 15–16.
[7] Dr Maung Maung, 1969: 15.
[8] Collis, 1938: 277.

royalty, he ordered his credulous followers to face down the police with home-made shotguns, crossbows, swords and spears.[9] The Saya San rebellion 'was an act of deep faith and great courage, but,' concedes Dr Maung Maung, 'it was doomed to defeat from the start'.[10] A 'medieval outburst against the modern world,' notes Tinker.[11]

Saya San and his followers' trials spawned more parties, some founded by their defence lawyers. Allegiances and party names changed almost as a matter of whim. Thakin Mya organized the Peasants and Workers' Party, then called it the Burma Revolutionary Party (BRP), then the National Party and then the People's Revolutionary Party.[12] Ba Pe, one of the founders of the YMBA and a twenty-oner, campaigned in successive elections under the banner of Home Rule Party, Nationalist Party and People's Party.[13] Some belonged to two or more parties simultaneously. Everyone, of course, fought under the flag of principle. In 1927, Westminster appointed another commission to examine the possibility of further progress towards 'self-governing institutions', and, in 1930, its chairman, Sir John Simon, published his report recommending that Burma be governed separately from India, triggering another realignment of parties, the separationists arguing that the proposed change would accelerate independence, the anti-separationists that it would deny Burma the advances accorded to India.

The Government of Burma Act 1935 implemented the recommendations of the Simon Report and in 1937 Burma was separated from India. Now there was a bicameral legislature, and all 132 members of its lower house were elected, 92 in general constituencies, 12 by Karens, 11 by commercial groups, eight by Indians, three by Europeans, two by Anglo-Burmans, two by Indian trade unions and one each by Burman labour and Rangoon University. The governor initiated money bills but, in practice, assented to all bills passed by the legislature. He was assisted by a council of ministers collectively responsible to the legislature and comprising the chief minister appointed by him, three ministers appointed by the chief minister, and 10 ministers chosen by the legislature. Technically, they held office during the governor's pleasure, but they resembled

[9] Lintner, 1994: 30; Pye, 1962: 259.
[10] Dr Maung Maung, 1969: 18.
[11] Tinker, 1959: 4.
[12] Trager, 1966: 57.
[13] Ibid.: 50.

the cabinet of a self-governing dominion with plenary powers save over defence, foreign affairs and the exchequer.[14] Nevertheless, nationalists dismissed the new constitution as diversionary, and it had powerful critics among the British:

> Burmans had the numerical majority but they had no place in industry and commerce, and capitalist interests, European, Indian and Chinese, dominated economic and social life. In the legislature it was an obvious move in political tactics for Europeans to support the numerically weakest section of the nationalists, with the paradoxical result, inherent in the system of communal representation, that politicians could obtain office only on terms that prevented them from exercising power. The Burmans had the men but Europeans had the money and the influence, and the leader of the British mercantile community was popularly regarded as the uncrowned king of Burma. Thus the constitutional reforms from 1923 onwards, though purporting to be an experiment in parliamentary democracy, were in practice an education in political corruption.[15]

In the first general election held under the provisions of the 1935 Act, Ba Pe's United GCBA won nearly three times as many seats as Ba Maw (46:16), but Ba Maw, who had formed his own party to contest the election, assembled enough support from other parties to form a government. The leading players in this final phase of prewar office-seeking were Ba Maw, U Pu, U Saw and Paw Tun.

Ba Maw (b. 1893), a Christian, widely believed to be part Armenian, had a BA degree from Cambridge and a PhD from the University of Bordeaux. He was a schoolmaster, then a barrister, led the most powerful group in the GCBA, and rose to national prominence as lead defence counsel for Saya San. He was elected to the legislative council in the anti-separation cause, served as minister for education in the governor's executive council in 1934 and founded in 1936 (reputedly with Japanese funding) the Sinyetha Wunthanu Party, popularly known as the Dama Party (from the *dama*, or peasants' hewing knife, a symbol that its members wore on their caps). It was the first party to issue a manifesto. Then, in October 1938, he collaborated with other politicians in organizing

---

[14] Ibid.: 52; Tinker, 1959: 4–5.
[15] John Sydenham Furnivall, introduction, Nu, 1954: xxii.

the Freedom Bloc[16] and became its *anashin* (lord of power, or dictator). He was chief minister from April 1937 to February 1939, but, after his government fell, resigned his seat in the legislature, declaring that the struggle for freedom must be waged throughout the nation. On 26 July 1940, he was arrested for sedition. 'He was a handsome man who looked good even in the eccentric dresses which he invented for himself. He spoke Burmese with an English accent and a little stutter which made his speeches sound musical. He had wit, charm, intellect, ambition, cunning. His French experience made him think and talk like a leftist.'[17]

U Pu (b. 1881) began his political career with the YMBA, which in 1919 sent him and two others to London to enlist Westminster's support for home rule.[18] He was a twenty-oner and, with his twenty-oner colleagues, Ba Pe and U Thein Maung, the Home Rule Party, the Nationalist Party and three independent members of the legislative council,[19] he founded the People's Party in the cause of separation. He was chief minister from February 1939 to September 1940, later joined the AFPFL, then resigned his post on its supreme council to accept appointment to the governor's postwar executive council.

U Saw (b. 1900) trained as a pleader and was an MP intermittently from 1928. In 1931, after assisting in the defence of the Saya San rebels, he styled himself *Galon* U Saw to prolong his links with this rebellion. He visited Japan in May 1935, then ran for and was elected to the legislature as a candidate for the Nga-Bwint-Saing (Five Flowers) Party. In 1938, he bought the *Thuriya* (Sun) newspaper (reputedly with Japanese financial support[20]), used it to further his political ambitions and, with backing from rich landowners and emerging industrialists,[21] formed the Myochit Party and the Galon Tat, a private army. He was a minister in Ba Maw's government. However, Ba Maw jailed him for sedition. On 30 May 1939, after his release from prison, he became minister for forests and agriculture in Pu's government. His Myochit Party exploited the weakness of Pu's coalition to demand ever more seats in cabinet, until he felt able to challenge Pu for the leadership. Then, in August 1940, half an hour before the debate of a no-confidence motion, he resigned his cabinet

[16] Named in obvious imitation of Subhas Chandra Bose's Forward Bloc.
[17] Dr Maung Maung, 1969: 34.
[18] The Pe–Pu–Shein mission.
[19] Pye, 1951: 43.
[20] It serialized a translation of *Mein Kampf*. Dr Maung Maung, 1969: 63.
[21] U Maung Maung, 1989: 8.

seat, cast his votes with the opposition and brought down the government. He was chief minister from September 1940 to January 1942, when he was banished to internment in Uganda for contacting the Japanese ambassador in Lisbon and promising his support for a Japanese invasion of Burma.[22] Ultimately, he would be tried and convicted for directing the murder of Aung San and six of his colleagues, but, as we shall see, reason exists for doubting the safeness of that verdict. Here it is important to note what Dr Maung Maung, Burman nationalist and Ne Win supporter, wrote of him:

> He did not have much formal education. He took out a lower grade pleader's licence but did not have a practice. He volunteered to defend Saya San, but . . . the other barristers, who rushed to offer their services, outshone him. . . . [H]e had the ability to recognize opportunity . . . and seize and exploit it with ruthlessness . . . [and] began without delay to bulldoze his way to power. . . . Only . . . silken, smooth-tongued barristers had attained ministerial office so far; there was no precedent of a lower grade pleader reaching that high. U Saw was determined to make a precedent with himself by becoming prime minister, not a minister merely.[23]

After gaining the top post, he 'sent several older politicians to jail: U Ba Pe, his mentor, U Ba U of Mandalay and U Ba Thi. The joke in town was that U Saw was not fond of people who had "Ba" in their names.'[24] His departure from Burma in October 1941 was theatrical:

> He flew up . . . in a private aeroplane . . . and circling round the Shwedagon pagoda, paid his respects from the air. People thought that was an unwise thing to do. One adopts the most humble posture, on hands and knees, to pay one's respects to the Buddha's image. U Saw did the reverse; he took to the air and worshipped from above.[25]

Paw Tun (b. 1883), Rakhine, was the headmaster of Methodist High School and Government High School, Rangoon (1904–8), a district official (1912–25), and a barrister and MP from 1925. As Sir

[22] Dr Maung Maung, 1962.
[23] Dr Maung Maung, 1969: 34.
[24] Ibid.: 68.
[25] Ibid.: 90.

Paw Tun, he sided with Chit Hlaing in opposing separation. In 1937, he was both the mayor of Rangoon and minister for home affairs; indeed, he served in every cabinet formed under the 1935 Act, and, from January to June 1942, was chief minister. He followed the government into exile and acted as adviser to the governor; then served as chief minister and member for home affairs in the governor's first postwar executive council.

Ba Maw wrote of the constitutional arrangements and politics of this era that they

> produced governments which did not govern, having little time or power to do so, but mostly shared the spoils of government among a few; and while these administrators or a large number of them were occupied with their deals to keep on in office the administration as a whole drifted just as ever before with nothing changed, nothing really done. It became more and more a government by deals and drifting.[26]

Thus two powerful but very different and conflicting traditions divided the nationalist movement as Aung San was about to go up to university. One looked back romantically to an idealized Burma ruled by its own king, Theravada Buddhism and the *sangha*. The other drew inspiration, naively, from the new values introduced by the colonial ruler, modern science, modern institutions and humanist rationalism. Nationalists who embraced the former had little influence in the legislature and the city. Those who embraced the latter forfeited support from Burma's monks and peasants.

The Dobama Asiayone, founded by veterans of the YMBA and GCBA[27] during the turbulence of the May 1930 Dock Workers Strike and ensuing Indo-Burmese Riots,[28] was an attempt to bridge the two traditions.[29] Its rallying cry was 'Burma for the Burmans', but the

[26] 'Burma at the Beginning of the Second World War', *The Guardian* magazine, October 1959. Quoted in Dr Maung Maung, 1969: 53.
[27] Ba Thaung, a magazine editor, English teacher and part-time book salesman, Kodaw Hmaing, Shin Ariya, U Soe Thein, Hteik Tin Kodaw Gyi and U Maung Gyi.
[28] Telegu-speaking Indian coolies struck for higher wages. The Scindia Steam Navigation Company replaced them with Burmans, then reached a settlement with the strikers without informing the Burmans, and, when the Burmans appeared for work, the reinstated coolies, 'the lowest stratum of the resident aliens in Rangoon', hurled insults at them. See Khin Yi, 1988: 4.
[29] See foreword by Robert Taylor, ibid.: ix.

name was usefully ambivalent, *Do* meaning 'We' or 'Our' and *Bama* meaning either 'Burman', 'Burmese' or 'Burma'; hence 'We Burmans', 'We Burmese' or 'Our Burma'—representing *all* Burmese but *led by Burmans*. Its motto was:

> Burma is our country
> Burmese is our literature
> Burmese is our language
> Love our country
> Cherish our literature
> Uphold our language.[30]

Burma's National Anthem today is a variant of the Dobama Song, which begins with allusions to the glorious days of the Burman kings, exhorts Burmans to be true to their kind by uniting in bravery, claims that Burmans 'are a race of masters', and repeats a tuneful, rousing chorus:

> For so long as the world will last,
> Burma is ours, Burma is ours.
> This is our country, this our land,
> This our country till the end.
> This is our country, this our land,
> This our country till the end.[31]

[30] Ibid.: 5.

[31] Adapted from a translation appearing in *The University College Magazine*, vol. xxii, no. 1, 1931, and quoted in Khin Yi, 1988: 9. The first stanza is:

> Long live, long live 'our Burma's' fame
> In history shines 'our Burma's' name.
> Our race well known the world over.
> Should we now prove inferior?
> Tut! Tut! Not we, not we,
> For Burman, Burman are we!
> Are we not Burman? We are, we are,
> Then unite and act, 'Father's sons' we are,
> Not for us, but for those of hereafter.
> Be brave, be brave, like a true Burman,
> Burma, Burma for us Burmans.
> Act and behave like Masters,
> For Burmans are a race of Masters,
> Under the heaven and on earth,
> High-minded and of Zamayi's blood.

Though small in numbers, the movement 'made a stir by the violence of its anti-British feeling and its revolutionary outlook'.[32] Its manifesto[33] urged Burmans to boycott Indian and Chinese shopkeepers, to trade only among themselves and to speak and write only in Burmese. Members were encouraged to 'mourn for their [lost] monarch',[34] to practise spinning and to patronize home-made goods. The 'clack-clack of their wooden slippers through the streets of Rangoon and Mandalay became a familiar sound of the nationalist movement',[35] whose emblem was 'a peasant marching towards the promised land of humming industries and abundant fields . . . behind him . . . the desolation of the royal palace of the Burmese kings, its spires down, its big drum shattered'.[36] The Dobama Song, especially its chorus, was hugely popular and attracted demands for recitals all over the country. It inspired students, and in the first batch to join the Dobama from Rangoon University were Nu, Ba Sein and Lay Maung.[37] They addressed each other as *thakin* (master), an honorific reserved previously for their rulers and, hence, the Dobama soon was known as the Thakin Movement. It resembled the freshman campus of an American university. Everyone agreed about the common enemy, but all else incited debate. Issues, such as whether Burmese literature, *lokaniti* (precepts for Right Living) and recitation of *payeikkyi* (daily chants to the Buddha) nurtured adequately the needs of modern life,[38] or whether *kan* (*karma*) meant 'fate' or 'work', aroused strong views. Some idolized heroes of Burma's past, such as Alaungpaya, Bandoola and Bayinnaung. Others drew inspiration from Rousseau, Voltaire, Nietzsche, Garibaldi, Mazzini, Marx, Lenin, Shaw, de Valera, Sun Yat-sen, John Strachey, M.N. Roy, Stalin, Gandhi, U Ottama, Nehru and Bose.[39] Nu translated Dale Carnegie's *How to Win Friends and Influence People*.[40] Rightist and leftist tendencies mirroring European

[32] Tinker, 1959: 7.
[33] Aung San is now generally credited with having drafted the Dobama's manifesto, but this seems doubtful. Compare Khin Yi, 1988: 5 (manifesto drafted soon after 30 May 1930) and Nu, in Dr Maung Maung (ed.), 1962: 18 (Aung San joined Dobama after Student Strike of 1936).
[34] Khin Yi, 1988: 27.
[35] Trager, 1966: 56.
[36] Dr Maung Maung, 1969: 55.
[37] Pye, 1962: 19.
[38] Khin Yi, 1988: 11.
[39] Ibid.: 43; Dr Maung Maung, 1969: 54.
[40] Ibid.

models were in rough equilibrium. 'The revival of Germany under Hitler suggested that leadership rather than democracy was the key to national progress, and Japan seemed to illustrate the same principle. In striking contrast, but equally effective, however, was the rise of Russia under communism with its new interpretation of democracy.'[41]

In September 1930 the first of numerous affiliated organizations, the All Burma Youth League (ABYL), was founded. About 5000 students and teachers met at the Shwedagon, declared their detestation of British rule, made a bonfire of imported British cigarettes and distributed leaflets urging people to smoke cheroots and to boycott British goods. In January 1931, in the wake of the Sino-Burmese riots, the thakins, inspired perhaps by fascist models, formed their own army, the Dobama Ye Tat (Our Brave Burman Army).

By 1936, however, leftist notions in the Dobama were in the ascendant. New recruits rejected the term 'thakin' as having a 'fascist' tint and claimed that the Dobama Song 'reeked of facism'.[42] They began calling the older thakins 'revisionists', and a crossed hammer and sickle replaced the peacock at the heart of the Dobama's tricolour. A motion proposed for the 1936 annual conference envisaged solidarity with 'workers' and 'peasants', and another motion, inspired by Lenin,[43] allowed members to contest elections to the new legislature to enable them to wreck the constitution.[44] Now, in addition to independence, the movement's goal was 'a socialistic heaven on earth in which all Burmans would enjoy equal opportunities', a 'Komin Kochin [one's own king, one's own kind] form of government' wherein the 'social and economic ills deriving from imperialism' and the 'class distinctions inherent in capitalism'

---

[41] Furnivall, introduction, Nu, 1954: xxii–iii. Ba Maw (1968: 6) states: 'Ideological niceties did not yet exist except perhaps among a very few. Fascism had not lost the war then, nor had the Western Allies won it, and all the talk about our postwar antifascists having always hated fascism is just not true. It is only a new policy seeking old roots in the past to gain a certain legitimacy. Most of the postwar antifascists were giving the fascist salute and shouting the fascist slogans in those days.'

[42] Khin Yi, 1988: 85.

[43] From an essay 'Should We Participate in Bourgeois Parliaments?', reprinted in G.D.F. Overstreet and M. Windmiller, *Communism in India* (Los Angeles: University of California Press, 1959), pp. 466–8. Redacted, Khin Yi, 1988: 36.

[44] Ibid.: 27, 31, 35.

would be eliminated. The tactics prescribed for achieving this heaven on earth, also inspired by Lenin, included agitating through trade unions and other front organizations.[45]

Historians, accordingly, tend to identify the split in the Dobama that brought about its demise in 1938 as one of left versus right, but the Dobama, as the nationalist movement in general, had always embraced and vacillated between ideologies of both right and left. Thakin Lay Maung's presidential speech at the National Day rally marking the sixteenth anniversary of the 1920 Student Boycott, for example, cited 'the examples of Alaungpaya, Hitler and Mussolini, who had risen from the common fold', and 'urged the people to overthrow the foreign capitalist yoke and set up a proletarian state as in Russia'.[46] No, what destroyed the Dobama was the perennial problem of who was to be the top man.

The Prome Conference of March 1938 opened without a president, who was in gaol for sedition. The election to replace him caused outrage. The chairman voted twice; first when the count resulted in a tie, then exercising his right as chairman to cast the deciding vote. Three months later the new president, Thein Maung, expelled the rival Ba Sein faction from the movement. Kodaw Hmaing called an executive committee meeting in an attempt to effect a reconciliation, but Thein Maung objected that Kodaw Hmaing was not an executive committee member and walked out, then proclaimed himself 'Hitler-Dictator' and barred Ba Sein and his supporters from Dobama headquarters. They responded by setting up their own headquarters, and accusations of dishonesty, corruption, incompetence, subversion, collaborating with the establishment, spying, inciting schism and rule violations flew back and forth between the two camps.[47] 'We deplored the division, particularly in those crucial times when unity was so vitally necessary. The Asiayone and the Thakin members were, after all, the best that we got in politics, and we did not want to see the party disintegrate due to lack of vision on the part of its leaders,' wrote Nu later of their endless bickerings.[48] Eventually, Kodaw Hmaing resigned his role as mediator and joined the majority Thein Maung camp, and,

---

[45] Ibid.: 44.
[46] Ibid.: 49.
[47] Ibid.: 84–9.
[48] Nu, in Dr Maung Maung (ed.), 1962: 18.

thereafter, the two camps were known as the Kodaw Hmaing faction and the minority Ba Sein–Tun Ok faction.

Aung San went up to university in 1933, 'a raw country lad, dour of expression and untidy of dress, quite out of place among the dapper students of Rangoon University who rather fancied themselves the cream of Burmese youth'.[49] Unfriendliness also set him apart. 'I don't think he is normal,'[50] Nu observed curtly. '[W]e would greet each other heartily when we met or passed in the street. Not so Aung San. Sometimes he would pass us in the street without a word or gesture of greeting.'[51]

There is a description of him with his mother, with whom he rarely communicated:

> [H]is mother came to [Rangoon to] see him. . . . [She] was anxious, and asked him many questions, looking at him tenderly all the time. . . . His replies were brief and curt and cold. He did not stay more than 15 or 20 minutes, and when he got up to go, he uttered no word of farewell . . . Aung San said to me as we walked back . . . 'She doesn't really mind my being in politics, but she doesn't like me to be so cold. I pity her.'[52]

He was singular also in his indifference to alcohol, the opposite sex and personal comfort:

> Once we had a few visitors from the district . . . and the boys at the headquarters gave them Thakin Aung San's room . . . because they did not want [them] to sleep in the corridor. The visitors were pleased to have [his] room, but only before the bugs started to make their presence felt. Around midnight, unable to take the torture any longer, our visitors fled from the room, carrying their sheets and blankets, and sought refuge in the corridor.[53]

His 'view of savages', states his daughter, 'was the romantic one of pure, honest, healthy beings revelling in their freedom'.[54]

[49] Aung San Suu Kyi, 1991: 6–7.
[50] Let Ya, in Dr Maung Maung (ed.), 1962: 15.
[51] Nu, in ibid.: 17.
[52] Let Ya, in ibid.: 9–10.
[53] Nu, in ibid.: 19.
[54] Aung San Suu Kyi, 1991: 11.
[55] Nu had returned to university to read for a law degree. Ba Sein had recently graduated.

Aung San's companions included Nu (b. 1907), Ba Sein (b. 1910),[55] Let Ya (b. 1911), Rashid (b. 1912), 'Tetpongyi' Thein Pe Myint (b. 1914), Ba Thein Tin (b. 1914), Kyaw Nyein (b. 1915), Ba Swe (b. 1915) and Ba Hein (b. 1913).[56] To the derision of their elders and the contempt of many of their contemporaries, who dismissed their antics as showmanship,[57] they wore *pinni* or *pinbyu* (homespun cotton) *longyis* (sarongs) and *gaungbaungs* (scarves tied about the head), tramped about on wooden sandals, smoked cheroots and affected the thakin form of address. They wrote inflammatory tracts on the strength of vacuous speculations culled from other inflammatory tracts and, like students in Britain, voiced their audacious opinions at the Rangoon University Students Union (RUSU). Of Aung San's maiden speech, the clumsy speech that caused his brother embarrassment, Let Ya noted: 'He was obviously trying to put on the airs of a Dr Ba Maw or Maung Maung Ji.[58] Later . . . he said, "I had to go on. If I didn't, I wouldn't get another chance to speak."'[59]

After a concerted campaign the young nationalists gained control of the RUSU's executive committee,[60] which previously had been conformist and conservative.[61] Then Nu exploited his position as the Union's president, attacked the university's principal, and Aung San, as editor of the Union's magazine, *Oway* (Fighting Peacock), attacked the bursar in an article alleging that the bursar (a Burman) was a visitor from the underworld who professed 'avuncular pretensions' to female students. These bold attacks set a new standard of disrespect,[62] and both men received expulsion notices. The entire student body declined to sit for their examinations in 'sympathy', but, instead of standing firm, the university authorities rescinded the notices, and the government appointed a committee to enquire into changes demanded by the students.[63]

Posterity has bestowed on these events a significance far exceeding the importance imputed to them at the time. To Dr Ba Maw, U Pu,

[56] Ba Hein had abandoned his place at university for want of financial means and taken employment with the Dobama.

[57] Dr Maung Maung, 1969: 38.

[58] U Saw's brother but possibly Sir J.A. Maung Gyi, one of the founders of the YMBA, a twenty-oner, acting-governor at the start of the Saya San Rebellion and independent Burma's first ambassador to the UK.

[59] Let Ya, in Dr Maung Maung (ed.), 1962: 7–8.

[60] U Nu, in ibid.: 17.

[61] Aung San Suu Kyi, 1991: 9.

[62] Dr Tha Hla, in Dr Maung Maung (ed.), 1962: 23.

[63] Aung San Suu Kyi, 1991: 10.

Galon U Saw, Sir Paw Tun, Sir J.A. Maung Gyi, Chit Hlaing and other actors in the real world, Aung San and his mates were like a litter of puppies playing Growl and Bark. The British were still very much in control. But in the hothouse of student politics of the mid-1930s this minor victory over authority catapulted Nu and Aung San to national notoriety, and, two years later, now reading for a law degree, Aung San was elected president of both the RUSU and another strike-generated organization that he helped to found, the All Burma Students Union (ABSU).[64]

Perhaps his early notoriety encouraged Aung San to believe that a political future on the national stage beckoned. At any rate, early in 1938, he abandoned his legal studies, left university and joined the Dobama,[65] joining the same day as his future brother-in-law, Than Tun (b. 1913).[66] To Ba Sein, Tun Ok and others who had contributed with penurious self-sacrifice to building the Dobama during its formative years, Aung San and his confederates were brash troublemakers[67] who needed a new organization to further their ambitions and wanted to start at the top, while they regarded Ba Sein and his confederates as 'not bold enough, not Burmese enough, not radical enough, or perhaps simply not young enough'[68] to prosecute the patriotic cause. Aung San backed Kodaw Hmaing, and soon became the Hmaing Dobama's secretary-general. Nu became its treasurer ('a treasurer without treasure,' he said of the office[69]), and Let Ya, Than Tun and Soe took over other important posts.[70] The following year the Dobama Ye Tat was renamed the Bama Let Yon

---

[64] Most studies of pre-war politics in Burma, e.g., Cady, Trager, Guyot, assume that the Burmese political elite believed that government was a purely administrative exercise and that mass politics were instituted and later dominated by student *thakins* 'untainted' by collaboration with the British. Taylor disputes this and contends persuasively that policies developed by pre-war politicians were 'little different in essence from those of independent Burma to 1962'. See Robert Taylor, 'Politics in Late Colonial Burma: The Case of U Saw', *Modern Asian Studies*, vol. 10, no. 2 (London: Cambridge University Press, 1978), pp. 161–93.

[65] Aung San Suu Kyi, 1991: 11.

[66] Nu, in Dr Maung Maung (ed.), 1962: 18. Pye, 1962: 19, however, states that Nu was among the first students to join the Dobama and that Aung San joined it a few years later.

[67] Let Ya, in Dr Maung Maung (ed.), 1962: 14; Aung San Suu Kyi, 1991: 11.

[68] Ibid.

[69] Tinker, 1959: 7.

[70] U Maung Maung, 1989: 21.

Shat Ni Tat (Strong-Fisted Red-Shirted Burma Army), popularly known as the Thanmani (Steel Corps).

The Student Strike of 1920, the Saya San Rebellion, the Dobama Movement, Aung San and the Student Strike of 1936 occupy centre stage in conventional accounts of Burman nationalism. What really galvanized it, however, began as an Indo-Burman labour dispute in the oilfields of Chauk and Yenangyaung in January 1938. A garage hand overstayed his leave. A suspension notice was served on him and within a week the oilfield workers were on strike. Although the garage hand was reinstated, the strikers' demands soon exceeded the first excuse for their strike. The thakins sought to exploit religious passions to create a political issue and 'student–worker solidarity'. Nevertheless, while the Dobama flag (hammer and sickle version), song and precept ('Master race we are, we Burmans!') were much in evidence, the Dobama central committee failed in its attempt to control the strike. It was led and managed locally.[71]

The strikers decided to march to Rangoon and lay their claims before the government, and, on 30 November, a 'workers' army' left Chauk, marching four abreast to the beat of the 'Victory Drum', cheered on by *thakinmas* (Dobama females), who baptised them with soaked *thabye* (Eugenia) leaves and shouted, 'Victory to you! Victory to you!' All along the 400-mile route people saluted them, performed theatricals for them, gave them food, drink, lengths of *pinni*, bamboo helmets, leather slippers and money. The Kodaw Hmaing central committee ordered them to turn back. When some of its student thakins were arrested at Magwe, however, the committee reversed tactics and sent *tatbo* (irregular militia) and other emissaries to 'protect and guide' the marchers. Ba Hein (ABSU president) taunted the police deployed to stop the marchers, proclaiming in the manner of Patrick Henry and Thomas Paine, 'One stamp of a hoof shall strike the spark that will set the whole country ablaze!' He was arrested, as were Ba Swe (ABSU secretary) and Thakin Soe.

The RUSU met on 14 December, explained why students needed to support the 'workers and peasants' (their parents), unanimously condemned the Ba Maw government and demanded the release of their leaders. The following day, All Rangoon Students Union cadres marched through Rangoon protesting against the government's ban on street manifestations and shouting 'Down with capitalism!'[72]

[71] See Khin Yi, 1988: 57 ff., and Dr Maung Maung, 1969: 55 ff, for these and other details of the Oilfield Strike of 1938 and its immediate consequences.
[72] Khin Yi, 1988: 108–9.

Rival politicians also sought to exploit the passions the march aroused. On 19 December, U Saw assembled some 10,000 supporters at the Shwedagon and, under a Myochit banner depicting a *galon* (Burma) gripping a dragon (Britain) in its claws, addressed them on the ineptitude of Ba Maw, then led a column to the Rangoon Corporation on Sule Pagoda Road, shouting 'Arise, galon! Arise!' and 'Master race we are, we Burmans!'[73]

The police ordered ABSU demonstrators picketing the secretariat building to disperse. They refused, and in the ensuing baton rush one of them, Aung Gyaw, was fatally wounded.[74] The funeral cortège took four hours to walk the half-mile from the RUSU to Kyandaw cemetery, and the funeral oration included the words: 'The sound of the baton with which the merciless police hit you shall serve as a clarion call. Just as your passive forbearance sent you to the land of death, so shall our future activities bring about self-government to Burma. Victory to the Revolution!'[75] Aung Gyaw's crew-cut hairstyle became a widely adopted nationalist emblem, and his *pinni* jacket would boost the wear-homespun campaign. Patriotic young ladies abandoned voile blouses for *pinni* jackets.

Meanwhile, a 'peasants' army' began a march to Rangoon to press their separate grievances on the government. They demanded the enactment of the Land Tenure and Land Alienation Acts, then pending before the legislature. During the preceding eight years, the Chettyars' share of the cultivable land in the principal rice-growing districts had grown from 6 to 25 per cent, and absentee landowners now owned nearly half of the 11,201,766 cultivable acres in Lower Burma.[76] Floods and storms threatened Burman cultivators with the loss of still more land.[77]

The 'workers' army' and the 'peasants' army' converged in Rangoon on 8 January 1939, the anniversary of the start of the Oilfield Strike. A vast crowd organized by the Kodaw Hmaing Dobama central committee had assembled to greet them. Standard bearers, heralds bearing pots of *thabye* leaves, pilots on bicycles, monks intoning *paritta* (prayer chants), Rangoon Dobama militia bands, bus company trade unionists, lapidarists, fire brigades, the Galon Tat, the Steel Corps, representatives of diverse other groups and parties, and some 3500 workers from the refineries at Syriam

[73] Ibid.: 119, 56.
[74] Ibid.: 111.
[75] Ibid.: 113–14.
[76] Ibid.: 96.
[77] Ibid.: 105–6.

joined them for the final procession to the Shwedagon, all marching to thunderous shouts of 'Dobama! Master race are we!' and 'Victory to the Revolution!' They stopped at Kyandaw Cemetery and laid wreaths at the grave of Aung Gyaw, then trooped in silence past the statue of U Wisara.[78]

On 23 January the police raided Dobama headquarters at the Swedagon, the holiest of all Buddhist shrines, *wearing boots*. We can understand their difficulties. Public order was under threat, and the immediate need was to avert a national strike planned by the Dobama. Footwear was not uppermost in their minds. Still, '[t]o enter the pagoda precincts without removing footwear is . . . an affront to all Buddhists!' fulminated *Sayadaw* Ledi U Zadila. The fact that the commissioner and deputy commissioner of police were British and most of the police were Indians exacerbated the offence. The outrage provoked many fiery orations and a proliferation of hunger strikes, but nothing more—until the authorities made further arrests and perpetrated another footwear sacrilege in Mandalay. A demonstration there led to the 'massacre of the 17', and seven of the dead were monks.

In the course of these tumultuous events, the Dobama split (22 March–23 November 1938), the Second Indo-Burmese Riots erupted (26 July–17 August 1938),[79] and the Ba Maw government fell (16 February 1939). What began as a 'glorious march' of thousands ended in July 1939 as an inglorious retreat of stragglers, for the government was still in control. But the Oilfield Strike succeeded where Saya San had failed in harnessing mob potential and demonstrating the nationalist passions of a broad mass of the Burman majority against continued foreign rule. Hegel's state might still be all-powerful, but it could rely no longer on the docility of the people.

Aung San's early yearning for ordination as a monk and training in a monastery did not translate into the wisdom of Aung San the adult. Indeed, he spoke against *sangha* participation in politics not only in his RUSU maiden speech, as we have seen, but also in his address to the League's convention the year before he died.[80] A more

[78] Ibid.: 106.
[79] 'The riots were deliberately caused by "a piece of unscrupulous political opportunism" which played upon and inflamed religious and nationalist sentiment and racial jealousy and dislike, in order to embarrass the ministry in power.' Donnison, 1970: 121, quoting 'Final Report Riot Inquiry Committee', p. 292.
[80] Aung San Suu Kyi, 1991: 7; Silverstein (ed.), 1993: 96.

potent influence was 'the smattering knowledge of leftism'[81] that passed for Marxism among his peers, as evidenced by his identification of *samsara* (Buddhist causality doctrine) with the Marxist thesis of capitalist-driven class exploitation and colonial conquest.[82]

Dr Maung Maung insists that use of communist slogans and gestures merely meant that 'the Dobama was marching in revolutionary directions, rather than that Marxism as an ideology was embraced'.[83] This might be said of the untutored masses who supported the Dobama, but not of the young radicals who now led it. The 'people's front' tactics they attempted in the Oilfield Strike came straight from Lenin. Nu opined that a child's death from starvation he had witnessed could not have happened in a communist state. Ba Swe extolled Stalin's love for all mankind and claimed that Marxism had the power to cure all human ills.[84] Although publication of Marxist-Leninist literature was prohibited in Burma, it was flooding into the country with every young Burman who returned from studies in India or Europe. Nu and several others founded the Naga Ni (Red Dragon) Book Club, one of a number of clandestine groups for the study of Marxism-Leninism, and Ba Hein translated Marxist-Leninist tracts into Burmese for mass circulation. Donnison offers another perspective on this development:

> Quite simply, what every Burman nationalist most desired was to get the foreigners out of his country, to step into their jobs, and to gain for himself and for Burma control of the country's resources. . . . It was scarcely to be expected that the Burm[ans] should do anything but adopt a political creed one of whose central tenets was that the people must own the means of production and that, to achieve this, capitalists must be expropriated. Here was a screen of respectable academic doctrine behind which the Burm[ans] could attain their very natural desires.[85]

---

[81] Khin Yi, 1988: 134, quoting Thakin Yi (of the Ba Sein Dobama), *Factional Struggle Among Thakins: An Exposition on Pseudo Thakins* [*Thakin Ayaydawbon Thakin Yaung Thakin War Mya Hnint Thakin Masit Thakin Mahnit Do le Tai Pwe Sadan*] (Rangoon: Shwe Pyi Nyunt Ponhneik Taik, *c*1939), page number not cited.

[82] Silverstein (ed.), 1993: 97–8.

[83] Dr Maung Maung, 1969: 55.

[84] Ibid.: 54.

[85] Donnison, 1970: 140.

At any rate, on 15 August 1939, Aung San, Ba Hein, Hamendranath Goshal (aka Ba Tin) and a Dr Nag met at Let Ya's lodgings on Barr Street and formed the Communist Party of Burma. Aung San was its general secretary.[86] Thakins Than Tun, Soe and 'Tetpongyi' Thein Pe Myint, who was its main theoretician, joined soon afterwards.[87]

Ba Maw was not a Marxist, but he found common ground with Marxists in 'Colonialism's difficulty is Freedom's opportunity'.[88] He resigned his seat in the legislature and, with Aung San, Mya and Nu of the Kodaw Hmaing Dobama, Thein Maung, ousted leader of the rival Dobama, secretly participating campus politicians, activist monks and various survivors of the GCBA, formed the Freedom Bloc, which now became the vanguard of the independence cause. Other veteran politicians, sensible to the fact that theirs was the art of the possible, were also shifting their positions. At the start of the decade, they had pressed for greater home rule. By the end of the decade, they were focusing their ambitions on a post-colonial Burma.

On 3 September 1939 war broke out in Europe. Europe was so remote it might have been on another planet. Ba Maw announced that the government could count on Burma's support if it pledged to grant Burma independence at the close of hostilities. If such a pledge was not forthcoming, he warned, the Freedom Bloc would urge the people to oppose Britain's foreign war. Aung San articulated the tactics they were prepared to use:

> a country-wide mass resistance movement against British imperialism on a progressive scale . . . co-existence with international and national developments in the form of a series of local and partial strikes of industrial and rural workers leading to the general and rent strike; and finally, all forms of militant propaganda such as mass demonstrations and people's marches leading to mass civil disobedience. Also, an economic campaign against British imperialism in the form of a boycott of British

[86] Whether the meeting at Barr Street was the Party's First Congress and who was present at it are matters of debate. See Lintner, 1990a: 3, fn 1; Aung San Suu Kyi, 1991: 13. The Party was 'an offshoot of the Communist movement in India'. 'Tetpongyi' Thein Pe Myint had studied law in Calcutta from 1936 to 1938, there met radical members of the Bengal Students' Federation and written his novel *Tet Hpongyi* (The Modern Monk), criticizing the traditional monastic hierarchy in Burma. Lintner, 1994: 22–3.

[87] Sources disagree as to whether Soe was present at the 'First Congress' at Barr Street. See Lintner, 1990a: 3, fn 1.

[88] Aung San Suu Kyi, 1991: 13.

goods leading to the mass non-payment of taxes, to be supported by developing guerrilla action against military and civil and police outposts, lines of communication, etc., leading to the complete paralysis of the British administration in Burma when we should be able along with the developing world situation, to make the final and ultimate bid for the capture of power.[89]

This was not the polemic of student debates, nor was Burma, now a few hundred miles from the expanding Empire of the Rising Sun, a student debating chamber. Hawking such messages about the country was the serious business of undermining public order at a moment of grave national peril. Within a year, most of the Freedom Bloc's leaders were in gaol. Nu went voluntarily, perceiving it as his duty to stand nobly and be counted. Aung San could not be found. He had gone to India and would return to Burma only to proceed to Tokyo.

We begin to notice here a Who's Who of pre- and postwar Burman politics, the contours of an old boys network that includes:

Aung San, RUSU general secretary, RUSU president, Kodaw Hmaing Dobama secretary-general, member of the executive committee of the All Burma Peasants' Organization, co-founder (with Let Ya and 'Tetpongyi' Thein Pe Myint) of the Naga Ni Book Club, CPB co-founder and general secretary, Freedom Bloc co-founder and general secretary, Thirty Comrade, BIA and BDA commander and war minister under the Japanese, co-founder of the People's Revolutionary Party (PRP), which combined with the CPB and the BNA in the coalition that became the League, League president, Interim Burmese Government (IBG) deputy chairman (chapter 5).

Nu, RUSU president, Kodaw Hmaing Dobama treasurer, Naga Ni Book Club co-founder, Freedom Bloc co-founder, Dobama delegate to the 1940 Indian National Congress session, foreign affairs minister and information minister under the Japanese, PRP co-founder, League vice-president, constituent assembly speaker, IBG deputy chairman and member for foreign affairs, prime minister 1948–58, 1960–2 (chapters 6 and 8).

Let Ya, Naga Ni Book Club co-founder, CPB co-founder, Freedom Bloc co-founder, Thirty Comrade, deputy commander-in-chief BNA and military affairs chief in the War Office under the Japanese, PRP

---

[89] Aung San, 1946; reprinted in Silverstein (ed.), 1993: 82.

co-founder, deputy inspector-general Burma Army, IBG member without portfolio and member for defence, deputy prime minister and minister of defence under Nu.

Ba Hein, Dobama leader, All Burma Trades Union Congress (ABTUC) activist (helped organize oil workers), ABSU president, Naga Ni Book Club activist and translator, Freedom Bloc leader, CPB co-founder, PRP co-founder.

Ba Sein, RUSU president, Dobama leader (sometimes credited with founding it), leader Ba Sein–Tun Ok Dobama, ambassador to Manchukuo under the Japanese, co-founder Burma Democratic Party (opposed to the League), revived and led Dobama.

'Tetpongyi' Thein Pe Myint, Naga Ni Book Club co-founder, CPB theoretician and general secretary, retreated to India rather than collaborate with the Japanese (but remained in touch with the collaborationists), CPB secretary, member of the League's communist wing, IBG member for agriculture and rural economy, left the CPB on the eve of its rebellion (although one of Burma's leading communists), MP for a short time in 1956, joined Burma Socialist Programme Party after Ne Win's 1962 coup (chapters 7 and 8) and became Ne Win's chief adviser.

Thakin Mya, MP, founder of the Workers' and Peasants' (later Burmese Revolutionary) Party (BRP), Freedom Bloc co-founder, deputy prime minister and foreign affairs minister under the Japanese, PRP co-founder, co-founder and president of the Revolutionary (later Socialist) Party, member of the League's supreme and executive councils, IBG member for first home and judicial affairs, then finance and revenue.

Kyaw Nyein, ABSU founder, BRP supreme council, vice-minister of foreign affairs under the Japanese, PRP co-founder, co-founder of the Revolutionary (later Socialist) Party, League secretary-general, IBG member for home and judicial affairs, and deputy prime minister, foreign minister, co-operatives minister, industries minister and acting foreign minister under Nu.

Ba Swe, ABSU secretary, Japanese *anashin* administration civil defence chief, PRP co-founder, co-founder and secretary general of the Revolutionary (later Socialist) Party, member of the League's supreme council, MP, defence and mines minister and deputy prime minister under Nu.

Than Tun (b. 1911), a leading player in the Dobama and the Freedom Bloc, agricultural minister under the Japanese, the League's general secretary and a member of its supreme and executive councils, Aung San's brother-in-law. He joined the CPB soon after it was founded and was its leader from 1945 until 1968, when he was assassinated. U Ba Win, Aung San's older brother, was serving in his IBG cabinet as the member for commerce and supplies when both men were assassinated. Tun Win and Hla Maung, Aung San's colleagues in the Dobama and Freedom Bloc, were respectively information minister and ambassador to Peking.

We find the same old boys network in the subsequent careers of the Thirty Comrades. Of the 23 who did not die during the war, 15 went on to occupy high positions in politics, the army or both.

Prominent under the Japanese were Aung San (*nom de guerre*, Bo Teza) and Hla Pe (Bo Let Ya); Tun Ok, head of the *Baho* government and forestry minister in Ba Maw's cabinet; Shu Maung (Bo Ne Win), BNA commander in chief; Aung Than (Bo Setkya), deputy defence minister, military attaché in Tokyo; Hla Maung (Bo Zeya, or Commander Success[90]), Military Academy principal; Tun Shein (Bo Yan Naing), the *adipati*'s aide-de-camp (he married Ba Maw's daughter); Ba Gyan (Bo La Yaung, or Commander Shining Moonlight), Tun Shein's assistant; Shwe (Bo Kyaw Zaw, or Commander Intensely Famous), Non-Commissioned Officers School principal; Hla Myaing (Bo Yan Aung, or Commander Conqueror), BNA chief of staff; and Saw Lwin (Bo Min Gaung, or Commander Supreme King), secretary to the war minister.

Prominent in post-war Burman politics were Aung San, Let Ya and Setkya; Zeya, Aung Thein (Ye Htut, or the Bravest), Ne Win and Kyaw Zaw, who commanded battalions in the reconstituted Burma Army; Tun Ok, who was a member of the legislative council; and La Yaung, who was a leader of the People's Volunteer Organization (PVO). Zeya was a Burma Army commander, then, with Yan Aung and Ye Htut, joined the communist insurrection. San Hlaing (Bohmu Aung, or Major Winner) was a PVO commander and Nu's defence minister. Saw Lwin (Bo Min Gaung) was a minister in several of Nu's cabinets. Ne Win was the Burma Army's commander in chief under Nu, then prime minister in the Caretaker Government (chapter 8), and, after 1962, 'Burma's undisputed strongman'.[91] Let Ya, Yan Naing and Bohmu Aung joined Nu's rebellious Parliamentary Democracy Party

---

[90] A rival view derives the name from Alaungpaya, whose original name was Aung Zeya; hence, Commander Alaungpaya.

[91] Lintner, 1994: 440.

after the 1962 coup. Tin Aye (Bo Phone Myint, or Commander of Inner Spiritual Power) was an MP and head of the Socialist Economy Construction Council under Ne Win's Revolutionary Council (RC) (chapter 8). Than Nyunt (Bo Zin Yaw, or Commander Seagull) was an MP and deputy manager of a parastatal under the RC. Thit (Bo Saw Naung, or Commander Early Brother) worked in the RC's trade department.

The colonial power ejected the Japanese in 1945. Burma's physical and administrative infrastructure was in ruins, and the provision for reconstruction contained in the White Paper[92] seemed to every British official concerned with Burma from the governor down and to almost every senior Burman politician and civil servant the sensible way forward. The governor would return, wind the clock back and resume the gradual process towards home rule with the support of a population grateful for their deliverance from the arrogant, face-slapping fascists. No one foresaw the power of Aung San's closed shop to alter the pace and course of events.

[92] 'Burma: Statement of Policy by His Majesty's Government, 1945' (London: HMSO, Cmd. 6635). This important document is reproduced in Dr Maung Maung, 1956: 176–84.

1. The last governor of British Burma, Sir Hubert Rance, bidding farewell to Thakin Nu, the first prime minister of independent Burma, on 4 January 1948

'Independence *now* was the one panacea for all Burma's ills.' – p. 118

2. Two of the astrologers who selected the most auspicious moment for transferring power and, when the moment arrived, enhanced auspiciousness by blowing on conch shells

Existing differences between the Burman majority and the ethnic minorities were 'only expressions of the same culture at different stages of development'. – p. 199

3. 1998: government poster

'What beyond demagogic platitudes . . . did the leaders have to offer to the people of Burma?' – p. 200.

4. Karen village incinerated by the Burma Army implementing Ne Win's 'Four Cuts' policy aimed at severing insurgents from the people supporting them with food, money, intelligence and fighting men

'The Karens, whose loyalty in war had been tested *against* the Burmans, were unenthusiastic.' – p. 121

5. Karen grandmother with grandchild orphaned by the Burma Army while implementing
Ne Win's 'Four Cuts' policy

'Who and what were to blame for all this bloodletting?' – p. 198

6. ABSDF recruits training near Thai border

'Institutions succeed only if supported by those charged with implementing them.' – p. 200

7. A KIA column fording a river

The Kachins, disillusioned of the hopes raised at Panglong, rebelled after U Nu established Buddhism as Burma's state religion. The Buddhist clergy already enjoyed privileges denied to their pastors, priests and teachers. – p. 185

8. Pickets posted during a KIA unit's crossing of a road controlled by the Burma Army

Aung San Suu Kyi: 'I would like every country in the world to recognize the fact that the people of Burma are being shot down for no reason at all.' – p. 228

9. Salween River, Karen State

The Salween provides 'an imposing natural barrier behind which hill peoples such as the Kokangs, Was, Akhas, Lahus, Karens and Mons have sheltered almost entirely free of external interference for most of Burma's recorded history'. – p. 8

10. Raw jade at KIA GHQ worth approximately $2 million

11. KIA convoy returning from delivering a consignment of jade to China

After his 1962 coup, Ne Win banned private exporters and confiscated the jade mines. – p. 190

12. Derelict house in Rangoon formerly owned by an Indian merchant

'By 1930, nearly half of the population of Rangoon was Indian. The business life of Rangoon was dominated by Indians, Mandalay by Chinese.' – p. 31

13. Public transport in Maymyo

'The initiative to shape the national economy must be kept in the hands of the state and the national people.' – p. 194

14–17. Houses formerly owned by British companies now owned by Burma Army officers

'Yet again, policy was beholden to the principle that whoever was loudest in blaming the colonial "exploiters" and their "capitalist minions" would inherit the spoils.' – p. 118

18. Opium addict

'The fortunes that [Burma Army] senior officers are making from narcotics is the main reason why the war continues.' – p. 179

19. Military Intelligence officers attached to Burmese Embassy in London photographing demonstrators on the first anniversary of Daw Aung San Suu Kyi's arrest

'We must be vigilant against various wily schemes of some neo-colonialists.' – p. 233

20. Left to right: Foreign Secretary U Peter Limbin, President U Sein Lwin and Finance Minister U Win Ko of the National Coalition Government of Burma with author in 1992 Six months after this picture was taken, U Win Ko was found with his throat slashed in a hotel room in Kunming.

5
Aung San Triumphant

IN NOVEMBER 1944, a group of young conservative MPs, in consultation with the governor of Burma, Reginald Dorman-Smith, then in exile in Simla, published a plan called 'The Blue Print for Burma', providing for a scheme of direct rule for a 'reconstruction period', and, six months later, on 17 May 1945, after prolonged cabinet deliberations in which labour members played a full part, HMG published its 'Statement of Policy', or White Paper, defining how this was to work in practice. The temporary military administration of the country known as Civil Affairs Services (Burma), or CAS(B), would end 'when operational requirements make it possible for civil government to function' and, for a period not exceeding three years, plenary power would vest in the governor. The governor might appoint a small executive council and a legislature to assist him in his duties, and, before the end of this period of direct rule, he would hold a general election to restore the council and legislature established by the 1935 Act. Then measures would be taken to prepare Burma for 'the attainment of full self-government within the British Commonwealth'. These would include soliciting contributions towards the drafting of a democratic constitution from all parties, and, when it was clear that such a constitution had general support, HMG would enact it. The Scheduled Areas, comprising most of the non-Burman minorities, would remain 'subject to a special regime under the governor until such time as the inhabitants signify their desire for some suitable form of amalgamation of their territories with Burma Proper'. It was hoped that Burma Proper, the Scheduled Areas and Karenni[1] would agree an arrangement allowing them to unite in an independent Burma in which Chins, Shans, Kachins and Karens would enjoy a measure of local autonomy and vetoes over matters affecting them.

As the White Paper suggested, there were sound practical reasons for such a stage-by-stage advance to independence. The country's commercial and transport infrastructure was in ruins. The railways'

---

[1] It will be recalled that, under the 1885 treaty between Calcutta and Mandalay, Karenni was a sovereign state voluntarily associating itself with the colonial power.

rolling stock comprised only 30 locomotives in working order, and such was the condition of the roads that it cost £200 to send a lorry of goods from Rangoon to Mandalay.[2] Millions of acres of rice land had reverted to jungle. The cattle population had declined by a third.[3] Dacoity was ubiquitous; in some areas the peasants feared working the fields. Prices were soaring, wages were too low,[4] and the currency, issued by the Japanese and denominating middle-class savings, was worthless.[5] Little remained of the oil business, once the most lucrative in Asia, and, with the flight of British management and Indian labour, the country's rice-milling, timber and mining industries were severely reduced. The country needed a moment of peace, political stability and order to reinstate a sound economy, and such was Dorman-Smith's sensible message when he presented the White Paper on the deck of HMS *Cumberland* on 20 June 1945. Direct rule need not last the full three years, he said, nor was there any reason why the enabling constitution should not be drafted very quickly if everyone cooperated in what, after all, was their common purpose, the speediest possible attainment of self-government. He repeated this message on 16 October, when his government was restored. 'Burma's fight for freedom is over,' he said cheerfully. 'Let's get on with the job!'

Get on with the job, he might, but his plea for cooperation went unheeded, for the young nationalists of the AFO saw matters differently. First, they were an alliance of the left, whose leaders 'moved back and forth within the socialist tradition' in the case of Aung San, Nu, Hla Pe, Mya, Kyaw Nyein and Thakin Ba Swe, and doctrinaire Marxists in the case of Than Tun, Ba Hein, 'Tetpongyi' Thein Pe Myint and Thakin Soe. 'Socialism, Communism, Marxism . . . were interchangeable terms in their minds';[6] colonial power was 'capitalist exploitation', pure and simple, and an 'interim period of reconstruction', a euphemism for restoring control of Burma's wealth to the very foreigners who had robbed them of it in the first place. Second, many of them had experienced the majesty of office;

[2] See Collis, 1956: 263–4.
[3] Cady, 1958: 485.
[4] Collis, 1956: 264.
[5] Tinker, 1959: 254–5; McEnery, 1990: 33.
[6] Dr Maung Maung, 1969: 54. *Accord*, Silverstein (ed.), 1993: 6–7, which suggests that the confusion owed something to the unavailability of study materials. 'They could not read systematically because much of the radical literature was proscribed.'

had acted and been treated as Burma's leaders under Dr Ba Maw and in the CAS(B). Relegating them to subordinate posts was retrograde. They wanted a provisional government of their own choosing, not 'direct' rule, and they wanted it now. Third, power and its benefits were up for grabs, and the thakin who failed to seize his opportunity effectively consigned it to a rival. 'Freedom' from 'imperialism' and 'capitalist exploitation', once tools of political analysis, now were more often crude slogans of vaulting ambition. Conflict between the two sides was inevitable.

Problems arose even before the war ended. Aung San, as we have seen, wanted to retain his Japanese-trained army as an intact and separate force. Mountbatten insisted on disbanding about half the PBF and integrating the other half as individual soldiers into the soon to be reconstituted Burma Army. Disbandment began on 30 June, but 'by 5 August only 789 of the PBF had been disbanded, with 169 arms handed in and 554 registrations of volunteers for future enlistment. . . . [T]housands of PBF were still armed in their own formations and were in some areas of lower Burma exercising control over the local population.'[7] Then Aung San ordered a halt to further disbandment. At a meeting at South East Asia Command Headquarters in Kandy in September, he 'explained his difficulty. . . . The incorporation of the PBF as individuals gave them the feeling that they had lost their soul [and were] giving up their own organization, a national institution, for nothing.'[8] The two sides struck a compromise. The Burma Army would accept up to 200 officers and 5200 other ranks from the PBF, who would form three new battalions (3rd, 4th and 5th Burma Rifles), comprising only PBF volunteers. Mountbatten characteristically viewed the compromise as a triumph of his personal powers of persuasion.

By the end of the year, 8324 PBF had passed through the demobilization centres; 4763 joined the Burma Army, and only 430 were not accounted for.[9] But these figures were perhaps more notional than real. Many who registered at the centres 'were probably

---

[7] McEnery, 1990: 32; Donnison, 1956: 364–5; 'Memorandum sent to Sir Henry Knight before commencement of his appointment as acting Governor of Burma, 21 May–14 June, 1946' (BL OIOC: M/5/103).

[8] McEnery, 1990: 32; report of meeting, headquarters, Supreme Allied Commander, South East Asia, Kandy, 6 September 1945 (BL OIOC: R/8/20); Tinker (ed.), 1984, vol. I, item 262: 443.

[9] McEnery, 1990: 32; 'Memorandum sent to Sir Henry Knight' (BL OIOC: M/5/103).

recruited into the PBF after hostilities were over'.[10] 3561 men did not volunteer, and 'did not quietly return to civil life but . . . formed the nucleus of what was represented as an "old comrades' association", *Pyithu Yebaw Ahphwe*, known in English as the People's Volunteer Organization (PVO). This was in fact a private army, with district formations throughout the country, all operating under a central headquarters controlled by Aung San.'[11] If Aung San thereby violated the spirit and letter of his Kandy compromise agreement, well, he explained, the violation enabled him 'to co-operate with and help government authorities and other organizations and the public in general in the suppression of crimes and in the maintenance of law and order in the country'.[12] By May 1946, the PVO was behaving as a 'parallel government',[13] while its nationalist allies, former BNA/PBF in the Burma Army, were receiving weapons and training and served as a useful counterpoise to the seven hill battalions there loyal to the British.

As Aung San built up his strength on the ground, the British debilitated theirs. Early in 1945, the four-year period of unbroken Far East service qualifying British troops for repatriation was reduced by four months, and, in June, by another four months. Demobilization began in June, and, by the end of 1945, was in full flood. All Indian Army fighting units (except Gurkhas) had left by 1 July 1947. 82 West African Division was repatriated between April and October 1946. 27 Field, 4 Field and 1 Medium, Royal Artillery, left in December 1946 and January 1947, while 2nd Worcester Regiment left in May 1947. By 19 July 1947—the date is important—the only British units left in the country were 2nd Durham Light Infantry (at Maymyo), 2nd Royal Berkshire Regiment (at Mingaladon) and 2nd Welch Regiment (at Kalaw), together comprising, with supporting elements, some 8530 troops. There were three Gurkha battalions of the Indian Army destined for transfer to the British Army, one at Mingaladon and two in Upper Burma. And there were another 20,580 men in the new Burma Army—including two battalions of Burma Regiment

---

[10] Tinker, 1959: 17, fn 2.

[11] Ibid.: 17.

[12] Aung San, 'Statement of General Aung San, Commander P.V.O., May 8, 1946'; reproduced with introduction in Silverstein (ed.), 1993: 43.

[13] McEnery, 1990: 51; telegram, Governor to Secretary of State, 22 May 1946 (BL OIOC: M/4/2619); Tinker (ed.), 1984, vol. I, item 576: 805.

Gurkhas,[14] six hill battalions of ex-levies,[15] one regular mixed battalion of Karens, Chins and Kachins,[16] and one Anti-Tank Regiment of mainly Chins, all of whom had fought with the British during the war and could be relied on in the event of a showdown with the PVO or a PVO-inspired insurrection.[17] But, as we shall see, the governor was constrained from using the much larger number of Indian troops still garrisoning Burma to maintain order.

Developments on the political side reflected the PVO's gaining strength on the ground. Complicating the prospects of local cooperation was the rivalry of the different parties. The governor's first intention, understandably, was to reward Sir Paw Tun and others of his pre-war administration who had remained loyal to him, but Aung San and his comrades were making all the running. Aung San had already pressed the AFO's claims to be treated as the government of Burma at his 16 May meeting with Slim, and, nine days later, in the AFO's first policy statement, it rejected the terms of the White Paper and organized the first of a series of mass meetings to enlist popular support. At a mass meeting at Naythuyein Hall on 19 August, a week after the Japanese surrender, the AFO re-named itself the Anti-Fascist People's Freedom League (AFPFL), and Aung San was elected its president. Surrounded on the podium by his commanders, 'who still had the mud of the fields on their boots',[18] he boasted of the achievements of the 'Resistance' and asked the people to rally behind them in a national front. He demanded the end of the military administration and the appointment of the League as a provisional government to supervise the elections to the constituent assembly, which would draft the constitution of a free Burma, 'because it is clear in the course of history that a Provisional Government should follow an armed insurrection before the convention of a Constituent Assembly'.[19] The League was expanded to embrace 'organizations and individuals representing a broad spectrum of social and political interests',[20]

[14] See McEnery, 1990: 130, 135.
[15] 1 and 2 Battalions, Kachin Rifles, 1 and 2 Battalions, Chin Rifles, and 1 and 2 Battalions, Karen Rifles. McEnery, 1990: 130, 135.
[16] 2 Burma Rifles, a pre-war regular battalion. Ibid.
[17] Formerly the Chin Hills Battalion of the Burma Regiment.
[18] Dr Maung Maung, 1959: 69.
[19] Dr Maung Maung, 1969: 54.
[20] Aung San Suu Kyi, 1991: 31. The English word 'freedom' masks the real meaning of *lut-lat-ye*, best translated as 'independence', while 'fascist' now signifies 'British'. Tinker, 1959: 18, fn 3.

including the ABTUC, formed on 1 June under Ba Hein's (communist) leadership, and the Revolutionary Party, which, on 1 September, emerged above ground as the Socialist Party.

Thus Dorman-Smith's task was not easy. He was bound by the carefully crafted, but perhaps myopic, terms of the White Paper, while Aung San was driven by the dynamics of the popular front and the impatient demagogy of his ambitious colleagues.

Issue was joined as soon as CAS(B) handed over to Dorman-Smith on 16 October.[21] In a gesture that the governor must have felt was generous, he offered seven of the 11 seats on his executive council to the League, which was as far as he dared go towards placating the young firebrands without abandoning those who had remained loyal to him. But, for Aung San, it was not enough. The League, and not the governor, he countered, would pick the nominees and decide their portfolios, which were to include the home portfolio. Moreover, the governor was to refer all business to the League to enable it to instruct its council members how to vote before referring it to the full council.[22] Effectively, Aung San was demanding independence under the League. It can be argued that Aung San acted out of principle; that he believed that the popular will should decide these matters and the League voiced the popular will. It is more likely that he was guided by his tactical sense, reasoning that such inherently unacceptable terms would force the governor to identify his administration with the has-beens of pre-war 'legislature politics'.[23] By such tactics, the Czar had been chased from power in 1917, and the Congress Party was advancing its claims to rule India. Dorman-Smith did not reject Aung San's audacious demands out of hand. He referred them to London, and Pethick-Lawrence, Secretary of State for India and Burma, ordered him to reject them.[24]

HMG advanced funds, reconstruction proceeded and, on 3 November, Dorman-Smith appointed his executive council, led by Sir Paw Tun and comprising two of Paw Tun's former Myochit allies.

[21] The area east of the Salween remained under military administration until 31 March 1946.
[22] Letter, T.L. Hughes to Sir Gilbert Laithwaite, 28 October 1945 (BL OIOC: M/4/2602); Tinker (ed.), 1984, vol. I, item 308: 525; Tinker, 1959: 19; Collis, 1956: 257; McEnery, 1990: 34; Dr Maung Maung, 1962: 3. Trager (1966: 70) mistakenly states that Dorman-Smith offered the League two seats on the Executive Council.
[23] Collis (1956: 257) and McEnery (1990: 34) share this view.
[24] Collis, 1956: 257.

Also included were four League representatives and three representatives from the minorities. Dorman-Smith called it a 'council of moderates' and believed that, as peacetime prosperity returned to Burma, sensible people would support it. But he was not indifferent to the widespread, rampant and daily more troublesome dacoity in the countryside and the threat that, at any moment, it might flare into a national uprising. Aung San warned him that Paw Tun 'does not know where the dumps of arms are hidden'.[25]

Notwithstanding the separation of Burma from India under the 1935 Act, responsibility for Burma remained with the same Whitehall office, which was of course preoccupied with India. As the war in the East drew to a close, this preoccupation intensified. Even Churchill's government had pledged HMG's commitment to Dominion status for India. The only issue was *when*, and this issue was resolved on 26 July 1945, when the Labour Party, which had campaigned on the promise of granting independence to India within the life of a single parliament, was elected to government in Westminster with a decisive majority. The result was a sea change in Whitehall. What was the point of holding a hard line in India, if Westminster was already pledged to grant India independence?

The Congress, having resumed its 'quit India' campaign after Nehru and six of its other leaders were released from detention in June, noisily protested the use of Indian troops to assist the French and Dutch in Indochina and Indonesia, and on 7 November Field Marshal Sir Claude Auchinleck, Commander-in-Chief, India, advised an inter-command conference in Delhi that he opposed using Indian Army units to suppress other nationalist movements in Southeast Asia and that future use should be only with Delhi's prior approval. Indian troops might be used to counter dacoity, but where to draw the line between dacoity and rebellion?

Dorman-Smith alone appears to have recognized the implications for Burma. On 11 November, when Major-General Symes, Commander South Burma District, informed him of Auchinleck's position, he cabled Whitehall: 'Either we carry out our policy or commit ourselves to complete surrender.'[26] Symes pointed out that

---

[25] Ibid.: 258.

[26] McEnery, 1990: 35; telegram, Governor of Burma to Secretary of State for Burma, 11 November 1945 (BL OIOC: M/4/2590); Tinker (ed.), 1984, vol. I, item 136: 536. After his dismissal Dorman-Smith would write, 'I was told that in the event of a rising I could not count on being allowed to use Indian troops to deal with it—in fact Indian units would be withdrawn to their

he was only reporting Auchinleck's view and not the official position of the government of India.[27] Nevertheless, the speed and nature of the evolving situation in India effectively destroyed any prospect of implementing the White Paper's carefully crafted scheme of an orderly, stage-by-stage transfer of power in Burma, since most units now garrisoning Burma were Indian Army remnants of the Fourteenth and Twelfth Armies.[28]

On the day Dorman-Smith learned of the proposed ban on use of Indian army troops in Burma, less than a month after he took over the administration of most of Burma from CAS(B), news reached him that Aung San might be charged with murder for the execution of the headman of Thebyugone village in Thaton District in 1942. The details were grisly. The murdered man, a Muslim, had assisted the British in suppressing the Thakins. The BIA had taken him to Thaton town in a bullock-cart with a pig for company, confined him for eight days without food while it advertised his pending execution, strapped him to a goal post in a football ground, and executed him before thousands of spectators. Aung San, flanked by two columns of BIA soldiers, had speared him to death with the victim's own bayonet.[29] The confidential Burma Police report of this gruesome

---

quarters if any rising in the sacred name of *freedom* broke out. Did not I understand the feeling in India about the use of Indian troops in Indonesia?' Letter, Reginald Dorman-Smith to G.F. Sayers, 8 February 1947, in Dorman-Smith archive at the India Office Library.

[27] McEnery, 1990: 35; telegram, Governor of Burma to Secretary of State for Burma, 12 November 1945 (BL OIOC: M/4/2589); Tinker (ed.), 1984, vol. I, item 137: 536.

[28] Consisting in January 1946 primarily of ten Indian battalions of 17 Indian Division. Reinforced by an extra brigade, the division disposed of 18 battalions, as well as artillery and one Indian armoured car regiment. Four of its battalions were Gurkha and the remaining four British. Such a large garrison was deemed necessary to defend Burma from *external* attack (by China). In September 1946, the operational requirement of defending against external attack was dropped, and the decision taken to reduce the force to three Indian Army brigades of three battalions each, one Indian, one Gurkha and one British, a level reached in January 1947. The remaining Indian Army units were recalled to India by the end of June 1947. John McEnery, correspondence with author, October 2000.

[29] Petition of Ma Ahma, wife of the late Abdul Raschid, 8 April 1946 (BL OIOC: M/5/102); Tinker (ed.), 1984, vol. 1, item 452: 728. Tun Ok, who stated that he was an eye-witness to the murder, maintained that Aung San used his own sword instead of the victim's bayonet. Telegram, Sir Reginald Dorman-Smith to Secretary of State for Burma, 25 February 1946 (BL OIOC: M/5/102); Tinker (ed.), 1984, vol. 1, item 406: 661.

crime was sent to Mountbatten, who, always the apologist for Aung San, responded: '[I]n the unsettled conditions which must have existed, it was only to be expected, I suppose, that summary justice would rule, and that old scores would be paid off.'[30]

Dorman-Smith again sought instructions from Whitehall. Whitehall equivocated (perhaps because Thaton remained under military government), their advice to the government alternating between suggesting to Aung San that he use the investigation as an opportunity to clear his name, or pressing ahead with a prosecution, or bringing Aung San into the executive council. The military took a consistently cautious line. There were forces enough even without the Indian Army units to put down a rebellion, they advised,[31] but did the government really want to embroil HM Forces in counter-insurgency of the kind that engaged the French and Dutch? Far better to conciliate the AFPFL, they said.

The League held its first congress in January 1946. Delegates from all over Burma and 100,000 supporters attended. 'Aung San, always frank to a fault, showed [Dorman-Smith] the agenda. The first item declared that the governor was unworthy to represent a democratic country like Britain. "It will be passed by acclamation," he explained.'[32] The League could not force the British to withdraw. But it could paralyse the government's activities. It could use the threat of a national uprising, without actually inciting an uprising. The policy 'would involve obstructing and slowing down the measures framed to restore the country. The people would suffer, their recovery be delayed, for the [reconstruction] programme admittedly had its good points. But liberty could not be purchased for nothing.'[33] To manifest its military potential, the PVO, already fomenting obstruction and organizing strikes, began drilling in public.

Dorman-Smith supported a League initiative to send a delegation led by Aung San to London, but Whitehall replied that the cabinet would not receive such a delegation.

---

[30] Cypher, Lieutenant General G.W. Symes to Sir Reginald Dorman-Smith, 18 November 1945 (BL OIOC: MSS Eur F 169/1); Tinker (ed.), 1984, vol. 1, item 324: 543.

[31] McEnery, 1990: 49–50; telegram, Lieutenant General Sir Montague Stopford to Lieutenant General F.E.W. Simpson, 10 May 1946 (BL OIOC: L/WS/1/1052); Tinker (ed.), 1984, vol. I, item 497: 781.

[32] Collis, 1956: 263.

[33] Ibid.: 264.

The governor pressed on with his plans for the economy regardless, enlisting the help of British firms who had managed the timber, rice milling, petroleum and mining industries to foster Burman enterprise, but this opened him to the charge of acting as a 'capitalist stooge' of the City of London, an allegation voiced at frequent mass meetings organized by the League and aired dramatically in the local press. Reconstruction even divided the governor from some of his supporters, who sought to outbid, not oppose, the League's demands.[34] Paw Tun, who lacked the power of arrest but wanted to remove Aung San from the political arena on a charge of sedition, tried to persuade the governor to arrest him. Dorman-Smith rejected the idea and decided instead to broaden participation in the political arena. He asked London to release U Saw and, moreover, to ask Washington to release Ba Maw and Ba Sein.

London continued to vacillate. On 19 January, with dacoity fast spreading in Pegu District, Mountbatten reminded Dorman-Smith of the decision taken against deployment of Indian troops, and he added that opinion in America would oppose propping up his government with an old-style British expeditionary force. At any rate, he said, such a despatch was doubtful, considering Britain's already huge debts and war-weariness and the number of British and Dominion troops available for deployment from SEAC. Yet London still refused to entertain the proposal to send a League delegation to Westminster: how could it deal with any one party claiming to represent Burmese nationalist opinion, while others the governor had appointed to his council ventured the same claim? The terms of the White Paper would have to be adhered to; there would have to be an election. Paw Tun advised that he could form the necessary front, and U Saw, that he could induce his party to join the front. Both counselled the governor that Aung San's popularity was waning. Dorman-Smith decided to press for an early election. If the electorate chose Aung San, then no one could accuse HMG of deserting its friends.

The first session of the legislative council envisaged by the White Paper began on 28 February. The League, having refused its cooperation, was not represented, and the members, all picked by the governor and encouraged to express their views freely, immediately rounded on the League. Tun Ok, former thakin, one of

[34] 'The difference between them . . . lay not in principle but in rivalry for power.' Ibid.: 267.

the Thirty Comrades, *ahnashin* of the *Baho* regime, and a minister in Dorman-Smith's executive council, exploited the moment to accuse Aung San of murder. He had been at Thebyugone village at the time of the murder, he declaimed, had witnessed the murder, and was prepared to testify so in court. The ensuing publicity both in London and Rangoon now confronted the government openly with the dilemma it had wanted most to avoid—whether to cave in to Aung San, or uphold the law and risk a Burman insurrection.

Procrastination satisfied everyone save Aung San's rivals and the widow of the murdered headman, but Aung San confronted the government squarely with the need to act by admitting the truth of the accusation.[35] Dorman-Smith recommended to Whitehall accordingly that the investigation proceed and that Aung San be arrested—but after 'Resistance Day',[36] when there might be trouble. Mountbatten, serving his twilight hours in Singapore as Supreme Commander Southeast Asia before assuming his responsibilities as Viceroy of India, weighed in with the view that arrest be postponed until there was a full investigation.

The matter was thrashed out at a meeting convened by Sir John Wise, the governor's chief adviser, at Government House on 27 March, while the governor was up-country. Mr Chettle, Inspector General of Police, Mr Orr, chief of the Criminal Investigation Department, General Briggs, General Officer Commanding-in-Chief, Burma Army, and Major-General Thomas, Inspector General of the Burma Army, attended. All accepted that arresting Aung San would trigger a rebellion. While there had been some defections from the League, Aung San remained popular, particularly in the rural population, they said, and the 3000–4000 strong ex-PBF contingent in the Burma Army would probably mutiny. Aung San himself, they thought, was too sensible to start a rebellion, as he had too much to lose and nothing to gain by a rebellion. His arrest would only eliminate his restraining influence,[37] nor would it ease matters on

[35] He published a rationalization in Burmese in the *Thadinsone Journal* of 12 April 1946. The *Hanthawaddy* published an English translation. 'All that I remember is that the headman was a wicked person who ill-treated his villagers. . . . It was also reported to me that the offences he committed merit no less a punishment than death.' Translation of extract from Hanthawaddy newspaper, 7 April 1946, forwarded by T.L. Hughes to Sir Gilbert Laithwaite, 10 April 1946 (BL OIOC: M/5/102); Tinker (ed.), 1984, vol. I, item 451: 726.
[36] 27 March, a national holiday in Burma commemorating the moment in 1945 when the BNA betrayed the Japanese.
[37] Collis, 1956: 275.

the political front. His rivals, all bidding to take over the League, would turn on the government with intensified fury as soon as he was behind bars. A book published by Tun Ok in 1943 showed him to be even more violently anti-British than was Aung San, and Tun Ok had committed darker deeds. The ban on use of Indian army troops, while not strictly applicable to containing an uprising, obliged them to do everything possible to avoid one. They recommended that Whitehall be asked to review the White Paper and specify a date for transferring power. Sir John Wise, who believed that rebellion was inevitable regardless of whether Aung San was arrested, said the country was awash with weapons and compared the situation to 'sitting on a barrel of gunpowder'. After Dorman-Smith returned to Rangoon and reviewed the notes of this meeting, he telegraphed Whitehall rescinding his previous advice.

The matter might have ended there. In early April, however, the murdered headman's widow formally pressed charges, engaging the governor's duty to enforce the law. Dorman-Smith reverted to his first position and recommended Aung San's arrest. If this entailed deployment of Indian troops, it could not be claimed they were being used to suppress a nationalist movement, and General Briggs agreed. Whitehall signalled its approval—and almost in the same breath rescinded, instructing the governor to 'suspend action on the arrest *pro tem* without prejudice'. London was under pressure from Delhi, then undergoing its own trials in setting up an interim government agreeable to both the Congress Party and the Muslim League. Delhi advised: 'the use of Indian troops to maintain the existing Government in Burma against the AFPFL would clearly not secure the assent of a new interim government'. Thenceforth, Aung San's arrest and prosecution was not an option.

The contradiction inherent in British policy that Dorman-Smith had foreseen in November—carry on with the scheme of the White Paper, while seriously undermining Britain's strength on the ground—was following its inexorable course. The governor tried to preserve what he could from the ruins, pressing new ideas on Whitehall almost every day and perhaps too energetically. By June, Prime Minister Attlee concluded that he had 'lost his grip'. Sir Henry Knight took over as acting governor, and Dorman-Smith left Burma for England on leave to recover from amoebic dysentery. He was never to return. Attlee decided to replace him and, on 19 July, the acting governor decreed that no one would be prosecuted for crimes committed during the war, save on the governor's instructions. The solution to the problem had been found, but at the cost of both Dorman-Smith and the White Paper. Aung San's victory was assured. It was left to the new governor, Sir Hubert Rance, to work through the details.

Rance was sworn in as governor on the last day of August 1946. Although he had full authority to reconstitute the executive council with a League majority, events would cast him as acting under the compulsion of the *vox populi*. Dacoits masquerading as patriots were pressing hard on the rural areas north and east of the capital, and, six days after he was sworn into office, union leaders brought the police out on strike over an issue of pay. Other government departments, posts and telegraphs, railway staff and government clerks, followed suit, and they were joined by employees of foreign firms, oilfield workers and students.[38] 'The People's Volunteer Organization, with brazen effrontery, took over the policing of Rangoon, and made a significant and very largely successful appeal to criminals to abstain from crime during the strikes in the national interest.'[39] The leaders of the 'White Flag' communists[40] and the Socialists,[41] who remained within the League in uneasy alliance, and Thakin Soe, who had led the 'Red Flag' communists underground in July, vied with each other and Aung San in deriving the maximum possible personal advantage from the general tension. Yet again, policy was beholden to the principle that whoever was loudest in blaming the colonial 'exploiters' and their 'capitalist minions' would inherit the spoils, and moderation had no voice. Countenancing gradualism would have meant political suicide. Independence *now* was the one panacea for all Burma's ills.[42]

Six of the nine seats in Rance's new executive council went to the League, one to the Karen leader, Saw Ba U Gyi, and, as a vestigial genuflection to the old order, one to Saw. Aung San was now the deputy chairman (equivalent to the position Nehru held in India),

[38] Tinker, 1959: 21.
[39] Donnison, 1970: 133.
[40] Thakin Than Tun.
[41] Thakin Mya, Thakin Kyaw Nyein and Thakin Ba Swe.
[42] Compare telegram, General Officer Commanding Burma Command to War Office, 13 December 1946 ('AFPFL, having taken office, and taunted as traitors by Communists whom they [subsequently] expelled [from the Executive Council and the AFPFL], must justify themselves as having expedited self-government or resign') (BL OIOC: M/4/2621); Tinker (ed.), 1984, vol. II, item 136: 189.

Thakin Mya the home member (displacing Sir Paw Tun) and Tin Tut (now retired from the civil service and Aung San's close ally, though not yet formally a member of the League) finance member (displacing Htoon Aung Gyaw, another pre-war veteran). Just as the League had demonstrated its authority by inciting the strikes, it now reaffirmed its authority by ending them—but only as a temporary relaxation of the pressure on HMG. On 10 November, as the country was returning to relative calm, it announced the following demands:

1. On or before April 1947, elections were to be held for a constituent assembly.
2. The elections were to embrace the Frontier Areas, as well as Burma Proper.
3. On or before 31 January 1947, the British government would pledge to give Burma full independence within a year.
4. There would be a review of the 'projects' scheme (reserving to British firms the contracts for rehabilitating Burma's economy).[43]

Overhanging these demands, as always, was the threat of rebellion.

Attlee, now almost eager to quit himself of the whole messy business of ruling these implacable young hotheads, announced in the House of Commons on 20 December that a 'Burmese' delegation was to be invited to London to discuss arrangements for a transfer of power. Aung San accepted the invitation. However, as even negotiating with the colonial masters comported a risk of loss of face, he announced at the same time that he would call out his troops if Westminster failed to satisfy his demands.[44] The delegation arrived in London on 9 January 1947, and discussions were conducted against the backdrop of communist manifestations and a League-organized civil servants strike in Burma, lest HMG forget what by now should have been plain, that the League's consent was indispensable to administering the country. The one sticking point in the negotiations was the fate of the Frontier Areas, and here Governor

---

[43] Donnison, 1970: 133.

[44] 'In accepting the [invitation] Bogyoke [Aung San] urged the [League's Executive] Committee . . . to start preparing the country for all eventualities including armed rising.' Pe Kin, 1994: 54. Pe Kin was a member of this committee. 'In his speech to the crowd, Aung San explained why the AFPFL had accepted the invitation from London. . . . However, the masses must be prepared for an armed struggle if things did not turn out as hoped.' U Maung Maung, 1989: 253, citing a report in *New Light of Myanmar*, 2 January 1947.

Rance indicated the way forward. He counselled Westminster not to leave the matter of HMG's financial contribution to the budget of the Frontier Areas Administration 'entirely in the hands of the Areas themselves. Theoretically the choice lies with them. In practice they have no option without our support'.[45] In short, if leverage was needed to extricate HMG from its wartime commitments to the hill peoples, it would be used. Noel Stevenson, director of the Frontier Areas Administration, warned Attlee of the implications of this policy and was ignored.

The Attlee–Aung San Agreement, signed on 27 January, mapped the way forward. Burma would receive its independence 'as soon as possible'. There would be a general election in April to establish a constituent assembly to settle the future constitution. Meanwhile, the executive council would act as the interim government of Burma, and the British military would continue its involvement with the Burma Army—that is to say, the British would assist the League in putting down the communists. London accepted that the 'objective of both His Majesty's Government and the Burmese Delegates [was] to achieve the early unification of the Frontier Areas and Ministerial Burma . . . with the free consent of the inhabitants of those areas', and to that end, the Government would remove all restrictions on Burman access to the Frontier Areas, a conference would be convened at Panglong to solicit the views of the 'leaders and representatives of the peoples of the Frontier Areas', and a Frontier Areas Committee of Enquiry (FACE) would take evidence and determine the wishes of the peoples of the Frontier Areas.

Aung San, having got all the terms he[46] wanted and won a clear victory over his communist rivals, whose cries of 'collaboration' and

---

[45] Telegram, Sir Hubert Rance to Lord Pethick-Lawrence, 23 January 1947 (BL: OIOC: M/4/2811); Tinker (ed.), 1984, vol. II, item 231: 347. For a brief discussion of HMG's vacillation over the issue, see U Maung Maung, 1989: 257. Aung San's views may be gauged by his speech at the opening session of his discussions with Attlee: 'When we speak of Burma, we envisage a Burma united and free. There are no insurmountable obstacles in the way of achieving that unity. If all the racial groups in the country are offered full freedom, and if they but meet together without outside interference, they will unite.' Quoted in Dr Maung Maung (ed.), 1962: 106.

[46] The two Karen members of the executive council were not included in the delegation, and Kachin and Shan leaders warned the parties they would not be bound by any arrangements between them, while U Saw and Ba Sein, each with his own political party, dissented from the Attlee–Aung San Agreement. See Smith, 1991: 77–8; Pe Kin, 1994: 55.

'neo-colonialism' were only dissonant noises in a fanfare of praise, now returned to Rangoon in triumph. But, as Noel Stevenson had forewarned, the Karens, whose loyalty in war had been tested *against* the Burmans, were unenthusiastic. British officers had assured them repeatedly that a victorious Britain would not hand them over to the Burmans; Mountbatten himself had made this pledge to them.[47] The previous August they had sent a delegation of lawyers to London to plead their case for separation—under British protection, if possible. Attlee had received them politely,[48] but counselled them to come to terms with Aung San.

The Rangoon dailies published the text of the Attlee–Aung San Agreement on 29 January. Exactly one week later, the KNU was formed, and its first resolution reaffirmed the Karens' aspirations for a separate state.[49] On 6 February, the Shans, Kachins and Chins advised the government that their demand to be represented at the London talks had been rejected and, hence, the Attlee–Aung San Agreement was not binding on them.[50] Nevertheless, the government pressed ahead with its new agenda, confident that it now had the tools it needed to disengage itself from Burma with honour.

An Aung San-led League delegation met with representatives from the Frontier Areas at Panglong, a market town in the Shan States, and the parties concluded the Panglong Agreement.

Burma now celebrates 12 February, the anniversary of the signing of this document, as Union Day, when the people of the Frontier Areas agreed to join a Greater Burma, but this document signified no such thing. Paragraph 8(b) of the Attlee–Aung San Agreement providing for the Panglong Agreement states:

> The leaders and representatives of the peoples of the Frontier Areas shall be asked . . . at the Panglong Conference . . . to express their views upon the form of association with the Government of

[47] Letter to the author from Colonel Ronald Kaulback, 8 February 1991, reproduced in Tucker, 2000: 367–70. See also Frontier Areas Committee of Enquiry, 1947 (FACE), *Report*: 17 (referring to the bitterness felt by the Karens on realizing that the letters received from Field Marshal Auchinleck and Admiral Mountbatten were 'meaningless, and such other assurances . . . empty').

[48] '[T]he most exciting event the British hosts arranged for their Karen visitors appears to have been a visit to the Sunlight Soap Factory outside London.' Lintner, 1994: 69.

[49] Ibid.: 70–1.

[50] Pe Kin, 1994: 76.

Burma which they consider acceptable *during the transition period* [to independence].[51]

The preamble of the Panglong Agreement states:

The Members of the [Panglong] Conference, believing that *freedom will be more speedily achieved* by the Shans, the Kachins and the Chins *by their immediate co-operation with the Interim Burmese Government* . . . have accordingly . . . agreed . . .

Clause 5 of the Panglong Agreement states:

Though *the Governor's* Executive Council will be augmented as agreed above [by the appointment of hill peoples representatives to advise it on matters pertaining to the Frontier Areas] *it will not operate in respect of the Frontier Areas in any manner which would deprive any portion of these areas of the autonomy which it now enjoys in internal administration. Full autonomy in internal administration for the Frontier Areas is accepted in principle.*[52]

It is thus clear that the signatories to the Panglong Agreement *believed* they were assenting to early independence from Britain *and* the perpetuation of their freedom from British and Burman interference in their internal affairs; that, whatever their commitment, it was not to permanent and irrevocable integration in an *independent* Union of Burma *ruled by Burmans*. Cooperation did not mean integration or submission; indeed, clause 5 preserved explicitly their existing 'autonomy . . . in internal administration'. The principles that would govern their relations with Burma *after* 'the period of transition to independence' were yet to be agreed.[53] The government

[51] London: HMSO, Cmd. 7029, 1947. Reproduced in Dr Maung Maung, 1956: 187, and Pe Kin, 1994: 150. Italics added. See also, Narrative, Arthur George Bottomley (BL OIOC: MSS EUR E 362/2); Tinker (ed.), 1984, vol. II: 846.
[52] Italics added. Panglong Agreement, telegram, Aung San to Lord Pethwick-Lawrence, 12 February 1947 (BL OIOC: M/4/2811); Tinker (ed.), 1984, vol. II, item 280: 404–5; also reproduced in FACE, *Report*: 16–17, and as appendix II in Dr Maung Maung, 1959: 229–30. The version printed in Pe Kin (1994: 83–4), published under the constraints of the military's censorship laws and sold in the streets in Burma, critically omits from clause 5 the words, 'Full autonomy in internal administration for the Frontier Areas is accepted in principle.'
[53] This point is confirmed explicitly in 'Note by John Leyden on the Panglong Conference, 1947', 20 February 1947 (BL OIOC: M/4/2811); Tinker (ed.), 1984, vol. II, item 294: 427, 429.

was still a British government, and the 'as soon as possible' for the proposed transfer of power still seemed remote. Nor did Panglong's signatories represent *all* 'the peoples of the Frontier Areas'. A delegation of four Karens arrived late at the conference, attended as observers and were not consulted,[54] Karennis were also there solely as observers and not consulted,[55] and the Chins of the Arakan Hill Tracts, Was, Nagas, Lushais, Palaungs, Paos, Akhas, Lahus and dozens of smaller tribes were not represented at all.[56]

The next device used to fudge Britain's wartime pledges to its allies was FACE. FACE's task, it is to be noted, was to 'report on the best method of associating the Frontier peoples with the working out of the new constitution for Burma'[57]—*not whether they desired such an association*—and the committee was to comprise

> equal numbers of persons from Ministerial Burma, nominated by the Executive Council, and of persons from the Frontier Areas, nominated by the Governor after consultation with the leaders of those areas, with a neutral Chairman from outside Burma selected by agreement.[58]

In the event, the 'neutral' Chairman was Lieutenant Colonel David Rees Rees-Williams, a Labour MP whose only previous involvment with Southeast Asia had been a spell of legal practice in Malaya in 1930–34.[59] His secretary was William Bernard John Ledwidge, who had made one previous trip to Burma lasting a few weeks,[60] while seven of the eight members, including three of the four representatives of the Frontier Areas, were League nominees.[61] The committee's remit included only the Frontier Areas; it thus

[54] FACE, *Appendices*: 124; Pe Kin, 1994: 68–70; Tinker, 1959: 24.

[55] Pe Kin, 1994: 68–70.

[56] Smith, 1991: 79. Compare, 'Note by John Leyden on the Panglong Conference, 1947', 20 February 1947 (BL OIOC: M/4/2811); Tinker (ed.), 1984, vol. I, item 294: 247. See also FACE, *Report*: 16 ('terms of the Panglong Agreement . . . regulated relationships between Burma and the major portion of the Frontier Areas').

[57] Paragraph 8(d), Attlee–Aung San Agreement. See also FACE, *Report*: 22.

[58] Attlee–Aung San Agreement, paragraph 8(d).

[59] Lintner, 1994: 72.

[60] He had assisted Arthur Bottomley the year before at the first Panglong conference. See Silverstein, 1980: 109.

[61] The members of the committee were Tin Tut (Aung San's ally and member of the executive council); U Nu (League vice-president); Khin Maung Gale (student union leader from Mandalay during the Nu-led Student Strike of

excluded Arakan, which was already in rebellion,[62] as well as the Delta, the Tenasserim and Salween District, home to nearly all Mons and most Karens.

FACE's whirlwind deliberations began in March and concluded in April. Its report noted tendentiously that 'in the minds of many of the witnesses from the Frontier Areas' participation in a constituent assembly was an issue 'inextricably intertwined' with the question of their future under the new constitution, and 'they appear[ed] to view the two questions as different facets of a single great problem'.[63] On the contrary, various witnesses indicated a clear preference to remain aloof from Central Burma.

> *Thakin Nu*: Do you think if Burma severs her connection from the British you will suffer?
> *Saw Marshall Schwin*: Certainly.
> *U Kyaw Nyein*: Supposing the world situation is such that Burma can stand on her own legs and can defend herself against any possible foreign aggression, would you object to Burma's secession from the British Empire and would you object to joining Burma?
> *Saw Marshall Schwin*: I do not think this is likely to be for a thousand years to come.

> Q. Do you want any sort of association with other people?
> A. We do not want to join anybody because in the past we have been very independent.
> Q. What do you want the future to be of the Wa states?

1936 and League member); Kyaw Nyein (League member and home member in the executive council), who participated during the Rangoon hearings and was replaced by Saw Myint Thein (Karen Youth Organization [KYO], which supported the League) for the Maymyo hearings; the Mongpawn *saohpa*, Sam Htun ('one of the few sawbwas who saw the writing on the wall and was prepared to go along with the people' [Pe Kin, 1994: 78], a signatory of the Panglong Agreement and member of the executive council); the Sama *duwa*, Sinwa Nawng ('the Kachin chief who had contacted Aung San since January 1946 and who stood up very strongly for union with Burma' [U Maung Maung, 1989: 289], a signatory of the Panglong Agreement and deputy counsellor for the Kachins under the Panglong Agreement); Vum Ko Hau (deputy counsellor for the Chins under the Panglong Agreement) and Saw Sankey (KNU).
[62] Labelled 'dacoity' at the time.
[63] FACE, *Report*: 22.

A. We have not thought about that because we are wild people. We never thought of the administrative future. We only think about ourselves.

Q. Don't you want education, clothing, good food, good houses, hospitals, etc.?

A. We are very wild people and we do not appreciate all these things.[64]

Others seemed baffled by the proceedings and wondered why their views were sought:

The chieftain told me that he had received orders from Government to come and listen to what the Committee had to say. . . . I do not know anything [about the committee]. . . . As for the future, we would like to remain as in the past, that is, independent of other people.[65]

The Yawnghwe *saohpa*, who was chairman of the Supreme Council of the United Hill Peoples, a coalition allied to the League, declared: 'We want to associate with Burma on the condition that full autonomy is guaranteed in our internal administration', a federalist view echoed by Kachin and Chin witnesses.[66] The Karennis reaffirmed their existing status as independent states and stated they would negotiate the terms of any association with Burma after examining its new constitution.[67] Nevertheless, the *selected evidence admitted into the record* presented opinion in the Frontier Areas as *divided* on the fundamental issue of union with Burma, with the 'weight of opinion' in favour.[68]

---

[64] FACE, *Appendices*: 37–9, 128–9; reproduced in Lintner, 1994: 73. All the other Delta Karens who testified were members of the KYO. FACE, *Report*: 20.

[65] FACE, *Appendices*: 37; Quoted in Tinker, 1959: 25, fn 1.

[66] Lintner, 1994: 72.

[67] U Maung Maung, 1989: 291–2.

[68] FACE, *Report*: 28. 'The selection of the main body of witnesses was carried out by the Councils in each area; but it was also announced that any individual or organization who was dissatisfied with the selected list of witnesses might apply to the Committee for a separate interview. A number of requests of this kind were received and all were accepted.' Ibid.:15. This seemed fair in principle, but, in fact, it allowed the more organized League to proffer testimony opposing whatever did not suit them. For example, after the witnesses selected to represent the Salween Karens had presented their views, the AFPFL/KYO sent other witnesses who controverted them. See U Maung Maung, 1989: 290–1, for a Burman justification for this practice.

The report was a model of its kind: concise, intelligible, internally consistent and ostensibly fair. It presented a scholarly and sympathetic account of the diverse histories of the hill peoples,[69] reciting faithfully the language of the Anglo-Burmese treaty of 1875 guaranteeing the independence and sovereignty of Western Karenni,[70] recording candidly that Burman pretensions of suzerainty over the Kachins had 'meant little in practice',[71] and confessing the desire of the Shan and Kachin witnesses for 'the fullest possible autonomy' within a federal Burma and the Chins' desire to continue 'to administer their tracts as at present'.[72] It suggested a number of measures to secure the proper representation of the hill peoples in the constituent assembly: they were to be eligible for places on all committees, their participation was to carry no implication of committing them to union with Burma, and no proposal affecting their governance was to be carried without a majority of the votes of their representatives.[73] However, the report stated misleadingly that almost 'all of the witnesses expressed without hesitation the desire that representatives of their States or local areas should take part' in the constituent assembly,[74] and, on the doubtful pretext of 'reduc[ing] the craziness of the patchwork quilt which the present administration of the Frontier Areas resembles', it recommended detaching large areas from these states and attaching these areas to Ministerial Burma. Kokang, whose representative, the report claimed, had assented to 'co-operation', should be administered as a sub-state of North Hsenwi, the Wa States either as part of the Federated Shan States or by a 'Federal Council' with reserved seats for the non-Burman States 'somewhat on the lines of a Legislature' under an 'interim Constitution', while the Naga Hills should be supervised 'by the Government of Burma proper'.[75] The question of Karen and Chin participation in the proposed federation, the report suggested, should be deferred. Rees-Williams, in short, crafted a document that

[69] FACE, *Report*: 6 ff.
[70] Ibid.: 11.
[71] Ibid.: 9.
[72] Ibid.: 26.
[73] Ibid.: 25–6.
[74] Ibid.: 22.
[75] Ibid.: 26–7, 29–31. Ministerial Burma, strictly, consisted of Burma Proper and some pockets of significant Burman presence in the Frontier Areas, such as Myitkyina, but 'Burma Proper' or 'proper' and 'Ministerial Burma' are often used interchangeably.

shielded Westminster from attack by critics disposed to accuse it of having sold out to Aung San.

Donnison served as chief secretary in the home department of all of the last three governors, and his observations concerning these developments bear repeating:

> Failure to gain the 'free consent' of the minorities was unthinkable, for this could only result in the rejection of the offer by the AFPFL. In this case insurrection and chaos would result. In the circumstances both British and Burm[ans] were deeply committed to obtaining that 'free consent'. Indeed it is pretty clear that the British government was not prepared to take no for an answer from the frontier areas. For the London agreement, although it referred to the 'free consent' of the inhabitants of these areas, went on to provide that the views of the inhabitants should be ascertained regarding the arrangements for the government of the areas both under the existing interim government and under the future independent government of Burma. The question that was to be put to the inhabitants about both these periods was not whether the frontier areas should or should not be unified with the rest of Burma. It was assumed that unification would take place. In regard to the interim government the minorities were to be asked 'to express their views upon the form of association with the Government of Burma which they consider acceptable during the transition period'. As far as independent Burma was concerned a committee was to be set up to inquire 'as to the best method of associating the frontier peoples with the working-out of the new constitution for Burma'. It is clear that it was not intended that the minorities should be consulted on the question that was really exercising them. . . . What [the minorities] agreed to was *co-operation*, and co-operation, not with independent Burma, but with the interim Burmese government, which still had a British governor, and under which they had been guaranteed that there would be no diminution in the independence they had hitherto enjoyed from control by the government set up under the constitution of 1937.[76]

Nevertheless, Donnison points out difficulties inherent in minority aspirations for independence from Burma and that Westminster's options were limited:

[76] Donnison, 1970: 135–7. Italics in the original.

In excuse for this burking of the real issue it may be argued that separate independent states for the minorities would not have been politically, militarily, or economically viable, and that the British could not in fact afford to oppose the Burm[ans] on this point. The Shans could have opted for inclusion in Thailand whose people are of similar race, though they probably would not have done so. . . . [I]t may be . . . that the unsophisticated leaders of the minority communities never had much choice or chance.[77]

Panglong's Shan, Kachin and Chin signatories left no record of their discussions,[78] but it seems inconceivable that they were not aware of Britain's predicament. Commissioner Stevenson had offered them the option of a protectorate now with the promise of a separate independence later,[79] but Stevenson, rumour had it, had been forced

---

[77] Ibid.: 136.

[78] See Smith, 1991: 78 (a 'complete account of what actually took place at Panglong has yet to be written'). Leyden compiled a lengthy report, 'Note by John Leyden on the Panglong Conference, 1947' (BL OIOC: M/4/2811); Tinker (ed.), 1984, vol. II, item 294: 423–30. Bottomley, who, as the under-secretary, Dominions Office, attended the conference, left a record (BL OIOC: MSS EUR E 362/2); Tinker (ed.), vol. II: 841–7. U Maung Maung (1989: 329, 330–1, notes 4, 20, 23–5, 27–9 and 31–5) refers to a document called 'Brief History of the Panglong Conference' that is at least 195 pages in length without, however, citing its author, publisher or place or date of publication. Pe Kin (1994: 13), without citing sources, states: 'Much has already been written about the Pinlon Conference and the historic Agreement it produced.'

[79] There was a conference in December 1946 at Manhkring, a part of Myitkyina, at which three Kachin leaders (Sinwa Nawng, Zau Rip and Dinra Tang) were selected to join with three others from Bhamo (Zau La, Zau Lawn and Labang Grong) to represent the Kachins in talks with the Burmans. Aung San met with Sinwa Nawng before the conference and promised to make him the first governor of Kachin State in return for his support. The promise was honoured. Sinwa Nawng also served in Nu's cabinet. As the Sama *duwa*, Sinwa Nawng was perhaps the most important of the Kachin's leaders, and the views he expressed at the Manhkring conference (and no doubt later in Kutkai and Panglong) carried great weight with Kachins there. He persuaded them to accept cooperation with the League and to reject Noel Stevenson's offer of protectorate status by defining the issue in terms of the most expeditious means of achieving their own independence. Sinwa Nawng's father had been killed during the 'pacification' of the Kachin Hills, and he was fiercely anti-British. He was one of the few Kachins, perhaps the only Kachin, who supported the Japanese during the war. He died a disillusioned man in 1971, after Ne Win refused to allow him to travel abroad to seek medical treatment for cancer. See Tucker, 2000: 167–8.

to resign.[80] Would Attlee, who had pointedly excluded them from the London talks, really give them a protectorate and risk a clash with the League? After a transfer of power, was such long-range protection feasible? Parallel developments in India, where HMG seemed about to renege on its treaty obligations to the princely states, were not encouraging. Was Aung San right in advising that their interests would be served best by *cooperating* with him in the *transition* to independence? Indeed, as Donnison suggests, perhaps 'the unsophisticated leaders of the minority communities' did perceive that they had neither 'choice' nor 'chance'.

The Attlee–Aung San Agreement adopted the reserved places scheme of the 1935 Act by which the constituent assembly would comprise non-communal and reserved constituencies, and elections for the assembly were held on 7 April. As the KNU, Karennis (soon to form their 'United Karenni Independent States'), the CPB, Saw's Myochit Party, Ba Sein's Dobama and Ba Maw and his Maha Bama (Greater Burma) Party all refused to participate, the result was a foregone conclusion. Widespread intimidation reinforced this certainty. Armed PVO units dragooned voters and escorted them to the polling booths that were guarded by other armed PVO units, while League supporters manned the government-provided electoral information facilities.[81] The opposition put up only 28 candidates, who were individual communists without the official backing of the CPB, and won only seven seats.[82]

PVO uniforms were much in evidence again when the 255 members of the constituent assembly convened on 9 June. Thakin Mya chaired the opening ceremonies, Nu was elected its president and, on 16 June, Aung San moved the resolution that decided that

[80] On 20 January. Pe Kin (1994: 75) states that he resigned, U Maung Maung (1989: 279 and 330, fn 18), that he was 'retired', alternatively, 'sacked'. He was succeeded as director of the Frontier Areas Administration by John Leyden, one of the few officers in the FAA who supported Attlee's policy of uniting Ministerial Burma and the Frontier Areas under one administration controlled by Burmans.

[81] Tinker, 1959: 26. Compare 'Latest Developments—Political Situation in Burma to 6th November 1947', a memorandum prepared by the Reverend J.W. Baldwin (BL OIOC: M/4/2756), pp. 2–3. Reproduced in pertinent part in chapter 6.

[82] The preponderance of the League's victory was: non-communal League members 175; Frontier Areas members (comprising mainly Panglong signatories) 45; Karen members (all nominated by the KYO) 24; Anglo-Burmans four; opposition members (communist independents) seven.

independent Burma was to be a republic outside the Commonwealth. He and his colleagues had already prepared a draft of what would become, with insignificant alterations, the first constitution of an independent Union of Burma.

6
A Hero's Death

A 'UNITED' BURMA under Burman domination was now assured, and Stevenson's plan for a separate Frontier Areas including the Arakan hill tracts, Karenni, Toungoo and Salween Districts, and parts of Thaton and Moulmein[1] was dead. The Karens and Karennis stood alone.

But not quite. The communists boiled with resentment. Unlike Aung San, they had identified fascism as the primary enemy and opposed the Japanese *throughout* the war, Soe and 'Tetpongyi' Thein Pe Myint openly and Than Tun clandestinely.[2] BNA units under their commanders had turned on the Japanese three weeks before BNA units under non-communist commanders.[3] Hence, they now expected the lion's share of the fruits of victory. If it suited Aung San to combine with them against the British, well, conceptually, it suited them to combine with him in their 'great national liberation struggle': the 'final seizure of power' by 'the People' (themselves) awaited the *departure* of the British. But this 'tactical cooperation' was under strain. It was becoming daily more obvious that 'bourgeois careerists' were gaining ascendancy in the League, formed at their initiative, and that Aung San was outmanoeuvring them.

In July 1946, 'bourgeois careerists' forced Than Tun's resignation as the League's general secretary, and, as seen, in September, Rance appointed Aung San deputy chairman of his executive council. The 'greatest general strike in the post-war period' now ended. Perhaps Aung San's appointment and the ending of the strike were not connected, but the Party believed otherwise and exploded, accusing the League's leaders of a sell-out. The League responded by expelling the Party, and, on 20 October, Aung San made a blistering attack on it from the steps of the Swedagon.

First, he claimed for himself and his faction within the BNA principal responsibility for having architected the AFO/AFPFL and

---

[1] U Maung Maung, 1989: 256.
[2] As minister of land and agriculture in Ba Maw's wartime cabinet.
[3] Smith, 1991: 61.

the Burman 'Resistance'[4]—but this was disingenuous. In 1944, as the BNA's Japanese and Indian allies crumbled, its leadership had

> to search for a means not only of redeeming their political popularity in Burma but also of making themselves acceptable to the Allies if they were to have a role in the post-war campaign for Burma's independence. Such a means appeared in the form of a coalition with the Burma Communist Party. The BCP had made contact with the Allies in 1942 and since that time had been organizing the peasantry in Burma to oppose fascism and take power in an anti-imperialist revolution. The Anti-Fascist Organization (AFO), formed under the leadership of General Aung San and Communist leader Thakin Soe . . . was the answer to the BNA's dilemma.[5]

Second, he accused the communists of acting dishonourably, of 'dirtiness . . . deceit . . . [and] crookedness', of breaking pledges, of betraying non-communists within the League to the British, of conspiring to advance their party interests at the expense of the League as a whole and the nation, and of discrediting non-communists with false rumours.[6] These strong words were a precisely accurate description of the Party's tactics from one of its founding fathers, but the important point here is that it was an insider's betrayal of confidences and former intimates.[7]

'Tetpongyi' Thein Pe Myint responded by denouncing his colleagues in the executive council as British stooges[8] and resigning

---

[4] See Silverstein (ed.), 1993: 47.
[5] Taylor, 1987: 234. The Burma Communist Party later split into the 'White Flags', or Communist Party of Burma, under Than Tun and the 'Red Flags' under Thakin Soe.
[6] See Silverstein (ed.), 1993: 47–50.
[7] The communists always reserved their keenest hatreds for those in the know. As a 'delegate' to the VIth World Youth Festival in Moscow in 1957, 40 other Americans and I were invited to visit the People's Republic of China. The other 'delegates' discovered that my political views differed from theirs, and this doctrinal divergence inspired them on the train bound for Peking to compose hymns of abuse. 'There'll be no more Shelby Tuckers, there'll be no more Shelby Tuckers, there'll be no more Shelby Tuckers when the Red Revolution comes!' they sang lustily to the tune of 'She'll be coming round the mountain'.
[8] 'They have surrendered to British duplicity. They are deplorably weak-kneed in their dealings with the Governor. And they are intolerant of criticism.' Reported in *New Times of Burma*, 30 October 1946, under the caption, 'Burmese Communists Bid for Success in General Elections'. Reproduced in Aung San Suu Kyi, 1991: 43.

his seat. Then, on 3 November, after further vitriolic attacks on the League's leaders, Than Tun and his following walked out of a meeting of its supreme council. Subsequent attempts at reconciliation[9] failed; the rift was final, and, from November 1946, 'the Socialist Party nominees, Kyaw Nyein, Nu, Ba Swe and Thakin Mya . . . dominated the AFPFL'.[10]

History's treatment of Aung San is an example of singling out individual protagonists to explain a complex chain of events. The Attlee–Aung San Agreement, the Panglong Agreement, the FACE report, the League's triumph in the elections to the constituent assembly, the constitution adopted by the constituent assembly, the merging of the Frontier Areas into a Union of Burma, independence itself: all are imputed to the actions of this one man, who was now scarcely 33 years old. Hugh Tinker's tribute is typical:

> It was Aung San's achievement that he, the raw ex-student, dictated the terms of Burma's independence. The British Government at Westminster, Admiral Mountbatten, commander of massive armed forces, the British Government of Burma with its shrewd and experienced officers: Aung San outfaced them all. From varying points of view these Englishmen in positions of responsibility and power aspired to put their mark upon Burma's attainment of independence. But in the end Aung San towered above them all, and imposed his will upon the acts and scenes that led up to the final British withdrawal.[11]

[9] By Than Tun, who, at a rally on 8 March 1947, urged Aung San to rejoin the masses in 'fighting the British Imperialists', and Nu, who invited the CPB to rejoin the League and participate in his provisional government. Smith, 1991: 70; Tinker, 1959: 28.

[10] Smith, 1991: 69.

[11] Tinker, 1959: 28. Donnison wrote of him: 'Aung San was to develop statesmanlike qualities which showed that his character could grow with events. For the last ten months of his life he was virtually prime minister, realizing, for the first time, the size of his country, the plurality of its races and the complexity of its problems; the volume of work told on his health and at times he was out of his depth but he was man enough to acknowledge it, winning the respect of the British administrators with whom he was now in daily contact.' Reproduced in Aung San Suu Kyi, 1991: 48. See also Trager, 1966: 89, and articles by San Po Thin, Vum Ko Hau, Sinwa Nawng, Donnison and Collis in Dr Maung Maung (ed.), 1962: 149–54.

Aung San's near-universal beatification, however, should not blind us to the hatred of many of his contemporaries—the communists,[12] older Burman politicians such as Saw, Ba Maw and Tun Ok, business magnates and owners of large estates who viewed the League as rabble-rousers and demagogues with no practical experience at running anything and deplored their fiery rhetoric about taking them into public ownership and breaking up their estates under the banner of 'land reform'.[13] Opinions among the British varied. Some traced their family connections with Burma back three generations, and not a few of their proud little community had given their lives for Burma. Burma was their country, too, and they would rather hand over to someone who, managerially, was rather more competent and less abrasive than this made-over Marxist. Having accepted the inevitability of independence, they were looking forward to looking back. Everything that represented order and the right way of doing things, a new and superior civilization, was to be their legacy to Burma. Not a few senior civil servants, perhaps even the governor himself, would have preferred Nu.

Dislike of Aung San was perhaps keenest among those closest to the hill peoples. The Attlee–Aung San and Panglong agreements and the cavalier FACE report disturbed them. Attlee, they felt, had tricked Britain's wartime allies into absolving Britain from its pledges, and they blamed the League, and Aung San in particular: power should not be transferred to him *as a matter of principle*. Major the Reverend James W. Baldwin, an Anglo-Indian padre who had parachuted into the Karen Hills with Force 136 and worked as a missionary to the Karens, prepared a memorandum and sent it to Attlee. Its summary of events between May 1945 and June 1947 reflects the feelings aroused by Aung San's methods not only among hill peoples but other minorities and many ordinary Burmans as well.

August 1945 to end of Dorman-Smith Government.

AFPFL Party under the leadership of U Aung San hold power gained through organization of Resistance Movement against Japanese. Fire-arms and AFPFL units stationed throughout country thus people are forced to recognize AFPFL in district areas where

---

[12] Save, possibly, Than Tun, who was his brother-in-law.

[13] In February 1946, shares in Burma Corporation stood at 18. On 7 July 1947, after one of Aung San's fiery speeches, they plunged to 7. Fowells, 2000: 18.

Military CAS(B) Government delayed to enter. No jubilation or rejoicing permitted at entry of Allies (14th Army) into Burma. Sympathetic allegiance to returned British by headmen or others severely crushed. Strong propaganda directed to belittling liberation of Burma by 14th Army—all made to believe AFPFL . . . routed Japanese.

On formation of Civil Government—October 1945—AFPFL organise again for rebellions—Mr. Dorman-Smith would not recognise AFPFL claim as majority party: funds and arms collected by political 'dacoity'. Police stations raided; treasury's looted, attacks become bolder and more widespread leading to crisis. Exit Dorman-Smith . . .

The end of Dorman-Smith government until Attlee–Aung Agreement.

Aung San launches independence demand in full force as soon as he gets official recognition in new cabinet. Countryside party drive for collection of more arms and funds by renewed 'dacoity'. New policies put into force—old Government civil servants unpopular. PVOs gain new place of power over [BNA]. . . . Mass meetings ordered countrywide. Large quantity of arms and PVO massed in Rangoon. Documents signed by AFPFL executive heads prove authority for collection of illegal arms. Sovereign independence demanded on threat of open revolt . . . dual Government set up. PVOs set up HQs in every district and mete out punishment to all and sundry found not cooperating. Great uncertainty and tension in country while Aung San delegation leave for London to demand sovereign independence. . . .

Attlee–Aung San Agreement to May 1947.

Preparations for elections. [PVO] reinforced. HQs set up in every Ward in Rangoon city and district towns and townships and village tracts. District civil officials powerless. Preparation for elections by all opposition parties crushed by violence, threat and intimidation—most opposition candidates forced to withdraw. 1st April 47. The great and infamous Public Order Preservation Act, section 5 and its later amendment is proclaimed—Arrests without trial or warrant—the policeman's knock rings loud. Result:

No opposition party to contest elections. Karen constituency . . . decide not to poll (out of 12 Karen constituencies only 3 disobeyed and polled but with only 8, 16 and 20 percent of electorate polling in Toungoo, Thaton Town West and West Bassein District respectively.)

Election Day polling booths suddenly armed by PVOs. Double lists checked at booths by AFPFL. Peep holes in booths to check electors.

Unrepresented Constituency Assembly formed by AFPFL. 100 seats uncontested, approximately 12–14% only of electorate vote.

May–June 1947.

First sign of trouble. Split in AFPFL. National Socialist section and Communists begin to openly criticize U Aung San and his new policies of rehabilitation and civil postings. A period of general unrest and uncertainty. U Aung San begins losing his hold on the 'mass'. Defiance strikes threaten to start and widespread non-cooperation with his policies, financial retrenchment and new administration schemes and projects. National Socialists under leadership of U Kyaw Nyein begin big scale 'dacoity' attacks in Delta areas under cover of Communist rebellion in Central Burma area. U Aung San strongly condemns 'dacoity', a political weapon of his own creation now being used by his new opponents—the National Socialists.

AFPFL [and] PVO compete in political 'dacoity' for party funds and arms. Bribery, corruption and jobbery rife. U Aung San's City Hall speech in mass rally strongly condemns corruption and removes U Ba Pe from Cabinet in connection with widely known Excise bribe scandal reported to involve U Ba Pe, U Tin Tut and Kyaw Nyein.

The latter two in UK. U Aung San expresses his disgust and strong determination to dismiss Kyaw Nyein from office on his return. Socialist followers in AFPFL resent this and determine to save their leader, Kyaw Nyein. Hence public widely believe [Kyaw Nyein] commenced plot of assassination. U Saw made scapegoat. True or otherwise, this is widely believed by public and some claim to have material evidence to support their views.[14]

---

[14] J.W. Baldwin, memorandum, 'Latest Development – Political Situation in Burma to 6th November 1947', attached to note, Lord Pethick-Lawrence to Sir Gilbert Laithwaite, 19 December 1947 (BL OIOC: M/4/2736), altered by minor orthographical corrections.

The Secretary of State for India and Burma dismissed Baldwin's memorandum as 'one-sided' and transferred it to a confidential Foreign Office file.[15] Still, a letter by M.A. Maybury, ex-Burma Civil Service, published in the *New Statesman* in 1949, confirms Baldwin's description of PVO intimidation in the election:

> The recognition of Aung San as Burmese leader made impossible the development of freedom of thought and speech because of the formidable private army he used to intimidate the opposition. The majority he received in the 'free' elections of April 1947, and the semblance of unity between the Burmese and the Minority races were obtained by methods with which Hitler and Stalin have made us familiar.[16]

Similarly, H.A. Stonor:

> I and several officers from the 2nd Bn The Welch Regiment walked down to Kalaw town to see how the Elections were going. We were just in time to witness the Frontier Constabulary, armed and carrying banners of the AFPFL with its logo the Hammer and Sickle march down the main street and take up positions on either side of the path leading to the polling booth, through which every voter had to pass. We were amazed at the flagrant intimidation and even more so when we spotted the British commander of the force, Capt. Jimmy Battle, standing in the crowd and doing absolutely nothing about it.[17]

And Kin Oung, who was an officer in the Burma Navy in 1947:

> I know something about the AFPFL-rigged April elections and can probably support some of Baldwin's account. There were senior naval officers backing top AFPFL socialists who actually arranged

---

[15] Note, Sir Gilbert Laithwaite to Lord Pethick-Lawrence, 19 December 1947 (BL OIOC: M/4/2736).

[16] 30 April 1949.

[17] Note appended to correspondence with H.A. Stonor, 17 June 2000. See also 'Note by R.E. McGuire', 13 August 1947, paragraph 2, attached to letter, Sir Hubert Rance to Sir Gilbert Laithwaite, 12 August 1947 (BL OIOC: M/4/2501); Tinker (ed.), 1984, vol. II, item 490: 718 ('[N]o Deputy Commissioner, if he has any sense, administers his District without the local AFPFL, or listening to their representations . . .')

ambushes of communists proceeding to the booths, and killed them.[18]

Nor did Aung San command the loyalty of those units in the Burma Army who regarded him as too soft on the Karens, or universal support within the League.

Baldwin refers to Aung San's City Hall speech. Other sources reveal that his accusations against Ba Pe, Tin Tut and Kyaw Nyein were based on rumour and were made without prior consultation with his colleagues. Ba Pe was widely regarded as the 'father of Burmese Nationalist movements and politics'.[19] He was the founder of *The Sun* newspaper, and had been the leader of the GCBA and a member of the legislature since 1923. Nevertheless, he was dismissed from the governor's executive council and the League's supreme council without being allowed to defend himself,[20] and, moreover, Aung San had declared his intention to dismiss Kyaw Nyein on his return from abroad.[21] As most politicians were corrupt,[22] a wave of fear spread among them. Ba Pe and Kyaw Nyein were the joint leaders of the Socialist Party, potential rivals to Aung San's majority within the League, and they had opposed building up the PVO as a private army loyal to Aung San. If Aung San could destroy men such as these, whom else might he eliminate? Kyaw Nyein's ally and supporter, Ne Win? A private army loyal to Kyaw Nyein (and Ne Win?) was already engaged in arms procurement 'dacoity' in the Delta, while the Burma Army, which had taken over responsibility for security in all Burma from the British Army from 15 June 1947, was preoccupied with the communists in central Burma. Men who were soon to compete in extolling their fallen hero's virtues were whispering in the corridors that the *Bogyoke* was too ambitious and too arrogant.

A room in the western block of the secretariat building, Rangoon, Saturday, 19 July 1947, about 1030 hours. Three tables at the western end of the room are joined at right angles in the shape of the Greek letter Π. Aung San, who has convened a meeting of the executive council of the Interim Burmese Government, is seated at the top of the Π, while at right angles to him, ranged along the other tables,

[18] Email, Kin Oung to author, 23 January 2000.
[19] U Maung Maung, 1989: 295.
[20] Ibid.
[21] Baldwin, memorandum, p. 2.
[22] U Maung Maung, 1989: 295.

are U Ba Win (the *Bogyoke*'s older brother and member for commerce and supplies), Thakin Mya (member for finance), 'Deedok'[23] U Ba Choe (information), Abdul Razak (education and national planning), Mahn Ba Khaing (industry and labour), U Ba Gyan (public works), U Aung Zan Wai (social services), Pyawbwe U Mya (agriculture and acting home member) and Sao Sam Htun, the Möng Pawn *saohpa* (frontier areas). Two of the councillors are absent: Kyaw Nyein (home affairs) is in Yugoslavia;[24] Tin Tut, having recently handed over the finance portfolio to Thakin Mya, is in London as high commissioner designate.[25] Behind Aung San, opening from the corridor and guarded by an unarmed peon named Thaung Sein,[26] is the one door in the room that has not been bolted from the inside. Suddenly, four men, Maung Soe, Maung Sein, Thet Hnin and Yan Gyi Aung, wearing jungle-green uniforms with Twelfth Army flashes ('Chinthe' badges) and bush hats and armed with three tommy-guns and a Sten gun, force their way past Thaung Sein into the room. They discharge their guns, then retreat into the corridor and quit the building. A getaway jeep driven by Thu Kha, awaiting them outside with engine running, spirits them to Saw's compound at 4 Ady Road on Inya Lake, where a police strike force apprehends them about four hours later. Aung San, Ba Win, Thakin Mya, Abdul Razak and Mahn Ba Khaing are already dead, and Ba Choe and Sao Sam Htun die the next day.

Five others besides the four gunmen and the driver were involved and tried for complicity in the murders. One of them, Ba Nyunt, turned 'approver', or King's evidence, named Saw as the person who conceived, planned and directed the killings, and the Special Crimes Tribunal that tried the case described his evidence as 'the principal piece of sworn testimony'.[27]

Ba Nyunt testified that he first met Saw when the Myochit Party leader addressed a meeting in Minhla and that, at Saw's invitation, he visited Saw's house on Ady Road and joined the Myochit Party.

---

[23] Nicknamed for *Deedok*, a magazine of which he was the editor.

[24] The other absent councillor is Saw San Po Thin (transport and communications), who is on tour. See U Maung Maung, 1989: 339, note 123, citing *Hanthawaddy*, 20 July 1947, pp. 1–2.

[25] Dr Maung Maung, 1962: 19.

[26] Telegram, R.W.D. Fowler to Sir Gilbert Laithwaite, 19 July 1947 (BL OIOC: M/4/2714); Tinker (ed.), 1984, vol. II, item 452: 673, refers to 'an armed PVO guard outside the door'.

[27] Dr Maung Maung, 1962: 76.

Five of the other accused were at Saw's house when he visited: they were collecting arms and ammunition. Saw first told him of his intention to murder Aung San on 15 July, stating that all other leaders would have to be killed as well if politics were to continue in Burma, then, on 18 July, Saw met him and three of the gunmen and Thu Kha and discussed the murder plan in detail. Ba Nyunt's task was to find and kill Thakin Nu after the others discharged their guns.[28] At about 0830 hours on the day of the killings, he heard Saw whispering instructions to three of the other accused, Khin Maung Yin, Maung Ni and Hmon Gyi, who then proceeded with him to the secretariat building in a Fordson truck. They parked the truck at the corner of Dalhousie Street and 41st Street, whereupon Khin Maung Yin and Hmon Gyi disappeared into the secretariat via the 'Out' gate on Sparks Street, while he, Ba Nyunt, proceeded to Nu's office in the constituent assembly building. Realizing that a man he saw there was not Nu, Ba Nyunt returned to the truck. Khin Maung Yin, who had returned to the truck by then, told him that Maung Ni had telephoned Saw to confirm that everything was in order. Then Ba Nyunt saw a jeep enter the secretariat compound via the 'In' gate on Sparks Street. The jeep stopped for a minute or so about 25 or 30 feet from the portico of the western block, then drove on to the portico, and, shortly afterwards, Ba Nyunt heard the reports of gun shots from within the secretariat compound and saw the jeep leave the compound via the 'Out' gate on Sparks Street. He saw the jeep again when it sped past him eastbound on Dalhousie Street. Ba Nyunt, Khin Maung Yin and Maung Ni then returned in the truck without Hmon Gyi to Saw's compound, where they found the jeep parked underneath the porch. The four gunmen and Thu Kha greeted them with shouts of '*Aung-byi* [victory]! *Aung-byi*!', and Ba Nyunt replied by shouting 'New Calendar', signalling thereby that a new era had begun in Burmese politics.

After Ba Nyunt turned 'approver', Maung Sein, Yan Gyi Aung, Thu Kha, Khin Maung Yin and Maung Ni proffered confessions corroborating his testimony and enlarging it with further details.

Maung Sein stated that Maung Soe had produced the shoulder badges and hats that they wore; that they had received their orders to leave in the jeep at about 1000 hours; that they concealed their uniforms beneath raincoats; that Hmon Gyi was waiting for them

---

[28] Thakin Nu was not a member of the Executive Council. He was, however, a close ally of Aung San and the speaker of the constituent assembly.

inside the western block and nodded his head as a pre-arranged signal to them to proceed; that Maung Soe forced open the door of the council chamber and gave the orders to shoot; that Yan Gyi Aung sat down to fire his Sten, and the other gunmen remained standing while firing their tommies; that, after shooting the councillors, Yan Gyi Aung shot someone in the corridor who was armed with a pistol; that they met Maung Ni as they were leaving the secretariat compound; that Saw embraced and kissed them when they reached his house; and that they put on other clothes and were talking with Saw when the Fordson truck returned with Ba Nyunt, Khin Maung Yin and Maung Ni.

Yan Gyi Aung confirmed that he had dropped to the floor and shot at the councillors under the table[29] and stated that Saw's table boy, Sein Maung, had relieved them of their weapons and hidden them when they reached Saw's house.

Thu Kha stated that the gunmen had with them in the jeep an extra tommy-gun for Ba Nyunt to use to kill Nu.

Maung Ni stated that Maung Soe had given him a revolver on the morning of the killings and showed him how to use it; that after venturing into the secretariat compound, Khin Maung Yin had instructed him to keep the 'Out' gate on Sparks Street open for the jeep; that he saw the jeep driven by Thu Kha arrive, heard shooting and saw Hmon Gyi running out of the compound; that he tried to get in the jeep as it was leaving the compound but was repulsed and went back to the truck and returned to Saw's house with Khin Maung Yin and Ba Nyunt.

Probative of motive, Khin Maung Yin described an attempt made on Saw's life the previous year,[30] and stated that, subsequently, he had disobeyed Saw's instruction to shoot Aung San at a party at the house of the general officer commanding.[31] Khin Maung Yin further stated that Saw had purchased a Sten gun, two tommy-guns and other weapons from a Major Young[32] and two tommy-guns and

[29] Aung Zan Wai and Ba Gyan. See Kin Oung, 1996: 13.
[30] Saw was widely reputed to have blamed Aung San for this attempt on his life.
[31] 'Interim Report on Situation in Burma', 20 August 1947, paragraph 11 (PRO: WO 208/4941).
[32] Major C. Henry Young occupied a house across Inya Lake from Saw, four miles by road but half an hour by row-boat. He was the commander of the Indian Army Electrical and Mechanical Workshop Company in Rangoon and in charge of a military transport camp situated on property owned by Saw. Kin Oung, 1996: 53, 56.

other weapons from a Major Lance;[33] that Saw had planned to rob a bank but good weather had frustrated the plan; that Saw had obtained Bren guns and ammunition from ordnance depots with the help of a Major Moore[34] and a Captain Vivian[35] and hidden some of this ordnance in the lake beside his house; that, on 17 July, Saw told him of his murder plan and despatched him to confirm that the executive council would meet on the 19th, as scheduled; that, on the 18th, Saw reminded him to keep ready the two vehicles to be used in the crime; that he put false number plates on the Fordson and painted false numbers on the jeep; that, after leaving the Fordson, he again verified that the executive council meeting would proceed as scheduled and reported thus to Saw from a telephone at the Sun Press, using code words previously agreed between them ('Piston rings have been received'); and that, after returning to Saw's house, he gave the truck's false number plates to one Tin Shwe[36] and painted fresh numbers on the jeep.

The prosecution produced other witnesses to corroborate the defendants' evidence. The deputy inspector general of police of the Criminal Investigation Department, Tun Hla Oung,[37] testified that he had posted 'watchers' to observe activities at Saw's house. After

[33] Major Peter Ernest Lancelot Daine was a grade 2 staff officer in X Branch, which was the signals branch of HQ Burma Command. Conversation with John McEnery (then on the staff of Burma Command), 5 November 1998; telegram, General Sir Neil Ritchie to Sir Henry MacGeagh, 29 August 1947 (BL OIOC: M/4/2/2715); Tinker (ed.), 1984, vol. II, item 504: 737. See also 'Statement by J.A. Moore' in telegram, Sir Hubert Rance to the Earl of Listowel, 28 July 1947 (BL OIOC: M/4/2715); Tinker (ed.), 1984, vol. II, item 470: 698. The biographical note on Daine in Tinker (ed.), 1984, vol. II: 903, erred in assigning him to the intelligence branch of Burma Command. Conversation with John McEnery, 28 September 2000.

[34] Major J.A. Moore, Indian Army Ordnance Corp, was the officer commanding, Base Ammunition Depot (Burma). Telegram, Sir Hubert Rance to the Earl of Listowel, 28 July 1947 (BL OIOC: M/4/2715); Tinker (ed.), 1984, vol. II, item 469: 696; ibid.: 909.

[35] Captain David Vivian was arms adviser to the Burma Police. Letter, governor's secretary to J.P. Gibson, 24 July 1947 (BL OIOC: M/4/2715); Tinker (ed.), 1984, vol. II, item 501: 732, note; ibid.: 917.

[36] The judgment of the Special Crimes Tribunal (reproduced in Dr Maung Maung, 1962: 71–117) describes Tin Shwe as a 'follower of U Saw living in his place'. He is referred to several times in the judgment but was not called as a witness.

[37] Kin Oung's father. His name is spelled 'Tun Hla Aung' in the Special Crimes Tribunal's judgment.

receiving reports implicating Saw in the theft of ordnance, two of the 'watchers', he stated, saw the Fordson leave Saw's compound on the day of the murder at about 0830 hours and recorded the particulars of its number plate. Sein Maung, an accountant for the *Thamada Daily*, saw a jeep leave the secretariat compound 'shortly after the sound of gun reports was heard from inside the building'[38] and noted its number plate on the back of a bank paying-in slip. At about 1100 hours, Saw's neighbour, a Mr Khan, encountered a jeep driving furiously up the road towards him and saw it turn into Saw's compound, then observed four or five men around the jeep, including Saw. A ballistics expert matched the spent cartridge shells and bullets found in the council chamber and the bullets in the bodies of the victims with tommy-guns and a Sten gun found in the lake beside Saw's shrine. Other witnesses testified to finding in the lake both false number plates and soft green hats of the kind allegedly worn by the accused and, in a fireplace in Saw's kitchen, a heap of unburnt cloth and the remains of an incinerated Twelfth Army shoulder badge. Tun Hla Oung and Khan testified that the numbers on the jeep they found in Saw's compound on the afternoon of the killings had been wet and freshly painted, while testimony was received from another witness excluding the possibility that the jeep legally bearing the number plates noted by Sein Maung was used by the killers.

Identifying the gunmen was never likely to present difficulty. Maung Sein, made no attempt to deny his guilt, and a peon with the Defence Department and a constable saw Thu Kha, who, in turn, named the gunmen in his confession. Two office superintendents saw the gunmen ascending the stairs seconds before the killing. Shwe Baw, the executive council's secretary who was seated next to Aung San when he was shot, and Thaung Sein and the three councillors who survived the attack could also identify them. A newspaper reporter saw the killers retreating down the corridor.

There was, however, no direct evidence of Saw's involvement, save for Ba Nyunt's and the other defendants' testimony. Nevertheless, Saw was convicted of 'the commission of murder in furtherance of common intention' and hanged, his case of guilty by association

---

[38] The words are those of the judgment, not necessarily those used by the witness. Kin Oung (1996: 13) states that Sein Maung was a reporter, but contemporary press reports of his testimony, such as that in *The Burman* (an English-language daily) of 23 October 1947, described him as an accountant.

never answered. Maung Soe, Maung Sein, Thet Hnin and Yan Gyi Aung were convicted of murder, and Hmon Gyi of abetment to murder, and hanged. Thu Kha, Khin Maung Yin and Maung Ni were convicted of abetment to murder, but their sentences were commuted to 20 years' imprisonment. The 'approver', Ba Nyunt, was granted a conditional pardon.

So goes the official version of the killing of Aung San and six of his cabinet colleagues. But the official version is not without difficulties.

The most obvious difficulty is one of inherent implausibility. To suppose that anyone masterminding the murders of almost the entire government would instruct the assassins to assemble at his house immediately afterwards is, simply, fantastical, especially so as Saw must have known that his house was under surveillance.[39] It is suggested that he expected Rance to call on him to replace Aung San, but, after 15 June, the government was the *League*, not just its leaders, and the only conceivable result of such murders would be the appointment of someone from within the League. Saw, a politician of vast experience, knew that his Myochit Party lacked popular support and would have understood this, and Rance rejected the notion as 'incredible'.[40] It is suggested that the attempt on his life had unhinged Saw,[41] but Galon U Saw was neither a fool nor a lunatic. If others directed the murders, we might expect *them* to instruct the killers to proceed to Saw's house.

Then there is the profoundly unsatisfactory nature of a conviction based principally on evidence purchased with offers of leniency for the witnesses. While this is common practice in British criminal proceedings, it amounts in effect to suborning the witnesses and

[39] 'It is difficult to believe that U Saw in his position had no suspicion that his house might be under observation.' 'Interim Report on Situation in Burma', 1 August 1947, paragraph 6 (PRO: WO 208/4941).

[40] 'Saw told his followers that it was certain that when the leaders of the AFPFL were removed HE [the governor] would send for Saw and ask him to form a Government. This seems incredible and all I can suggest if the information is true is that Saw anticipated that suspicion for the crime would fall on one or other of the Communist parties.' Telegram, Sir Hubert Rance to Earl of Listowel, 2 August 1947 (PRO: WO 208/4941); Tinker (ed.), 1984, vol. II, item 481: 709.

[41] See 'Interim Report on Situation in Burma', 1 August 1947, paragraph 9, suggesting the possibility of 'mental disturbance built up on his urgent desire for revenge after the attack on his life in January 1947 [*sic*]'. The attempt on Saw's life occurred on 21 September 1946. Telegram, Sir Hubert Rance to Lord Pethick-Lawrence, 21 September 1946 (BL OIOC: M/4/2504); Tinker (ed.), 1984, vol. II, item 36: 55.

would be a crime, were it done by the defence. Ba Nyunt, Thu Kha, Khin Maung Yin and Maung Ni were all spared. After examining the evidence, Saw's defence counsel, Derek Curtis-Bennet, KC, declared unequivocally that it was 'cooked',[42] and it is perhaps relevant that Saw protested his innocence even as he went to the gallows. One has to bear in mind that neither the British nor the League wanted a disruption in completing the transition to independence, and, after the handing over of power to the interim government, its home member, Kyaw Nyein, was *in charge of the police*[43] *and the courts*. Saw knew this and urged the governor to 'approach His Majesty's Government to send out Special Police Officers to this Country for the purpose of investigating into the Case'.

> To have a case tried by an impartial Court or Tribunal sounds very grand but at the same time the Court or Tribunal has to go according to the evidence produced by the Police. There were many cases in the past where the Court had no alternative but to accept the evidence produced by the Police although the Judge or Judges knew perfectly well that the evidence so produced was as false as it was fabricated or concocted by the Police. The point I am trying to submit to your Excellency is that the present stage at which the Police officers obviously, under direct pressure of the Member or Members of the Party in Power, trying to smash us [the Myochit Party] by all possible means, is an early but very important stage.[44]

Rance presented this letter to the 'Member of the Party in Power', Kyaw Nyein, who replied, 'There is no need to make a reply.'[45] Contemporary British intelligence reports paint 'a depressing picture of . . . the adverse effect of "political" direction on hitherto impartial Government servants'.[46]

Yan Gyi Aung withdrew his confession because it had been extracted from him by 'ill-treatment', and, on 8 May 1948, the day

[42] *Keesing's Contemporary Archives*, 28 February–6 March 1948.
[43] 'Interim Report on Situation in Burma', 1 August 1947, paragraph 12, and 'Interim Report on Situation in Burma', 20 August 1947, paragraph 13.
[44] Letter, Saw to Sir Hubert Rance, 29 July 1947 (BL OIOC: M/4/2721); Tinker (ed.), 1984, vol. II, item 475: 703–4.
[45] U Saw to Sir Herbert Rance, 28 July 1947 (BL OIOC: M/4/2721); Tinker (ed.), 1984, vol. II, item 475: 704, note.
[46] 'Situation in Burma—September 1947', part I, paragraph 7, attaching a report of Major de Hamel (PRO: WO 208/4941). See also 'Interim Report on Situation in Burma', 20 August 1947, paragraph 13.

after Saw was hanged, we find the new British ambassador to a now independent Burma writing to one M.E. Dening in the Foreign Office about someone of importance in the League or the police, '[H]e has undoubtedly taken the major part in bringing Saw to the gallows, and that too by methods *not entirely in accord with Queensbury rules*.'[47] Although the Foreign Office has censored the name of this party, an index in its files suggests he *may* have been Tun Hla Oung,[48] the CID chief who had been in overall charge of the investigation, and Tun Hla Oung's record of service with SOE reflects a disquieting question concerning his 'trustworthiness'.[49] In January 1947, he was a modest district superintendent of police with a past record of hostility to the League, and, on 28 March 1947, after the Attlee–Aung San Agreement, he tendered his application for early retirement—only to withdraw it soon afterwards when Kyaw Nyein offered him the plum job of deputy inspector general of police.[50]

Then there is the court that tried the case. The case should, and ordinarily would, have been tried in the High Court of Justice. Burma was a British colony still, and the courts were British courts.[51] Nevertheless, the interim government wanted a special forum for this trial, and the governor meekly complied, enacting on 30 August 1947 the Special Crimes (Tribunal) Act, a retroactive measure unprecedented, surely, in the history of British justice, domestic or colonial. Selection of the judges was entrusted to the officiating chief justice of the High Court, Dr Ba U, who later would write: 'There was no problem as far as the chairmanship of the Tribunal was concerned. I asked U Kyaw Myint to take on the job, and he readily consented.' Kyaw Myint, was the brother of Tin Tut, whom Aung San had attacked for involvement with Ba Pe and Kyaw Nyein in the excise bribes scandal and who had just returned to his former post as finance member in the interim government.[52] Kyaw Myint

[47] Letter from Ambassador Bowker to M.E. Dening, 8 May 1948 (PRO: FO 371/69472). Italics added.

[48] Ambassador Bowker's 8 May 1948 letter was originally filed as FO F7454/17/79. The Foreign Office file index for 1948, p. 389, identifies the censored party in FO F7454/17/79 as the inspector-general of police.

[49] PRO: HS/1/24; BL OIOC M/4/2032.

[50] Ibid.

[51] The case was *The King v. U Saw, et al.*

[52] *Keesing's Contemporary Archives*, 28 February–6 March 1948. Tin Tut returned to his former position as finance member after the assassination. Telegram, Sir Hubert Rance to Earl of Listowel, 2 August 1947 (BL OIOC: M/4/2714); Tinker (ed.), 1984, vol. II, item 481: 709.

also had the right political credentials, having supported both student strikers and the thakins.[53] 'But,' Ba U continues, 'I had considerable difficulty in choosing the [other] two members of the Tribunal. The judges so chosen had to be . . . *acceptable to the Government*.'[54] After the Special Crimes Tribunal rendered its guilty verdict, Kyaw Myint was elevated to the bench of Burma's highest court and its court of last resort,[55] while Aung Tha Gyaw and Si Bu, the judges he had selected to serve on the Special Crimes Tribunal, were appointed to the High Court.[56] The choice of a lawyer to lead the prosecution at first fell on U Myint Thein. However, this choice 'would have looked a little improper . . . in a trial over which his older brother . . . presided',[57] so U Tun Byu was selected as lead counsel. Nevertheless, 'U Myint Thein rendered service throughout the trial advising U Tun Byu'.[58]

An intelligence report of 1 August states that the escape vehicle was an 'unnumbered jeep',[59] but Sein Maung testified that he noted its number on the back of a Grindley's bank passbook. Although Sein Maung 'heard sounds of bricks falling down and gun-reports [and] knew that the sounds came from the secretariat and . . . saw people running about in the compound' and was sufficiently suspicious to note the jeep's number, he refrained from tendering this vital evidence to the police until 'two or three days later',[60] a delay that the tribunal was at some pains to explain ('news of the real tragedy was of such a shocking character that it was hardly possible for an ordinary man in the street like Sein Maung to think and act in as strictly a consistent manner as might ordinarily be expected of him in his normal life'[61]). When Sein Maung returned to the *Thamadi Daily*, he told his employer, U Ba Gale, about the jeep's number, but neither did U Ba Gale report this vital evidence to the police, which the tribunal again condoned ('During the period of public anxiety and excitement which prevailed immediately after the assassination became known, one could hardly expect either U Sein Maung or U

[53] Dr Maung Maung, 1962: 22.
[54] Ba U, 1959: 195; quoted in Dr Maung Maung, 1962: 22. Emphasis added.
[55] Right of appeal to the Privy Council having been abolished.
[56] Dr Maung Maung, 1962: 22–3.
[57] Ibid.: 24.
[58] Ibid.
[59] 'Interim Report on Situation in Burma', 1 August 1947, part I, paragraph 1.
[60] *The Burman*, 23 October 1947.
[61] Dr Maung Maung, 1962: 85.

Ba Gale to make use of the knowledge which they had in their possession regarding the suspected jeep in the manner in which they subsequently did after the excitement had subsided to some extent.'[62]). It was established on cross-examination that Ba Gale had once managed *The Sun* newspaper, controlled by Saw, and that Saw had accused him of dishonesty, but the tribunal merely observed that this was not a fact 'sufficient to vitiate' his testimony.[63]

The striking force led by S.D. Jupp in the search of Saw's house and adjoining lake did not find the number plate on the *day of the arrest*. A search party of the 7th Field Company of the Royal Engineers led by Lieutenant J.S. Coulson found it while dredging the lake *11 days later*. Meanwhile, no one *save the police* was allowed access to the house.

The particular 'ballistics expert' used to match spent cartridges with weapons recovered, one Hla Baw, principal of the Detective Training School at Insein, was chosen, according to the Crown's lead witness, because:

> We do not have any instrument with which to conduct ballistic experiments and tests regarding bullets. We lost them during the war. I made attempts to get such instruments from abroad. We enquired from Lawrence and Mayo in India for a bullet comparison microscope with lighting arrangements and bullet-holders. They replied they had no stock. I also tried to get one from England, without success. We have not been able to get the experiments done in India, firstly because at the time we intended to send out the exhibits there were air accidents due to bad weather, and secondly, communal riots were raging in India. Also, owing to the great political significance attached to the case, we consider that sending out the exhibits would be too risky. We had to think of delays and substitution and tampering of exhibits.[64]

At about 1100 hours on 19 July 1947, before news of the assassinations reached Burma Command headquarters, Major Hugh Toye, an intelligence officer from Singapore filling in temporarily for a sick colleague, rang Saw in the ordinary course of his duties to ask if he could come and see him. They had met once before. Toye recalls:

[62] Ibid.
[63] Ibid.: 84.
[64] Ibid.: 34.

The phone was answered promptly and U Saw seemed unhurried, normal and relaxed, with nothing particular on his mind. Judging from what I could hear, the house too seemed normal and undisturbed. U Saw said he had a bad cold and was keeping his feet up, but he would be glad to see me the next day, Sunday. It was later alleged that the assassins reached U Saw's compound at about the time of the telephone call. I left Burma two months later and did not see the prosecution's case, which must have been completed after I left, but it seems to me extraordinary, if not impossible, that someone who had just welcomed, or was about to welcome, the murderers to his house could have been so absolutely relaxed and calm. I have never thought U Saw guilty.[65]

Then there is the bizarre matter of Colin Tooke, a senior police officer stationed in Rangoon at the time of the assassination. The investigation of Saw's case disturbed him. Suspecting that the police were setting Saw up, he made his own investigation and, to ensure secrecy, kept the file in his home, which was guarded by a fierce Alsatian. One evening on returning home, his servant told him that the dog had been put down for rabies and thrown in a river. Tooke was suspicious. Rabies does not come on that suddenly, and the dog had been perfectly healthy that morning. Tooke retrieved the carcass and at post-mortem a veterinary surgeon found no sign of rabies. Tooke then learned that his file on Saw's case was missing. Seriously alarmed, he resumed his investigation and, several months later, died suddenly of Landry's acute paralysis, 'a mysterious paralysis of the body that is caused by a toxin, or poison'.[66]

Other tantalizing facts bear on the case. A telegram from the acting governor's secretary to Sir Gilbert Laithwaite transmitted several hours after the killings states, 'An armed PVO on guard outside the door tried to stop [the assassins] and was shot. He has identified the armed men as members of the 4th Burma Rifles.'[67]

---

[65] Telephone conversation with Toye, 5 October 2000; Toye, correspondence with author, 25 March 2001.

[66] Anonymous, 'Who really killed Aung San?', *Karen National Union Bulletin*, April 1986 (to which I am indebted also for other details in this paragraph). Alasdair McCrae, formerly of the Irrawaddy Flotilla Company, told this story to H.A. Stonor at a meeting of the Burma Luncheon Club in 1985. Kin Oung (1996: 61, 142) reports the same story with minor variant details, citing Stonor and Michael Busk as his sources.

[67] Telegram, R.W.D. Fowler to Sir Gilbert Laithwaite, 19 July 1947 (BL OIOC: M/4/2714); Tinker (ed.), 1984, vol. II, item 452: 673.

However, this PVO guard is not called as a witness, and Dr Maung Maung, author of the most comprehensive account of the investigation and trial, does not allude to him. He merely vanishes from the scene, and nothing further is said linking the assassins to 4th Burma Rifles—commanded by Ne Win, whose biographer is Dr Maung Maung.

Tin Tut's murder raises further questions. Born in 1895, son of a deputy commissioner, educated at Dulwich College, Queen's College, Cambridge, and Dublin University, barrister of the Middle Temple, first Burman member of the Indian Civil Service, adviser for reconstruction to (Dorman-Smith's) Burma government in exile, administrator in Rance's CAS(B), Aung San's deputy at Kandy, member for finance and revenues in the executive council, principal Burman negotiator and draughtsman of the Attlee–Aung San and Panglong Agreements, member of FACE, principal draughtsman of the 1947 constitution,[68] council (later cabinet) member for finance and revenues, then foreign affairs under Nu, led Burma Financial Mission to London in September 1947, Let Ya's deputy in the mission to London that negotiated the Freeman–Let Ya Defence Agreement, inspector general of auxiliary forces, founder and editor of *The New Times of Burma*, he was assassinated on 18 September 1948—14 months after Aung San's killing—by 'the hirelings of a political opponent in circumstances which have never been satisfactorily explained'.[69] Did Tin Tut know too much? As seen, Kyaw Myint, president of the Special Crimes Tribunal, was his brother.

Again, what did Tun Hla Oung know? The first Burman to attend Sandhurst, he was deputy inspector general and chief of the Criminal Investigation Department in July 1947 and assigned men to conduct a surveillance of Saw's house two days before the assassination. He was in the secretariat building when the killings happened and is credited with despatching the police unit that arrested Saw and the gunmen. He was involved in the police investigation of the case and, jointly with his brother-in-law, Justice Thaung Sein, was responsible for protecting Saw during Saw's imprisonment.[70] In August 1948, Nu appointed him deputy supreme commander of the armed forces with the rank of major-general, but, a few months later, he was spirited off to serve as military attaché at the Burmese embassy in London. In 1951 he embarked for home.

[68] Nu, obituary, *The Nation*, 20 September 1948.
[69] Tinker, 1959: 38.
[70] Kin Oung, 1996: xiii.

Burmese intelligence officers boarded the ship at Colombo, however, and revoked his passport.[71]

Finally, and this perhaps is the most disturbing feature of Saw's case—where is the transcript of the court proceedings? The defendants were tried for the murders of the country's national hero and six of his colleagues—seven of the nine members of the interim government. Are we to believe that in proceedings of such importance no transcript was made? Conversely, if no was transcript was made, why not? Are we to believe that Saw, who distrusted both the investigating police and the tribunal and who must have understood that an accurate record was critical to his chances on appeal, did not engage his own stenographer? One competent and generally reliable source confirms that there was a transcript and that it 'was last checked out to Dr Maung Maung and never returned'.[72] A 'Mr Justice Mya Thein' made a 'personal copy of the records of the trial and proceedings',[73] but where is it? And where are the police reports? All records pertaining to the most important crime in modern Burmese history have *disappeared*.[74]

Saw's culpability for these murders is thus uncertain. But, if he did not hire and direct the assassins, then who did? Who, we must ask ourselves, might have gained from the murders?

The Karens, or individual British concerned about their welfare? None of the League's leaders was more sympathetic to Karen aspirations than Aung San. While he stopped short of conceding their desire for full independence, he favoured a broad measure of regional autonomy and constitutional safeguards for ethnic rights and was at odds with colleagues precisely because he rejected Burman hegemony, stating in a speech to a meeting of the Anglo-Burman Council on 8 December 1946: 'The welfare of all people of this country irrespective of race or religion has always been the one

[71] Ibid.: 70.
[72] The party that made this statement has requested anonymity for his own protection.
[73] Dr Maung Maung, 1962: 25n.
[74] Accessing court records normally entails making application to the clerk of the court having custody of the record. I once obtained from the clerk of the United States Court of Appeals for the Fifth Circuit a transcript comprising 12 folders that was shipped to me in New Orleans from Dallas free of charge. As the Special Crimes Tribunal was disbanded after trying the Saw case, the court having custody of the transcript should be the High Court of Burma. When I sought the transcript there, however, I was told to discontinue this quest.

purpose that I have set out to fulfil.'[75] He elaborated his ideas in a speech made to a League convention on 23 May 1947, less than two months before his death:

> Only true democracy can work for the real good of the people, real equality of status and opportunity for everyone, irrespective of class or race or religion or sex. . . . There must be provisions [in the Constitution] for the fundamental rights of citizens irrespective of race, religion or sex. . . . [N]obody can deny that the Karens are . . . a national minority. . . . Therefore, we must concede to them the rights of a national minority. . . . Now, when we build our new Burma shall we build it as a Union [federation] or a Unitary State? In my opinion, it will not be feasible to set up a Unitary State. We must set up a Union with properly regulated provisions as should be made to safeguard the rights of National Minorities. We must take care that 'United we stand' not 'United we fall'.[76]

Again, he delivered the same message in a speech to the constituent assembly on 17 June 1947, just over a month before his death, 'Burma should consist of specified Autonomous States . . . with adequate safeguards for Minorities',[77] and offered to the assembly a seven-point resolution that included these provisions:

> the Union shall comprise such units as shall be specified by the constitution and the units so specified shall exercise such autonomy as shall be defined in the constitution. . . . [T]he constitution shall guarantee and secure to all the peoples of the Union justice, social, economic and political; equality of status, of opportunity, and before the law freedom of thought, expression, belief, worship, subject to law and public morality [and] provide adequate safeguards for minorities.[78]

By contrast, a few months after Aung San's assassination, his successor stated, 'I am cent per cent against the creation of Autonomous States for Karens, Mons and Arakanese.'[79] The Karens

[75] Aung San, 1946: 189; reproduced in Silverstein (ed.), 1993: 148.
[76] Ibid.: 153–4, 158.
[77] Letter, H.A. Stonor to Martin Smith, September 1997.
[78] Silverstein (ed.), 1993: 72–3.
[79] Anonymous, 'Who really killed Aung San?'; letter, H.A. Stonor to Martin Smith, September 1997.

knew that Aung San was the only Burman with the clout to deliver on a deal acceptable to them. Clearly, they had nothing to gain and all to lose by exchanging Nu for Aung San as the League's leader.

On the fiftieth anniversary of Aung San's death, the BBC (which is responsible to neither anyone nor anything, and least of all to the truth) broadcast a programme echoing an allegation promoted by the CPB immediately following the assassination—the 'British' were behind the killings.[80] Not only did the programme offer no evidence to support this allegation, but the allegation is inherently implausible. After British rule was restored, Whitehall's overriding concern, as we have seen, was to avoid a League-induced rebellion. Had it wished to remove Aung San, his admission of guilt in respect of the Thebyugone headman's murder afforded sound legal grounds. Why resort to assassination? Why wait until the British garrison was reduced to an almost token force of three British and three Gurkha battalions? The murders of Aung San and his colleagues threatened the peaceful withdrawal of the remaining garrison and endangered the lives of many Britons who were still in Burma. Again, why mount a major military operation in central Burma, 'Operation Flush', in March 1947, ostensibly to suppress 'dacoits' and facilitate election to a constituent assembly, but effectively to support Aung San against the communists and done at his request?

The BBC repeated another allegation of communist provenance, that British commercial interests were behind the killings, but here the only evidence it adduced were innuendoes drawn from the activities of Majors Young and Moore and Captain Vivian, a Major Daine, an Indian named Malhotra, who worked for a British company, and a certain John Stewart Bingley, who worked for the British Council. The four officers knew Saw and were on friendly terms with him. Vivian appears to have frequented his compound fairly often, and Saw wrote to Vivian when both men were in prison. Saw purchased guns from Vivian, but they were *Bren* guns, not Thompson sub-machine guns and Sten guns of the type used in the killings.[81] Vivian and Young were convicted of illegal arms trading.[82]

---

[80] *Who* Really *Killed Aung San*, BBC 2, 19 July 1997.
[81] All pertinent testimony in Saw's trial, including that of the assassins themselves and the ballistics expert, concurred in the type of weapons used. The .45 shells found in Aung San's body were of a type fired from tommy-guns; Bren guns fire a 9 mm round. McEnery, 1990: 113. See also note from Sir Gilbert Laithwaite to Secretary of State, 11 August 1947 (BL OIOC: M/4/2715); Tinker (ed.), 1984, vol. II, item 489: 716.
[82] Smith, 1991: 114.

Selling arms, however, is not evidence of abetment to murder. Every player in the civil war that had been gathering force since prior to the Second World War and would break out eight months after Aung San's assassination was scurrying for weapons:[83] the Karen National Defence Organization (KNDO), Thakin Soe's 'Red Flag' communists, Than Tun's 'White Flag' communists, Aung San's PVO, U Saw's Galon Tat, Ba Sein's Dobama Tat, Ba Maw's Maha-Bama Tat, the Students' Revolutionary Front and ubiquitous gangs of bandits masquerading as patriots. Young's conviction was based on Khin Maung Yin's fabricated confession, he was acquitted on appeal,[84] and no charges were pressed against the other two officers. Malhotra lived in the same block of flats as Vivian and was on friendly terms with both Vivian and Saw[85]—nothing more, scarcely evidence enough to connect him with the killings. Bingley was seen in the company of a Donald Burman Petch a few weeks before the killings, and Petch was 'a senior civil servant known to be an incorrigible British imperialist, out to thwart Burmese nationalist programmes by every means'.[86] Bingley had attended a party at Saw's house, where he was heard to boast, '[W]e're all prepared to help you fully.'[87] He would regret that hollow nod and wink to Saw. It led Saw to write to him from prison to enlist his help. But none of this remotely approaches proof of abetment to murder, and no such charge was ever made against any of these men.

The question arises, then, was Aung San murdered by one of his own? Drawing from Dorman-Smith's papers, Collis tells us that Aung San prophesied his own murder:

> He began to speak of his loneliness. He had always been lonely, he said. He had wanted friends, but found it very hard to make them. 'How can you say you have no friends,' said Dorman-Smith, 'when you are the people's idol?' 'I did not seek to be that,' said Aung San, 'but only to free my country. How lonely a task it would be, I never guessed.' And saying this he wept. Dorman-Smith sought to comfort him, but he was not comforted. 'How long do national heroes last?' he said bitterly. 'Not long in this country; they have too many enemies. Three years is the most they can

---

[83] Kin Oung, 1996: 51–2.
[84] By a Burman judge. See McEnery, 1990: 114, note 3; Kin Oung, 1996: 54.
[85] Kin Oung, 1996: 54.
[86] Ibid.: 95.
[87] Ibid.: 52, 95.

hope to survive. I do not give myself more than another eighteen months of life.'[88]

Aung San's prophesy does not specify who these homicidal 'enemies' were, but it is clear that he was thinking of his fellow Burmans, and, 18 months almost to the day after this conversation, he was dead.

It is here that the identification of the gunmen as belonging to 4th Burma Rifles comes into sharp relief, for, as noted, the officer commanding 4th Burma Rifles was Ne Win. The top military post, on Aung San's recommendation, had gone to Let Ya—*not* Ne Win. Aung San even recommended replacing Ne Win as officer commanding 4th Burma Rifles with Kya Doe, a Karen.[89] Ne Win was only a lieutenant colonel—a steep plunge from the dizzying heights inhabited as BNA, then PBF commander-in-chief,[90] yet he fancied himself a better soldier than Let Ya, Tun Hla Oung, Kya Doe, Smith Dun and others who outranked him. The Karens' seniority and Aung San's choice of Smith Dun to lead the post-independence Burma Army rankled him in particular. Ne Win was close to several senior British officers and may have known of Aung San's recommendations. Moreover, Aung San, although four years younger than he, had dressed him down in front of his men for womanizing, drunkenness and gambling. He knew he would never get the top post so long as Aung San was in charge.

Also suggesting a link with Ne Win is this curious tale emanating from Mya Hlaing, Let Ya's younger brother. Mya Hlaing was working as a clerk at the War Office in the summer of 1946, when his *saya*, Bo Aung Gyi, Ne Win's close confederate,[91] invited him to his house, stating, 'There is an important matter we have to discuss.' According to the story, Mya Hlaing stayed at Bo Aung Gyi's house for two months, while a sharp-shooter named Yangon Ba Swe lodged with Ne Win, and, during that time, Mya Hlaing and Ba Swe underwent training for 'a certain duty' they had 'to perform'. They studied Saw's movements in 'minute detail . . . when he left his house to go to his office and when he returned'. On the day of the attack, Mya Hlaing

[88] Collis, 1956: 270.
[89] Kin Oung, 1996: 104.
[90] Ba Maw, 1968: 329, 444.
[91] Brigadier Aung Gyi was Ne Win's main co-conspirator in engineering the events that brought the Caretaker Government to power in 1958 and the coup that overthrew Nu in 1962 and Ne Win's deputy in the Revolutionary Council. Later, Ne Win arrested him. See Smith, 1991: 8, 201, 212.

drove a vehicle they used and Ba Swe handled the gun, which Ne Win owned and provided:

> U Saw . . . came in his big black car, sitting by the side of his driver. We followed them from behind. When we reached a good spot, I overtook his car. It was then that Rangoon Ba Swe pulled the trigger. The first shot grazed U Saw's forehead. That was the most important shot. Rangoon Ba Swe then fired a second shot. It did not hit U Saw, as he had slid off his seat. A third shot was fired into the air. . . . U Saw never knew that Rangoon Ba Swe and I had carried out the plot . . . this was a matter that only four of us—Bo Ne Win, Bo Aung Gyi, Rangoon Ba Swe and myself—knew about.

The two men wore PVO uniforms to induce Saw to impute blame to Aung San and seek revenge, Mya Hlaing claimed.[92]

Ne Win and Yangon Ba Swe make another appearance in this context. Early in July 1947, Michael Busk, assistant commissioner of police for Rangoon, noted that 'some 60 Bren guns had gone missing' and 'made a case for additional security precautions to be taken at the secretariat. The case I put,' states Busk, 'was rejected by [Aung San] who felt he was secure in the affections of his people. Following the theft of the Bren guns I understood that we asked for a warrant to search the house of U Saw. This was turned down on political grounds, so I understood from a fellow officer investigating the case who was living in my house.'[93] However, as rumours of Aung San's pending assassination spread, colleagues became concerned for his safety.[94] Ne Win *volunteered* to assume responsibility for guarding him, but instead of assigning this task to ordinary army personnel, he assigned it to Yangon Ba Swe, who engaged two

---

[92] Mya Hlaing, as told to Dr Kyin Ho (aka Naing Win) in 1987. Kyin Ho wrote up this story in a pamphlet published in Burmese in 1992, and Mya Hlaing translated it into English. The English translation is reproduced in part in Kin Oung, 1996: 70–1. 'The journalist Tin Maung Win wrote in a review of Kin Oung's book: "persons claiming to be disciples of this or that leader began to conspire against those they imagined as their master's political enemies, at times acting on their own. Writer Yangon Ba Swe himself had confessed in Bangkok in 1972 that he and Mya Hlaing had engaged in foolhardy exploits."' Email, Kin Oung to author, 18 January 2000. Both Mya Hlaing and Yangon Ba Swe are now dead.

[93] Letter, M.E. Busk to H.A. Stonor, 24 October 1983.

[94] Email, Kin Oung to author, 23 January 2000.

subordinates, Ye Myint and Ba Tok, who guarded Aung San sedulously day and night *until the day of the killings.*[95]

There is evidence of Ne Win involvement from still another source. In October 1947, the Reverend James W. Baldwin was arrested and detained in Insein Prison for supporting the Karens' claim for independence.[96] After his release from prison and deportation, Stonor contacted him. He told Stonor he had learned the true story of Aung San's assassination while in Insein Prison from the assassins themselves. Saw had played no part in it, Baldwin told Stonor. The people responsible were Ne Win, Kyaw Nyein, Nu and Khin Maung Gale.[97] Baldwin repeated this story to Lieutenant Colonel John Cromarty Tulloch and Stonor in a taxi *en route* to the first meeting of the Friends of the Burma Hill Peoples organized by Frank Owen, then editor of the *Daily Mail*.[98] Stonor also remembers Baldwin telling him that he had written to the *Daily Mail* concerning Aung San's assassination,[99] but there is no trace of the document Baldwin sent to the *Daily Mail* in the relevant files.[100]

Finally, there is this claim by Saw Samson, based on what his 'boss', General Sein Hmon, district superintendent of police in Insein, told him. Sein Hmon, who was investigating Saw's arms deals, assigned a surveillance team to monitor Saw's compound. No 'outside' car was seen to enter or leave the compound during the several days preceding the killings. When the police had evidence of Saw's arms purchases sufficient to convict him of high treason, an arrest warrant issued, and Sein Hmon arrested Saw on 19 July at 0900 hours—an hour and a half *before* the killings—and, when arrested, Saw was *alone with his family*. That same evening, shortly after dark, Sein Hmon received a report of some Burmans in a car

[95] Email, U Thaung to author, 11 January 2000. U Thaung stated, 'I even knew the two men [Ye Myint and Ba Tok] and talk to them on occasions.'

[96] For 'preventing agreement . . . between the Karens and Burmese'. See 'Situation in Burma—September 1947', part I, paragraph 12.

[97] A founder member of the Socialist Party who had served with Nu on FACE. Tinker, 1959: 392; U Maung Maung, 1989: 289, 293, 296.

[98] H.A. Stonor, correspondence with author, February 2000.

[99] This is a matter of record. See note to Sir Gilbert Laithwaite, 19 December 1947 (BL OIOC: M/4/2736).

[100] An annotation of the relevant Foreign and Commonwealth Office file, PRO: FO 371/63266, appearing between documents dated 28 November and 8 December 1947, states that a document was 'returned to the FCO under reference F15969/8793/79', but no such document appears in that file, suggesting that the Foreign and Commonwealth Office has classified it.

shouting at the tops of their voices, 'Triumph! Triumph!' He despatched a team to investigate and was transferred to Pegu the next day. Sein Hmon did not expose the 'blundering lie to the whole public of Burma' following the killings, because 'both groups of Burm[ans were] killing each other . . . like reducing the strength of evil'.[101] The time of Saw's arrest, 0900 hours according to this story, conflicts with Toye's statement that he rang Saw at his house about two hours later. Moreover, when Saw Samson reported the story, he was Karen National Union ambassador at large and Sein Hmon was a Karen. The story stands alone and is uncorroborated. If true, though, it is further evidence of Saw's false conviction.

We now confront the critical question—who stood to gain by Aung San's murder?

If we exclude from culpability the British government and the Karens for lack of evidence and motivation, and exclude Saw, British commercial houses and communists for lack of evidence, we are left with Nu, Ne Win, Kyaw Nyein and Khin Maung Gale. Nu became the first prime minister of independent Burma and remained prime minister for most of the succeeding 13 years, when he was overthrown by Ne Win. Three months after the killings, Ne Win was promoted to the rank of full colonel and, two months after that, he was a brigadier.[102] On 1 February 1949, he replaced Smith-Dun as chief of general staff and supreme commander of the armed forces,[103] and, two months later, he was admitted to Nu's cabinet as deputy prime minister, minister of home affairs and minister of defence.[104] 'The inclusion of . . . Ne Win in the cabinet [in these three capacities] made official for a brief period what was unofficial throughout the first fourteen years of Burma's independence,' observes the American historian, Robert Taylor.[105] Khin Maung Gale was minister of home affairs from 1952 to 1956 and minister of finance and revenues in 1956, then served for a time as the vice-president of the All-Burma Peasants' Organization. Kyaw Nyein was not dismissed from the cabinet for his reputed involvement with Ba Pe and Tin Tut in the Excise Bribes scandal. Instead, he stayed on as home member and, after independence, became the richest man in Burma.

[101] Letter, Saw Samson to H.A. Stonor, 27 January 1983.
[102] Tinker (ed.), 1984, vol. I: 1050.
[103] Dr Maung Maung, 1969: 209.
[104] Ibid.: 214.
[105] Taylor, 1987: 237.

Aung San's supporters insist that the *Bogyoke*'s premature death robbed Burma of its best chance of unity, stability and prosperity, and this may well be so, for the sufficient reason that it transformed Ne Win's career prospects. His death certainly did not help to resolve the many difficult issues that faced the new nation on 4 January 1948.

7
The Narcocrats

THE POPPY I saw during my trek into the Shan State and across the Kachin hill country is a plant having a green tubular main stem with several branches standing four to five feet high when fully grown. It is sown in October or November on the slopes and summits of hills, both in village gardens and in clearings slashed out of the jungle. Depending upon its latitude and elevation, the plant blooms from late December to late March,[1] each branch producing a bright red, violet, purple, white, white tipped with red or purple and red flower.

As the flowers mature, green, golf ball-size seed capsules form. When the capsules are scored with a three- or four-bladed, pencil-thin instrument, a milky white latex oozes from them. This latex is the raw opium. It congeals, is left on the capsules overnight to harden further, then, with a crescent-shaped blade, is scooped into pots attached to the farmer's waist. After standing for three weeks or so, by when it is the colour and consistency of treacle, it is kneaded into round, grapefruit-size cakes weighing about 1.6 kg that are packed in plaintain leaves.

In 1989, each of these packets sold for about 9600 kyats (approximately $1000 at the then official exchange rate, and about $150 at the then free market rate), old opium fetching a higher price than new because it contained less water. A pellet about half a thumbnail in size sufficed for a sedation, but an habitué might indulge double or treble that amount up to seven times a day, and, hence, it was too valuable for local consumption. The villagers sold it to itinerant Chinese traders for a fraction of the price the traders received on reselling it. There were no morphine factories or heroin refineries in Kachin State. The traders sold most Kachin opium in Myitkyina, while that produced further south had various outlets. Kokang and most Wa opium went to the Shan villages of Möng Ko, Möng Hom, Nam Kyaun, Kunlong and Kang Möng, where it was refined into heroin, then transported to Mandalay or Hong Kong. Factories near the Shan village of Loi Hi took some Wa and most Akha and Lahu

[1] The opium in the Wa lands visited by Scott and Hardiman was sown in November, sprouted early in January, flowered at the end of January or the beginning of February, and was harvested in April.

160

opium for trans-shipment to Hong Kong or Thailand. Opium produced in the hill country south of Kengtung was processed in refineries along the Thai border.[2]

In its raw state, the drug is a mild, sleep-inducing substance, a narcotic in the proper sense. Apart from recreational use, it is a remedy for diarrhoea, dysentery and various fevers and has veterinary applications. It has a reputation for enhancing capacity for hard work, and porters charged with heavy burdens sometimes consume small amounts as a balm on long, steep hauls. Used occasionally and in modest amounts, it is quite harmless. My one experiment with it produced no rockets in the sky or hallucinatory dreams, nothing intense; simply the slowly dulling comatosity of *papaver somniferum*.[3] It had no enduring consequence and was certainly not addictive. Used more often, its adverse effects are a tendency to emaciation and, when supply fails, lassitude. Since their conversion to Christianity, the Kachins have reprobated it save for medical or veterinary applications, but have condoned its cultivation, because alternative cash crops, such as tea and coffee, take longer to establish and require venture capital beyond the average farmer's means. Heroin, or, as it is known in Southeast Asia, 'number four', is another substance altogether.

The poppy's anaesthetic properties were known to both Hippocrates and Galen, but it was left to modern science to exploit the deleterious potential of extracting morphine from the resin and bonding it with acetic anhydride. In 1898, Bayer Pharmaceutical Company began marketing this synthesis under the trade name heroin as a panacea for common respiratory complaints such as asthma, bronchitis and tuberculosis. Available over the counter, it soon succeeded the milder opiates in popularity, and its popularity increased still further when, in 1908, the Congress prohibited doctors from prescribing opium. Heroin use in the United States had claimed at least 200,000 addicts when, in 1914, the Congress responded with the Harrison Narcotics Act, licensing dealers in opiates and requiring them to pay a penny duty on every ounce sold. Nevertheless, thousands of wounded soldiers returned from the First World War as morphine addicts.[4] A ruling of the United States Supreme Court in 1922, prohibiting prescriptions of morphine or

[2] *Far Eastern Economic Review*, Lintner, 'The new dealer', 28 June 1990: 22–3.
[3] See Tucker, 2000: 150–1.
[4] The author's great aunt was a morphine addict, the victim of doctors prescribing the drug for protracted pain relief.

heroin to 'addicts' under 'any circumstances',[5] seemed to redress the problem, and for the next 40 years addiction declined.[6] Then hundreds of thousands of young men were drafted into combat in Vietnam, and, in 1971, the *New York Times* reported medical researchers' studies showing that from 10 to 14 per cent of American soldiers in Vietnam tested used heroin and that 7 per cent of factory workers tested were addicts.[7]

Arabs introduced opium to India a millennium before its properties were known in America. In the sixteenth century, Portuguese traffickers cultivated a taste among indentured Chinese in Java for smoking it blended with tobacco from Brazil. From Java, the habit spread to China. Later, the East India Company asserted a monopoly over poppy grown in Bengal and stole the China trade from the Portuguese.[8] Bengal's exports, mainly to China, ballooned from 270 tons in 1821 to 2400 tons in 1838,[9] and the average annual tonnage for the decade preceding 1839 was almost six times that for the decade preceding 1821.[10]

The First Opium War (1839–42), fought by Britain to defend the principles of 'free trade' and 'diplomatic equality', followed China's attempt to close its ports to this flood of poison, but China lost the war[11] and its ports remained open. China then tried to ban use of

[5] *United States v. Behrman*, 258 U.S. 280, 42 S.Ct. 303, 66 L.Ed. 619 (1922).

[6] By 1965, there were only 57,000 known users in the entire United States. McCoy, 1972: 1. McCoy's book is essential reading for the innocent at heart.

[7] McCoy, 1972: 1, citing *The New York Times*, 16 May 1971, p. 1, and 23 July 1971, p. 1.

[8] Opium was 'a pernicious article of luxury', admitted Governor Warren Hastings responding to criticism from his peers—but, he added, its cultivation served 'purposes of foreign commerce'. Exports of 'Bengal', 'Benares' and 'Patna' provided one-seventh of government revenues. McCoy, 1972: 358, citing Owen, 1934: 7, 23. Another interesting defence to criticism (whose echoes are heard today in the context of the arms trade) is that foreign suppliers would meet demand if Britain had not. McCoy, 1972: 359, citing Owen, 1934: 87.

[9] McCoy, 1972: 60.

[10] Ibid.: 360.

[11] 'Opium not only provoked the war, it helped China [to] lose it. . . . During one battle, for example, an officer named Chang, who was in charge of important reserves, took time off to satisfy his craving.' While 'the sound of cannon and musketry-fire drew closer and closer', his aides debated whether to advance or retreat. When panic 'seized his troops and with one accord they fled . . . Chang himself was still puffing away at his opium pipe. At last he staggered into a litter and was carried away.' McCoy, 1972: 360–1, citing Waley, 1958: 176.

opium, but this only further weakened the ruling Ch'ing dynasty by exacerbating the corruption endemic among officials charged with enforcing the ban. Addicts' lips were slit so they could not smoke their pipes[12]—in vain. In the 1860s, China lifted its ban and began to grow local, cheaper produce. Imports declined to half their 1880 peak of 6500 tons but were more than offset by home supplies. When Sun Yat Sen overthrew the emperor in 1911, the Middle Kingdom's annual crop exceeded 22,000 tons.[13]

Merchants had been encouraging Yunnan hill tribes to grow poppy even before the emperor lifted the ban, and opium cultivation spread from Yunnan to the adjoining Kokang and Wa highlands. James George Scott, who travelled through Wa country in the 1890s, found 'miles and miles' of it. 'One can make several days' journey through nothing but opium fields.'[14] In 1930, when the Kuomintang (KMT) restricted its cultivation in China, merchants began buying the Kokang and Wa sap and refining it, both for Chinese use and exporting to Indo-China, Europe and the United States. As the hill farmers' only experience with the drug was raw opium, which appeared to them to be less deleterious than alcohol, they were ignorant of the wider impact of this commerce. The British banned opium cultivation west of the Salween, but allowed it east of the Salween, bought part of the harvest at fixed rates that varied from year to year,[15] and restricted its use to licensed addicts. A former assistant superintendent of the Northern Shan States charged with responsibility for purchasing the opium recalls that Kokang wives would encourage their husbands to use it to slacken sexual demands made on them.[16] Poppy was also farmed in the Kachin Hills, illicitly, in small quantities and solely for local consumption. Units of Force 136, the Northern Kachin Levies and the Burma Regiment used opium air-dropped to them behind Japanese lines for small transactions like engaging porters during the Second World War, and the Kachin Rangers and Merrill's Marauders used it to finance intelligence-gathering.

[12] McCoy, 1972: 362, citing the Reverend Hudson Taylor's testimony to the Royal Commission on Opium, Minutes of Evidence and Appendices, vol. 1 (1894), p. 30.
[13] McCoy, 1972: 361, citing Morse, 1913: 378.
[14] Scott and Hardiman, 1900–1, part I, vol. I: 509.
[15] Saimong Mangrai, 1965: 7.
[16] Conversation with Patrick Reginald Molloy, 5 March 2000.

When Burma received its independence in 1948, the nation's raw opium yield was about 30 metric tons. By 1996, it was 2560 metric tons[17]—an 8533 per cent increase that admits few rivals in the history of commerce. The eradication of opium in the People's Republic of China (PRC) under Mao was partly responsible, as was the rise in world demand for heroin. The main force driving this commerce for the past four decades, however, has been the Burmese Civil War.

In late March 1948, less than 12 weeks after Burma became independent, the CPB led an armed rebellion against the government. They were joined by other communists, by irregular forces that had not been integrated into the PVO, by mutinous ex-PBF Burma Army battalions and by disaffected Muslims in Arakan (Rohingyas). In August, the Union's paramilitary police (UMP) attacked Karenni National Organization headquarters and murdered a prominent Karenni nationalist, provoking the defection to the KNDO of Karen, Padaung and Pao policemen posted to the Shan State and an attack by KNDO and Mon National Defence Organization (MNDO) units on government positions in the Thaton–Moulmein area. On Christmas Eve, Burman territorials under Ne Win's general command hurled grenades into Karen churches in Mergui District, killing 80 Karens and triggering the defection from the Burma Army to the KNDO of Karen battalions and a battalion of the Kachin Rifles. A KNDO/MNDO offensive then began, which very nearly captured Rangoon.

As Burma's civil war began, China's drew to an end. Chiang Kai-shek and most of his Nationalist forces were already in Taiwan by May 1949. On 1 October, Mao proclaimed the People's Republic of China, and, two months later, the People's Liberation Army (PLA)

[17] Lintner (1994: vii) provides the 1948 figure. Although Lintner does not cite his source, the figure tallies broadly with Patrick Molloy's purchases (7000 vis, or 11.2 metric tons in both 1940 and 1941) and may represent data supplied by the Burma government, which continued British practice of buying in Wa and Kokang stocks for two years following independence. The 1996 figure is found in Bureau for International Narcotics and Law Enforcement Affairs, US Department of State, 'International Narcotics Control Strategy Report, 1998'; reproduced in *Burma Debate*, 'Online Discussion on Drugs in Burma', vol. VI, no. 1, spring, 1999: 4–12. The figure is arrived at by multiplying a notional average yield of 15 kg per hectare by the number of hectares under cultivation, as established by aerial photography and satellite imagery.

took Kunming. Stragglers from the KMT's defeated armies in Yunnan fled into Burma. The Burma Army captured about 200 of them, but 1000 others under Chen Wei-chen, commander of 93 Division of the KMT's 26th Army, and Ting Tsuo-shou, a French-educated ideologue, trekked down the Mekong to Möng Pong in the extreme southeast corner of Shan State, where they established radio contact with Taipei. Their declared intention was to form, with some 5000 other KMT remnants who had fled to Laos, the nucleus of an expanded and re-equipped force that would reconquer Chiang's lost provinces, starting with Yunnan, where, they believed, the grateful mainlanders, having experienced a spell of communist tyranny, would welcome them back. Chiang decided to reinforce them.[18]

In June 1950 Chen and Ting's strengthened force demanded the release of the 200 men captured by the Burma Army. The Kengtung District commander responded with an ultimatum to leave Burma. The KMT force seized Tachilek, an important Shan border town on the Chiang Rai–Kengtung road, and a Burma Army counter-offensive recaptured it. The KMT force then moved west to Möng Hsat and began rehabilitating an airstrip built during the Second World War to supply Force 136.[19] Enter the Americans with their focus on the bigger issue: to many in Washington in 1950, the rapid spread of world communism was the *only* issue. On 25 June 130,000 North Korean soldiers crossed the 38th parallel and swept through South Korea, and 400,000 PLA 'volunteers' reinforced them when the Americans counter-attacked. Officially, Washington was not involved with the KMT in Burma, but the Korean development probably resolved any unofficial misgivings about aiding it clandestinely.[20] General Claire Chennault, of 'Flying Tigers' renown, led the way. He was close to Chiang, and his airline, Civil Air Transport (CAT), was already running supplies to Möng Hsat from Taipei and Bangkok. By early 1951, Burma Army intelligence officers were reporting at least five drops a week from unmarked C-46s and C-47s.[21]

[18] Lintner, 1994: 93–5.
[19] Ibid.: 95–6.
[20] A 10 April 1950 memorandum from the joint chiefs of staff to the secretary of defense proposed 'a program of special covert operations designed to interfere with Communist activities in Southeast Asia'. McCoy, 1972: 128–9, citing *The Pentagon Papers* (Boston: The Beacon Press, Senator Gravel edn., 1971), vol. I, p. 366.
[21] Government of the Union of Burma, 1953: 15.

Secure in their new headquarters, Chen and Ting's CIA-supplied forces began consolidating other KMT survivors scattered about the Kokang, Wa and Kengtung hills. They also began recruiting and training the local Kokangs (Han Chinese), Was, Lahus, Akhas, Shans, Palaungs and Hmongs (Miaus or Meos). Chinese living on the Yunnan side of the border and a small Kokang force led by Yang Kyin Hsiu (Olive Yang) supported them.[22] Thus, by December 1951, a 6000-strong, well-armed 'Yunnan Province Anti-Communist National Salvation Army' was concentrated at Möng Hsat, Pangyang (in the Wa hills) and Lungtangchai (in central Kokang). Two bold moves into Yunnan ended in disaster (Ting's anticipated popular welcome did not materialize), but, undaunted, the CIA increased its assistance, and the CAT shuttle service to Möng Hsat intensified.[23] The American-piloted C-46s and C-47s brought in 'instructors' from Taiwan, machine guns, bazookas, mortars, anti-aircraft guns, M-1 carbines, ammunition and medical supplies, while outbound planes flew out opium.[24] A new base was established at Möng Yang, north of Kengtung. A further attempt at liberating the enslaved Yunnanese masses in August 1952 also ended in disaster.[25]

The KMT's forces in Burma, commanded now by General Li Mi, switched to an interim strategy congenial to their American sponsors. They would 'hold the line against the reds' in Burma. Recruiting more hill people, they trebled the number of their forces[26] and soon were ready to move west and south to exploit opportunities of forming alliances with rebellious groups fighting the Burma Army. Their strategic objective was to open a deep-water port on the Sea of Martaban to allow bringing in really serious supplies. Combined KMT, Karen and Karenni forces seized Mawchi, an important mining town on the southward extension of the Shan Plateau straddling the road from Toungoo, and supplied the then

---

[22] Lintner, 1994: 99–100; Yang Li, 1997: 71.

[23] McCoy, 1972: 130.

[24] Lintner, 1994: 108–9, citing an interview with Mika Rolley, who led a KNU mission to Möng Hsat in 1952.

[25] McCoy, 1972: 130.

[26] Ibid., citing an interview with the Reverend Paul Lewis, a missionary who had worked with the Lahu. Lintner (1994: 103, citing Lamour, 1975: 80) states that the number was '13,000 well-equipped troops'. Lamour's figures, based on an interview with General Li Mi, present a different proportion of KMT survivors (8000) to local hill tribe recruits and refugees from China (4000). Locally recruited Sino-Burmese (2500), she says, were mostly muleteers.

Mon leader, Nai Aung Tun, and helped him to reorganize and re-invigorate the MNDO. A KMT force of 700 men in the Dawna Range then marched on to the Andaman Sea south of Amherst. Ships from Taiwan bearing KMT regulars and 4500 tons of ammunition arrived offshore and were only prevented from discharging their cargoes by the vigilance of the local Burma Army commander, 'Thirty Comrade' Kyaw Zaw.[27] KMT and KNDO forces then attacked Loikaw, Loipuk, Bawlake and Nam Hpe.

These various operations, of course, required financing, but the KMT now controlled the trans-Salween highlands.[28] No finer opium grew anywhere, and Yunnanese opium farmers were flooding there to escape Mao's ban on opium cultivation in the PRC.[29] Facilitating the KMT's task, moreover, the traders were all Chinese. The KMT imposed an opium tax on farmers, regardless of the crops they grew, and to pay the tax, the farmers grew more opium. Opportunity, experience and necessity thus combined to produce ever increasing yields. Poppy, with KMT encouragement, spread to the hills west of the Salween. Then the Burma Army found morphine factories near one of the KMT's airstrips, marking an altogether new and more sinister phase in Burma's drugs trade.

The CIA-backed 'secret war' in Burma continued until 26 January 1961, when six Burma Army battalions and three PLA divisions took the KMT base at Möng Pa Liao, seized five tons of US-supplied ammunition and drove most of the remaining invaders across the

[27] Lintner, 1994: 109–10. Had the ships succeeded in landing their cargoes, Lintner suggests, the entire fate of the Burmese Civil War would have been different. Ne Win subsequently charged Kyaw Zaw with passing intelligence to the communists and dismissed him from the army. He lived quietly in Rangoon for two decades, then joined the CPB.

[28] Harry J. Anslinger, chief of the US Federal Bureau of Narcotics, provided public relations cover with 'seemingly meticulously detailed reports claiming that the US and the West were being flooded by "Yunnan opium" and heroin manufactured in China [as a] Communist plot to subvert the morals of Western youths.' Lintner, 1994: 332, citing Peter Dale Scott and Jonathan Marshall, *Cocaine Politics: Drugs, Armies and the CIA in Central America* (Berkeley, CA: University of California Press, 1991), p. 172. See also McCoy, 1972: 146. Anslinger elaborated his 'Communist plot' accusations. See Anslinger, 1961. The Bureau of Narcotics has since repudiated his accusations. See McCoy, 1972: 127.

[29] Lewis, 1957; Lintner, 1994: 473, n. 60. See also Tucker, 2000: 116 (opium farmers at 'Freedom Hill' village who called themselves '*wu bana*', or fifty-eighters, after the year they fled from Yunnan).

Mekong into Laos.[30] By now, though, the KMT's decade-long presence in Burma had created a narcotics industry and a trading infrastructure that the KMT continued to exploit from bases in Thailand and through proxies such as Yang Kyin Hsui, her older brother, Yang Kyein Sein (Jimmy Yang), Lo Hsin Han, Maha San, Moh Heng and Khun Sa.[31]

When Chen and Ting's column trekked out of Yunnan and down the Mekong with their grandiose plans of regrouping and returning north as liberators, Rangoon was at war with six armed insurgencies.[32] Almost no opium grew in the rebellious areas, and none of the rebels dealt in narcotics. Their rebellion was a simply defined clash of ethnic, political and personal adversaries. In November 1959, the Shans rebelled, outraged by Rangoon's abuse of Panglong's equal treatment provisions and its hostility to Shan secessionist rights guaranteed by chapter 10 of the 1947 constitution, and, by 1968, 'in virtually every valley and on every mountain top a different ethnic army, [government] militia or local warlord force was fighting to gain control'.[33] When I trekked into the Shan State near Möng Ko

[30] Where the CIA recruited them to fight the Pathet Lao. See McCoy, 1972: 134–5.

[31] After its defeat at Möng Pa Liao, the KMT split into two factions. The 5th Army, comprising about 1800 men and led by General Tuan Shi-wen (variant spellings, Tuan Shee Wen, Duan Xiwen), operated from Mount Mae Salong, about 30 miles northwest of Chiang Rai. The 3rd Army, comprising about 1400 men and led by Li Wen-huan (variant spellings, Ly Wen-huan, Lee Wen Huan, Li Wenhuan), operated from Tam Ngop, a mountain redoubt near Fang, about 50 miles west of Chiangmai. McCoy, 1972: 318–19; Smith, 1991: 224. But see Belanger, 1989: 19, which assesses Tuan's force as 1000 men. After Tuan's death in 1980, his subordinates formed their own groups or joined rival groups. Boucaud and Boucaud, 1985: 36.

[32] Thakin Soe's Red Flag communists, the monk Sein Da's Arakan People's Liberation Party and Jafar Kawwal's *mujahids* in Arakan; the CPB and its PVO and mutinous ex-PBF Burma Army units in central Burma; the Kawthoolei Armed Forces (KAF), MNDO and various individual Kachin, Karenni, Pao and Palaung soldiers fighting under the KAF's colours in Tenasserim and the eastern hills; and the PNO in the hills around Taunggyi. In 1952, the Red Flags, White Flags (CPB) and PVOs entered a 'Tri-Partite Alliance', and, in 1957, Taw Plo established the KNPP. In 1958, Nai Shwe Kyin revitalized the Mon rebellion by launching the NMSP after most of the MNDO accepted a government amnesty and 'returned to the legal fold'. The tally disregards a short-lived 'Pawng Yang National Defence Force' that had captured and briefly held Lashio and Namhkam.

[33] Smith, 1991: 190–1, 251.

in 1989, the diverse groups that were or had been active there against each other or the Burma Army included all of the following:

Group	Year founded
Noom Suk Harn	1958
Shan State Independence Army (SSIA)	1960
KIO/KIA	1961
Shan National United Front (SNUF)	1961
Shan National Army (SNA)	1961
Palaung National Front	1963
Kokang Revolutionary (or Resistance) Force (KRF)	1963
SSPP/SSA	1964
Shan National Independence Army	1966
Shan State Nationalities Liberation Organization	1966
Shan United Army (SUA)	c1967
CPB	1968[34]
Shan United Revolutionary Army (SURA)	1969
Maha San's Vingngün[35] government militia	1969
Lahu National United Party	1973
WNO/WNA	1974
Shan People's Liberation Army Front	1974
PSLP	1976, 1985
PNO	1976[36]
Tai Independence Army	1978
Wa National Council (WNC)	1982
Tai (or Tai-land) Revolutionary Council (TRC)	1984
Möng Tai Army (MTA)[37]	1985
LNO	1985, 1987
United Shan Patriotic Council (USPC)	1987
United Wa State Party/Army (UWSP/A)	1988
ABSDF	1988

While most of these insurgencies were ideologically inspired, all depended in some measure on the drugs trade to finance their armies, and some, such as the SUA, SURA, WNC, TRC and USPC,

[34] Date of invasion of Shan State.
[35] A place in the southern Wa Hills where silver was mined during colonial times. The name in Shan means 'silver town'.
[36] The PNO disbanded in 1958 and reformed in 1976. Smith, 1991: 168–9, 338.
[37] The TRC's military wing.

were little more than armed gangs led by drug barons masquerading as Wa and Shan patriots. One of the most ideological was the SNA, yet Adrian Cowell and Chris Menges, who spent five months with the SNA in 1964–65,[38] reported that it sold opium smuggled into Thailand from Kengtung and used the proceeds to buy guns smuggled from Laos.[39]

Further complicating the picture was the 1968 invasion of northern Shan State by a heavily armed force of CPB 'volunteers'. By 1974, the CPB's North East Command (NEC) controlled most of the Kokang, Wa and Kengtung highlands east of the Salween—the 8000 square miles of poppy belt more or less coterminous with that previously dominated by the KMT. At its peak, the NEC numbered about 20,000 troops.[40] The PRC supplied them abundantly with sophisticated arms, communications equipment, transport, uniforms and food.[41] Only the political cadres were Burmans;[42] the fighting men were Was, Kokangs, Palaungs, Kachins, Shans, Akhas and Lahus. The NEC tried to eradicate poppy through crop-substitution measures,[43] but the local farmers distrusted the new, alien crops, and a rat invasion in 1976 seemed to vindicate their suspicions. The NEC then resolved to license poppy, which led to taxing it and, eventually, to accepting produce in lieu of cash.[44] Individual commanders began growing opium, then trading it; ultimately, they were refining it.[45] In 1980–81, the PRC ceased

---

[38] *Opium Warlords*, London, ATV, 1976.

[39] Lintner, 1994: 182–3.

[40] Including village militias. Interview with General Kyi Myint (aka Zhang Zhiming), Möng Ko, January 1989.

[41] Lintner, 1990a: 26.

[42] They were Maoists to whom the PRC had given sanctuary in the 1950s and early 1960s. See *Burma Debate*, Lintner, 'Ethnic Insurgents & Narcotics', vol. II, no. 1, February/March, 1995: 18–21.

[43] At Möng Ko in 1989, my companion and I were shown a video of happy hill people destroying poppy and harvesting wheat while singing anthems extolling collectivization, but the video even then was already an artifact of a dead fantasy.

[44] 'Visitors to the party's general headquarters at Panghsang in 1973, shortly after the [People's Army] took control of the area, were impressed at the scale of the CPB's eradication programmes; a few years later they found poppy fields lining the route.' Smith, 1991: 315.

[45] The KIA also had difficulties in its efforts to eliminate opium farming. 'In 1964, we banned poppy growing in all our areas except the Southern and Eastern Divisions, where other crops could not be grown. But our people saw this as discriminatory, and we had no completely satisfactory answer to their

supporting the NEC and its revenues from excise on cross-border commerce[46] fell sharply, as smugglers were no longer obliged to use its tollgates,[47] begetting yet greater dependence on revenues from the drugs trade. The resulting ideological contradictions proved too great a strain, and, on 12–14 March 1989, six weeks after my companion and I left Möng Ko, Kokang mutineers seized Möng Ko, including its heroin factories. A month later, Chao Ngi Lai's Was seized the NEC's GHQ at Panghsang, including its opium stocks. This was to expose to public scrutiny what, hitherto, had been obscure—Rangoon's involvement in the trade.

In April 1948, Kyaw Nyein's Ministry of Home Affairs began raising 'special police reserves', later named *sitwundan* (lit. military personnel).[48] Drawing upon the organizational structures of the resistance cells formed under the Minami Organ, they were pocket armies loyal to the League's socialist wing and Ne Win's 4th Burma Rifles. Ne Win seconded 173 officers and other ranks to train them, and Nu, Kyaw Nyein, Ba Swe and other socialists were prominent in the committee appointed to administer them. Their ostensible role was to combat the CPB's threat to the Union. In fact, they provided a power base for Ne Win and Kyaw Nyein against the PVO and leftist ex-PBF battalions in the Burma Army.[49] After the PVO and two of

-----

criticism, since there were also places in the Northern and Western Divisions unsuitable for other crops. The farmers there petitioned us, and we granted them an exception, and soon there were so many exceptions that we had to stop enforcing the ban altogether. Opium is like a small hole in a tree. A termite enters the hole, makes more holes, and, before long, the tree dies.' Conversation with Major-General Zau Mai, chief of staff, KIA, and vice-chairman (after 1992 chairman) KIO, Pajau Bum, 1989. See Tucker, 2000: 92–3.

[46] Excise taxes collected at the CPB's toll gates at one time amounted to 67 per cent of its revenues. See Lintner, 1994: 291.

[47] Opinions differ as to why Chinese support for its Burmese surrogate ended. Compare Lintner, 1990b: 261, and Smith, 1991: 248.

[48] Callahan, 1996: 351.

[49] The *sitwundans'* politically partisan purpose is shown in Let Ya's criticism of its recruitment practices. 'It was rather surprising to note that the personnel appointed to lead these levies are either dacoits, ex-dacoits or people familiar in police registers. Some of them are either known criminals or political chameleons. . . . What will be the impression of the public to see a criminal or a political chameleon with gazetted rank of deputy SP? How will police subordinates feel to find a criminal as their senior officer?' Weekly report for week ended 28 August 1948, telegram, British Embassy, Rangoon, to Foreign Office, 5 September 1948 (PRO: FO 371/69484). Quoted in Callahan, 1996: 353.

the three ex-PBF battalions joined the CPB's rebellion in the summer of 1948, the *sitwundan* were expanded, strengthened and officially transferred to the authority of the War Office. Now acting under Ne Win, they distinguished themselves (and proved their pro-Burman fervour) by senseless acts of brutality on minorities.[50] When General Smith Dun resigned as commander-in-chief of the Burma Army after the attacks on the churches in Mergui District and an attempt to assassinate him,[51] Ne Win assumed command of the Burma Army as well, and the *sitwundan* declined in importance. In 1955, they were reformed as *pyu saw hti tat*, forces recruited from local communities tasked to defend specific areas.[52]

Variants of the *sitwundan* and *pyu saw hti* pocket army territorials were the *ka kwe yei* (lit., 'defence affairs'),[53] established in 1963. They provided Rangoon with the means of participating in and, as we shall see, ultimately controlling the drugs trade, for they were military alliances *cum* business partnerships with drug barons, the most notorious of whom were Lo Hsin Han,[54] Moh Heng[55] and Zhang Qifu.[56] These gangsters all have profiles of baffling complexity.

---

[50] Let Ya broke with Nu over the issue. 'Does not the Government trust the army . . . and police? Have not they shown adequate proof of their loyalty?' Quoted in Callahan, 1996: 352–3. Tun Hla Oung's misgivings about the scheme provided the pretext for assigning him to the Burmese embassy in London. See telegram, Foreign Office to British Embassy, Rangoon, 25 September 1948 (PRO: FO 371/69484).

[51] Smith, 1991: 117–18.

[52] The scheme was modelled on Israel's policy of establishing armed settlements at strategic sites. See Smith, 1991: 95. Pyu Saw Hti was the title of a traditional chief at Pagan and the founder of a quasi-legendary Pagan dynasty who was reputed to have found a way to get rid of *bu*, a gourd-like climbing plant infesting river banks. Conversation with Peter Zan, 16 October 1998. There is irony in the choice of name for a force allied to Rangoon. Saw is the same word as *saohpa*, *sawbwa* and *chao*, respectively Shan, Burmese and Nanchao for king, while Hti is a Burmese rendering of *ti*, Chinese for king, evincing early Nanchao (Chinese Shan) conquest of the Burmans (Pyus). See Harvey, 1967: 15, 308.

[53] The *ka kwe yei* are sometimes referred to as 'government militias' or 'home guards'. See Smith, 1991: 221.

[54] Variant spellings include Lo-Hsing Han and Luo Xinghan. Chinese names are spelled according to whether the writer's intention is to render them phonetically or in Pinyin. Where possible, I have used the spellings preferred by Yang Li (1997: esp. 132–6) and included the most common variants in footnotes.

[55] Aka Gon Jerng.

[56] Variant spellings include Chang Qifu, Chang Shi-fu and Chan Shee-fu.

Lo Hsin Han is a Yunnan-born player who displaces the Kokang *sawbwa*'s son, Jimmy Yang, as the leader of the Kokang Revolutionary Force after the CPB established the NEC. As his *ka kwe yei* privileges include use of government roads to transport his opium, giving him a competitive edge over rivals still dependent on mules, he soon acquires the reputation of being the 'kingpin of the heroin traffic in Southeast Asia'.[57] His assistance to the Burma Army in repelling the CPB at the decisive battle at Kunlong Bridge so pleases the Burman commanders that they assign troops to him to use as extra security for his convoys, but he then accuses them of not exerting themselves sufficiently to prevent the SSA from taxing his convoys and merges his operations with the SSA. In 1973, Adrian Cowell delivers to the US Embassy in Bangkok an offer made by Lo and the SSA to sell to the United States all the opium they control ('a third of the world's heroin for approximately $12 million') if the US will lend its help in resolving their dispute with Rangoon. A few hours later, Thai police arrest Lo,[58] and Washington hails the arrest as a 'big victory in the war against drugs'. But the Thais extradite Lo to Burma and Rangoon pardons him, even helps him to recruit, train and equip a new army, and, by 1981, Lo is back in the narcotics business. When Bertil Lintner travelled through Kokang in 1987, Lo's 'agents were busy making deals with their erstwhile enemies, the CPB'.[59]

Moh Heng, a Shan of leftist leanings from the Lai Hka–Möng Küng area north of Taunggyi, joins the CPB in the 1950s and goes underground, then leaves the CPB and establishes his own Shan State Communist Party. In May 1958, he surrenders to the government, but, a few months later, joins the general Shan rebellion. The SSIA wants his support but recognizes that Moh's political orientation presents ideological difficulties and, hence, establishes the SNUF, with Moh as its chairman, to serve as the SSIA's political arm. The Mahadevi of Yawnghwe[60] forms the SSA, hoping thereby to unite all the various Shan armies and factions, and the SSIA, SNUF and KRF

---

[57] Nelson Gross, US narcotics adviser, 1972. Quoted in Lintner, 1990b: 225.
[58] Lintner, 1994: 227–8. An alternative view is that Lo exposed Rangoon's complicity in the trade, and Li Wen-huan betrayed him to the Thais. See *Burma Debate*, Yawnghwe, 'Shan Opium Politics: The Khun Sa Factor', vol. II, no. 1, February/March 1995: 26; Belanger, 1985: 99.
[59] Lintner, 1990b: 226.
[60] Whose husband, Sao Shwe Thaike, the first president of Burma, died in prison after the Burma Army shot their son.

merge with the SSA, Moh now commanding its 3 Brigade. Moh, however, soon tires of his relatively humble position in this combination and forms the SURA, supported by General Li Wenhuan's KMT Third Army based at Tam Ngop on the Thai side of the border north of Chiang Mai. The SSA's 2 Brigade defects to Moh and, on April Fool's Day 1984, merges with SURA to form the TRC.

Khun Sa (Prince Pleasant) is the adopted Shan name of Zhang Qifu.[61] He forms his own army to fight the KMT, and, later, negotiates *ka kwe yei* status. In 1964, Ne Win invalidates (demonetizes) much of the national currency, so inflaming Khun Sa that he defects to the insurgents and renames his army the Loimaw Anti-Socialist Army.[62] A few months later, however, he realigns it with Rangoon and builds the first morphine factory in Burma at Vingngün.[63] All goes smoothly, Khun Sa's forces expanding in tandem with the profits from his drug operations until 1967, when he announces that he will pay no further transit taxes to the KMT save on a reciprocal basis, provoking the KMT to attack one of his mule convoys. In the ensuing battle, the Lao Army chief, General Ouane, consignee of the convoy's cargo, sends T-28 prop fighters to bomb the feuding warlords, moves in his troops and makes off with the opium.[64] The publicity embarrasses Rangoon, and Khun Sa falls from grace—but not for long. Six months later, now contending with a revitalized CPB in the north and needing Khun Sa's help in defending the Loimaw heights above an important crossing point on the Salween, Rangoon renews its support, and Khun Sa resumes trucking his product south over government roads. About this time, he makes his first big, laundered money investment in Thailand. Then, on 29 October 1969, the Burma Army arrests him.[65]

Mounting international criticism forced Ne Win in 1973 temporarily to abandon his *ka kwe yei* tactics, and Lo's Kokangs, Khun Sa's SUA, Maha San's Vingngün Was and the many other warlord armies shifted their allegiances back to Shan nationalism.[66]

[61] A variant spelling is Chan Shee-fu.

[62] *Burma Debate*, Yawnghwe, 'Shan Opium Politics: The Khun Sa Factor', vol. II, no. 1, February/March 1995: 26.

[63] McCoy, 1972: 338.

[64] Ibid.: 322–8; Belanger, 1989: 100; Lintner, 1994: 245.

[65] Ibid.: 211.

[66] In 1986, Khun Sa merged the SUA, the TRC's military wing, with Moh Heng's SURA to form the MTA. The MTA's forces were deployed escorting Khun Sa's and Moh Heng's mule caravans and protecting their heroin refineries near the Thai border. See Lintner, 1990a: 108. In an interview with

The reader need not burden himself with the fine detail of these shifting alliances. The point to note is the interdependence of the Burmese Civil War and the trade.

In 1986, Washington began supplying Rangoon with Bell 205 helicopters, fixed-wing Thrust aircraft, pilot-training and agent 2,4-D, a herbicide banned in the United States, to assist the Burma Army in its professed intention of eradicating opium. It was a grave miscalculation. The hill farmers' only cash-crop possibilities were tea, coffee and opium, and, of these, opium alone provided a return in a single growing season.[67] The longer their crops stood in the field, the greater the risk of destruction, and providing this capability to the Burma Army effectively *forced* them to grow opium.[68] The Burma Army used the herbicide to assist its partners in the trade by spraying only their competitors' opium.[69] It also discovered that the herbicide was ideal for ethnic cleansing. The herbicide entered rivers and streams and spread beyond its target areas. People who drank from the rivers or ate food poisoned by the herbicide became violently ill. Its toxicity persisted in the soil. Nevertheless, the programme had its advocates in the National Security Council and the Congress. No American lives were at risk, the programme was cheap to administer and, above all, its proponents were seen to be doing something. Washington's counter-narcotics and Southeast Asia experts, still under the illusion that Rangoon was on-side, even claimed it was reducing the amount of opium produced. In fact, it had precisely the opposite result.

Washington changed its policy after the massacres of 'democracy summer' 1988, and Rangoon resumed forming home guards, now called '*pyithu sit*' (people's militias). The CPB's collapse was the catalyst.

Andrew Drummond published in *Observer Magazine* (16 July 1989), Khun Sa is reported to have said: 'The Burmese government want me to fight the Communists. As long as I am doing that, it's not to their advantage to attack me.'

[67] See Overholt, 'The Wrong Enemy', *Foreign Affairs*, no. 77, winter 1989–90.

[68] 'Even if our farmers could manage the capital to grow crops like coffee and tea, the Burma Army would destroy them—just as they cut down the orange trees along the Myitkyina–Bhamo road. . . . In 1978 the Central Committee sent me to Nam Hkam Pa in Kachin State to supervise an irrigation scheme for paddies costing seven lakhs and involving 300 families. The Burma Army sent a company of soldiers and destroyed the entire scheme.' Interview with Zau Mai, Pajau Bum, February 1989. Quoted in Tucker, 2000: 93.

[69] Ibid.: 55, 93–4.

A week after the Kokang CPB commander, Peng Kya Shen,[70] mutinied and seized Möng Ko on 12 March 1989, Lo dined with him and his younger brother, Peng Kya Fu.[71] A series of high-level meetings followed: in Lashio between Brigadier Aung Gyi, accompanied by Olive Yang, representing Rangoon, and Peng Kya Fu and other ex-CPB commanders representing the mutineers; in Kunlong between Major-General Khin Nyunt, the Directorate of Defence Services Intelligence (DDSI) chief, Colonel Maung Tin, commander of the Burma Army's northeastern command, and Peng Kya Fu; in Lashio between Khin Nyunt, Maung Tin, Brigadier General Maung Aye, Brigadier General Tin Oo and Chao Ngi Lai.[72] In December, Peng Kya Fu and the CPB's former treasurer, Liu Guo Chi,[73] led a delegation who met with Khin Nyunt in Rangoon, and, the following May, the regime's *Working People's Daily* depicted Peng Kya Shen's son-in-law, Lin Mingxian,[74] commander of the former CPB Mekong River Division, in friendly conversation with another senior Burma Army commander.[75] The deals concluded with these men, called 'border areas development agreements', allowed them to retain their armies intact, produce their drugs and use the Army's roads for transporting their drugs, and, within a year of the mutinies, according to erstwhile CPB comrades who fled to China, at least 17 heroin factories were operating in their former fiefdoms.[76]

Pyithu sit trafficking in narcotics with Rangoon's encouragement and assistance now included:

Group	Year founded
Burma National Democratic Alliance Army[77]	14 March 1989
Myanmar National Solidarity Party[78]	8 May 1989

[70] Variant spellings include Pheung Kya-shin and Peng Jiasheng.
[71] Variant spellings include Peng Jiafu and Pheung Kya-fu.
[72] *Far Eastern Economic Review*, Lintner, 'A fix in the making', 28 June 1990: 22. See also Lintner, 1994: 297–8.
[73] Variant spellings include Liu Guo Qi and Liu Go Shi.
[74] Variant spellings include Lin Ming Xiang and Sai Lin. The Mekong River Division operated in the 815 War Zone, named for the month and day of the founding of the CPB, August 15 (1939), in the extreme northeast corner of Shan State, about 40 linear miles south of Jing Hong.
[75] Ibid., Lintner, 'Triangular ties', 28 March 1991: 23.
[76] Ibid., Lintner, 'A fix in the making', 28 June 1990: 22. See also Lintner, 1994: 299.
[77] Aka Brave Nationalist Democratic Alliance Army, later called Myanmar National Democratic Alliance Army.
[78] Aka Burma Democracy Solidarity Party or Burma National United Party, since absorbed into the United Wa State Army.

Noom Suk Harn[79]	15 May 1989
SSA	24 September 1989[80]
National Democratic Army[81]	15 December 1989
Kachin Defence Army	11 January 1991[82]
Pao National Organization	18 February 1991
Palaung State Liberation Front/Army	21 April 1991
Shan State Nationalities People's Liberation Organization	9 October 1994[83]

Meanwhile, Khun Sa, having returned to the jungle in 1975 after six years in gaol, now controlled almost the entire Shan State border abutting Thailand and perhaps two-thirds of the opium production of Shan State.[84] Every mile-long caravan fetched enough opium to buy at least 1000 new carbines,[85] and, from his new headquarters at Homöng on the Thai border, he continued to build and direct his empire. In 1987, André and Louis Boucaud estimated his strength at 6000 men,[86] and, by December 1995, it was more than double that size, its numbers swollen by defectors from *pyithu sits* formed after the CPB's collapse. Equipped with some of the world's most lethal weapons, including SAM-7 missiles,[87] it was perhaps the most potent narcotics force ever assembled. Then something altogether extraordinary happened. Khun Sa handed over his army and the city of

[79] From the earlier Shan rebel group of that name, now defunct. It was later called the Eastern Shan National Democratic Alliance, and its military arm, the Eastern Shan State Army.

[80] A faction that broke away from Sai Lek's SSPP/SSA.

[81] Later called the New Democratic Force (Ting Ying and Zalum's Kachins operating in the CPB's former 101 Military District, a 50-mile strip along the Kachin State–China border crossed by the Kambaiti, Panwa and Hpimaw passes).

[82] Formerly KIA 4 Brigade, led into mutiny by Mahtu Naw.

[83] Letters to author from KIO foreign secretary Zau Zeng, 15 November 1989, and Kyi Myint, 27 July 1990; Lintner, 1990a: 39–53, appendix II; Lintner, 1994: esp. 292–9; *Far Eastern Economic Review*, Lintner, 'A fix in the making', 28 June 1990: 20 ff., and 'Fields of dreams', 20 February 1992: 23 ff.; Smith, 1991: 374–81; *Burma Alert*, vol. 5, no. 12, December 1994; *Burma Debate*, Lintner, 'Ethnic Insurgents & Narcotics', vol. II, no. 1, February 1995: 20–1; Bureau for International Narcotics and Law Enforcement Affairs, US Department of State, 'International Narcotics Control Strategy Report, 1998'.

[84] Smith, 1991: 343.

[85] McCoy, 1972: 323.

[86] Boucaud and Boucaud, 1985: 178.

[87] Lintner, 1999: 411.

Homöng, with its video halls, karaoke bars, brothels, discos and golf course, to Burma's generals and retired to Rangoon.[88]

Underlying Washington's Burma policy from the mid-1970s until the end of the 1980s was the assumption that Rangoon was engaged in a war against narco-terrorists. In September 1989, the US General Accounting Office questioned this article of faith, pointing out that 'corruption [in Burma] facilitates illicit trafficking and makes effective action against narcotics difficult to sustain'. Others had voiced similar concerns before,[89] and Washington began to heed their warnings.

In February 1992, Senator Jesse Helms testified to the Senate Foreign Relations Committee that Rangoon was financing arms procurements with money earned from the heroin trade,[90] and the following month the US Drug Enforcement Administration (DEA)'s annual report (for 1991) described Burma as 'the world's largest producer of heroin' and imputed to it 56 per cent of the heroin consumed in the United States.[91] In June 1994, US deputy assistant secretary of state for East Asian and Pacific affairs, Thomas Hubbard, told the House of Representatives sub-committee on Asian and Pacific Affairs that 'it is unlikely that the heroin trade can be curtailed without fundamental political change in Burma' and that 'heroin from Burma is a threat not only to the US but also to . . . China, India, Thailand and Malaysia'. Hubbard then led a delegation to Rangoon and advised the generals that improved relations between the US and Burma presupposed curtailment of the drugs trade. A 1996 article by Robert Gelbard, US assistant secretary of state for international narcotics and law enforcement affairs, stated: 'The lawlessness of authoritarian rule . . . results in the corruption and criminalization of the state and the entrenchment of the drugs trade in Burma's political and economic life.'[92] President Clinton echoed this view: 'The role of drugs in Burma's economic and political life

---

[88] Smith, 1999: 447.

[89] As one example, I raised the matter of the Burma Army's involvement in the trade at a meeting with the directors of the Southeast Asia, counter-terrorism and narcotics desks at the National Security Council in July 1989. See Tucker, 2000: 332–3.

[90] *Burma Alert*, vol. 3, no. 3, March 1992.

[91] Ibid.

[92] *Far Eastern Economic Review*, Gelbard, 'Slorc's Drug Links', 21 November 1996: 35.

and the regime's refusal to honour its own pledge to move to multi-party democracy are really two sides of the same coin, for both represent the absence of the rule of law,'[93] and, citing the regime's continued failure to act against the drugs trade, in May 1997 signed into law a ban on new US investment in Burma. The State Department's most recent report states that there 'are persistent and reliable reports that officials, particularly corrupt army personnel posted in outlying areas, are either involved in the drug business or are paid to allow the drug business to be conducted by others'.[94]

The report goes on to assert, however, that there is 'no evidence that the *government* [of Burma], on an institutional level, is involved in the drug trade'.[95] Furthermore, the White House has endorsed this view.[96] This seems to me an astonishing assertion. I suggest that there is very considerable evidence of Rangoon's involvement in the trade.

First, there is the regime's condonation of individual Burma Army officers' involvement. Seng Hpung told me in 1989, 'The fortunes that [Burma Army] senior officers are making from narcotics is the main reason why the war continues,'[97] and Kyi Myint, various other KIA and CPB commanders, the SSA's commander,[98] Burman soldiers with the ABSDF, captured Burma Army soldiers,[99] the opium merchants themselves, and everyone else I interviewed concurred. The merchants, they said, delivered the sap to Burma Army posts on the Namhpakka–Kutkai sector of the Burma Road for transport to Mandalay or Rangoon, where it fetched 100 times what the farmers had received, and most, if not all, front-line Burma Army commanders were traffickers.[100] Farmers around Lashio, an area

[93] BBC World Service, 11 November 1996. Quoted in *Burma Alert*, vol. 7, no. 12, December 1996.
[94] Bureau for International Narcotics and Law Enforcement Affairs, US Department of State, 'International Narcotics Control Strategy Report, 1999'.
[95] Ibid. Italics added.
[96] Clinton, 'Report to Congress on Conditions in Burma and U.S. Policy toward Burma for the period March 28, 1999–September 28, 1999'. There would appear to be dissenting voices in Washington on this issue. See *Far Eastern Economic Review*, Lutterbeck, 'Dollar Diplomacy', 7 May 1998: 20, imputing to a 'senior official' the statement that 'everything indicates that the [Burmese] government is deeply involved in the drug trade'.
[97] Tucker, 2000: 55, 57–8.
[98] Sai Lek, who said that his Shan State Army was, and for the preceding two years had been, fighting both the Burma Army *and* Khun Sa. Tucker, 2000: 55–6.
[99] Ibid.
[100] Ibid.: 55.

controlled by the Burma Army accessed by Lo and Khun Sa's caravans, have grown opium for the past three decades, and poppy still grows abundantly around Lashio, where Lo lives in lordly grandeur. Even if we allow for the corruption of local army commanders, the production of opium and trafficking in opium could not have continued *on such a scale* without Rangoon's connivance.[101]

Second, there are the regime's partnerships with drug traffickers. The CPB's disintegration deactivated 15,000–20,000 battle-hardened, well-equipped insurgents and eliminated the main source of arms to its former allies. The reduced combined strength of the remaining insurgents amounted to less than a twentieth that of the Burma Army, their widely scattered disposition greatly exacerbated the difficulties of coordinating a common strategy, and the CPB's Kokang and Wa mutineers now threatened no one save rival warlords and their convoys. *Ka kwei ye/pyithu sit* partnerships, therefore, had no further tactical *raison d'être*. Why, then, exempt the mutineers from Burma's narcotic drugs and psychotropic substances law if Rangoon did not *want* them to continue producing drugs? The generals who negotiated the agreement with Chao Ngi Lai's United Wa State Army (UWSA) included two of the three most powerful men in the junta, Khin Nyunt and Tin Oo.[102]

Third, the DDSI headed by Khin Nyunt is the body simultaneously responsible for all 'military intelligence' (police surveillance) operations and enforcement of Burma's anti-narcotics laws,[103] a combination of powers that, I suggest, is inherently suspect, as the curious case of U Saw Lu (Ta Pluik) shows. The missionary-educated

---

[101] Patricia Callahan, in Pedersen, Rudland and May (eds), 2000: 38–49, contends that the Army's regional field commanders have operated semi-independently of Rangoon and that this centrifugal tendency has been more marked since 1988, to the extent that 'several regional commanders . . . have refused to be transferred to cabinet positions in Rangoon after their scheduled [three-year] tour of duty ended'. See also, Callahan, 1996: 405 ff. But, as Callahan observes, whatever the regional commanders' power, it has never been absolute.

[102] The State Department's most recent report states: 'Ceasefire agreements with insurgent ethnic groups dependent on the narcotics trade involve an implicit tolerance of continued involvement in narcotics.' Bureau for International Narcotics and Law Enforcement Affairs, US Department of State, 'International Narcotics Control Strategy Report, 1999'. *Tolerance?*

[103] Ibid.

Saw Lu remained loyal to Rangoon for nearly 30 years, even serving as an official in Ne Win's Burma Socialist Programme Party (BSPP). As the commander of a *ka kwe yei*, he had fought against Chao Ngi Lai, then a CPB commander. In 1992, he reported to his superiors that the DDSI office chief in Lashio, Major Than Aye, was trading drugs. Than Aye's agents intercepted the report, jailed Saw Lu, his wife, their two sons and two adopted sons, hanged Saw Lu upside down and administered electric shock treatment to him. He was not released until Chao Ngi Lai, his former adversary but fellow Wa, threatened to end the 'border areas development' agreement the UWSA had concluded with Khin Nyunt.[104]

Fourth, where is the funding for Burma's foreign procurements if not from 'hard currency generated from narcotics production'?[105] In 1987, servicing Burma's external debt absorbed 90 per cent of its hard currency earnings,[106] and, in December 1987, the UN granted Burma least developed country status, ranking it economically with countries like Chad and Ethiopia.[107] Eleven months later, the International Monetary Fund (IMF) reported that Burma's foreign exchange reserves were approximately $28 million, insufficient to meet the cost of one month's imports. Yet, between 1988 and 1998, Burma's armed forces grew from 186,000–195,000 to 350,000–400,000 men.[108] In 1990, it began receiving from China small arms, F7 jet fighters, gunboats, tanks and armoured personnel carriers, purchased at a cost exceeding $1.4 billion,[109] and, by 1996,

---

[104] Lintner, 1994: 327–8, citing a May 1993 interview with Saw Lu.

[105] Selth, in Pedersen, Rudland and May (eds), 2000: 62, citing Ball, 1999: 7. See also *Far Eastern Economic Review*, Lintner, 'Safe at Home', 14 August 1997: 18–19; Davis and Hawke, 1998: 26–31; and Callahan, in Pedersen, Rudland and May (eds), 2000: 23, note.

[106] David Isaac Steinberg, 'Neither Silver Nor Gold', in Silverstein (ed.), 1989: 40.

[107] Ibid.: 35.

[108] This is seven-tenths as large as the US armed forces excluding National Guard and other reserve units. See Maung Aung Myoe, 1998: 27; Andrew Selth, 'The Future of the Burmese Armed Forces', in Pedersen, Rudland and May (eds), 2000: 56, citing Maung Aung Myoe and William Ashton, 'Burma's armed forces: preparing for the 21st century', *Jane's Intelligence Review*, Surrey: Jane's Information Group, vol. 10, no. 11, 1998: 28–31; Callahan, in Pedersen, Rudland and May (eds), 2000: 23; *Far Eastern Economic Review*, Lintner, 'Army of occupation', 23 May 1991: 13.

[109] Mya Maung, 1998: 67.

the cost of such procurements soared to approximately $2 billion.[110] However, a remittance to China of $400 million from Burma's account with the Charter Bank of Singapore in 1991 did not shrink its official foreign currency reserves.[111] Notwithstanding recurrent trade deficits,[112] the exchange rate between the dollar and the kyat from 1990 to 1998 remained more or less stable.[113]

Fifth, there is the regime's grace and favour treatment of Lo Hsin Han and Khun Sa. The drug don was in detention, and his organization had 'collapsed', crowed the DEA at the news of Khun Sa's January 1996 'surrender'.[114] '[T]he Burmese . . . made a major dent in the drugs trade, and we gave them no credit,' decreed a former Rangoon CIA station head.[115] But the don lives with his four teenage wives in a swanky new house in the DDSI compound and torture centre at Yay Kyi Aing, a millionaire quarter of Rangoon near the airport, while his children look after the 'collapsed organization'. Third son, Sam Seun (Thai: Pairot Changtrakul), runs the family's tourist complex in Tachilek. The reputed cost of building the Las Vegas-style hotels, nightclubs and casinos near the junction of the Burmese, Thai and Lao borders where traffickers have traditionally exchanged their cargoes for gold bars (whence the term 'Golden Triangle') was $20 million. Sam Seun also manages the family's jade interests at Hpakan in Kachin State and collaborates with second son, Sam Heung (Patai Changtrakul), in overseeing its new island gambling venture in the Mergui archipelago. Second daughter, Mi

---

[110] The weapons and equipment purchased are specified in Selth, in Pedersen, Rudland and May (eds), 2000: 57–8, citing Brooke, 1998: 11–16; Selth, 1998: 388–415; and Ball, 1998. The cost of the procurements is speculative. See Callahan, 1996: 23 ('The Burmese regime does not publish reliable statistics on defence spending. [They are] considered too sensitive for disclosure'), and to the same effect, Selth, in Pedersen, Rudland and May (eds), 2000: 54.

[111] *Far Eastern Economic Review*, Lintner, 'Hidden reserves', 6 June 1991: 12–13.

[112] $1 billion in 1998, the last year for which Rangoon has supplied official data.

[113] Lintner, 'Drugs and Economic Growth in Burma Today', in Pedersen, Rudland and May (eds), 2000: 187–9. Figures are those provided by 'the government . . . before it ceased publishing data on the money supply and foreign exchange reserves'. See also Clinton, 'Report to Congress on Conditions in Burma and U.S. Policy toward Burma for the period March 28, 1999–September 28, 1999', and Callahan, in Pedersen, Rudland and May (eds), 2000: 23n.

[114] Lintner, 1999: 412, citing a DEA press release dated 20 August 1997.

[115] Ibid., citing *Asia Times*, 3 June 1997.

Dawn (Kanitha Changtrakul), is the family's financial comptroller. By the end of 1998, seven family refineries were operating around Homöng. Ex-TRC/MTA personnel with ties to the junta managed five of them for the Changtrakuls, while a local militia chief closely associated with the regime's second secretary, General Tin Oo, managed the other two. The Burma Army has taken over responsibility for harranguing local farmers to grow opium instead of rice and beans and guards the routes leading to both the family's and the UWSA's refineries in the Doi Sam Sao, Soi Loilem and Doi Makon hills and Nam Yawn valley. As Khun Sa's family covets the UWSA's refineries,[116] the resulting tension has sparked another drugs war that, in March 1998, was blazing and continues still. Effectively, it is an undeclared drugs war between the UWSA and the Burma Army. The family also runs seven heroin and amphetamine laboratories in former CPB commander Lin Mingxian's 'government special zone' fiefdom in the hills southeast of Kengtung.[117] Khun Sa's brother, Khun Hseng (Ronald Chang), Khun Sa's accountant and aide-de-camp, Lao Tai, and the MTA's former chief of staff, ex-KMT officer Chang Chu-chuan, have invested their portions of the family pile in Rangoon real estate and transport businesses.[118]

Finally, there is the regime's termination of Project Old Soldier. During the Second World War, the US Tenth Army Air Force flew the 'hump' shuttling men and materiel between India and China, while the US Office of Strategic Services (OSS-101) operated behind enemy lines. After hostilities ended, the men who served in these dangerous roles, many of whom owed their lives to Kachins and other hill people, wanted to express gratitude for the help they had

---

[116] L'Observatoire Géopolitique des Drogues, '1998 Report, III. South East Asia, Far East and Pacific Ocean, Burma': 65–6. The Doi Sam Sao, Soi Loilem and Doi Mak-on hills and Nam Yawn valley were areas occupied by Khun Sa's MTA until 1990–1, when the UWSA, with Burma Army encouragement and assistance, seized them. 'The Burma dictatorship told the Wa that if they could drive Khun Sa's Shan army out of the [Nam] Yawn valley . . . the Wa could settle that area.' Email from David Eubank, 25 October 2000.

[117] Lin Mingxian 'has [now] successfully rid his area of opium cultivation. There are [now] no current, confirmed reports of [Lin Mingxian] or [his Eastern Shan State Army] still being involved in narcotics trafficking.' Bureau for International Narcotics and Law Enforcement Affairs, US Department of State, 'International Narcotics Control Strategy Report, 1999'.

[118] L'Observatoire Géopolitique des Drogues, '1998 Report, III. South East Asia, Far East and Pacific Ocean, Burma': 64–5; *Far Eastern Economic Review*, Lintner, 'Heroin Haven', 27 March 1997: 25.

received. Project Old Soldier was thus born. The Congress appropriated funds, OSS-101 veterans with agricultural experience volunteered their labour, and two sites were found for establishing an agricultural college to teach Kachins how to grow 'economically-viable crops'. Both sites, alas, were in areas controlled by the Burma Army, and hardly had the volunteers arrived before the army escorted them back to the airport. Washington sought to keep the project alive under the auspices of the UN Drug Control Program, but Rangoon refused.[119] On 21–22 March 2001, the Burma Army arrested, tortured and murdered nine KIA soldiers and two Kachin civilians supervising crop-substitution projects near the Old Soldier site, then tried to conceal the murders by burning and burying the corpses.[120] Opium grew on all the surrounding hills,[121] and the presence of foreigners or insurgents in ceasefire mode who might blow the whistle or adversely affect production was, evidently, unacceptable.

These matters taken together, I submit, raise what L'Observatoire Géopolitique des Drogues has called '*présomptions convergeantes*',[122] a body of circumstantial evidence demonstrating Rangoon's involvement with Burma's booming narcotics industry 'on an institutional level' extending beyond condoning its field commanders' corruption. We turn now to the generals' role in the Burmese economy generally.

[119] Interview with Peter Lutken, Jr., trustee of OSS-101 Association, Inc., and an on-the-ground participant in Project Old Soldier, November 1999; Clinton, 'Report to Congress on Conditions in Burma and U.S. Policy toward Burma for the period March 28, 1999–September 28, 1999'. See also Bureau for International Narcotics and Law Enforcement Affairs, US Department of State, 'International Narcotics Control Strategy Report, 1999'.
[120] http://www.karen.org/bbs/wwwboardt/messages/6805.html;
  http://www.karen.org/news/wwwboardt/messages/1101.html.
[121] Interview with Peter Lutken, Jr., February 2000.
[122] *Burma Debate*, 'Online Discussion on Drugs in Burma', vol. VI, no. 1, spring, 1999: 22.

8
The Kleptocrats

WE HAVE SEEN how the Union of Burma's fate hung in the balance at the début of its independence. Rebels controlled most of the country, including a large part of Arakan (*mujahids* and Rakhines), Magwe, Minbu, Pakokku, Myingyan, Henzada, Pyinmana, Yamethin, Prome, Thayetmyo, Tharrawaddy, the oilfields at Yenangyaung and Chauk (CPB/PVO), Einme, Insein, Twante, Toungoo, Nyaunglebin, Thaton, Kawkareik, Papun, Kyauksè, Myingyan, Myitnge, Mandalay, Pantanaw (KNDO), Loikaw, Mawchi (KNDO/Karennis), and Meiktila, Maymyo, Taunggyi, Lashio, Kutkai and Namhkam (Naw Seng's Kachins). By February 1949—13 months after independence—Karen rebels were within four miles of Rangoon, and only a battalion of Burma Regiment Gurkhas and scratch units of *sitwundan* stood between them and the capital.[1] Nu's AFPFL administration of Rangoon and its immediate suburbs, was, in a precisely geographical sense, the 'Rangoon Government'. Burmans who had supported Aung San and still supported the League credited the military's BIA/BDA/BNA/PBF antecedents with having delivered their *Bama* from the Japanese and pinned their hopes on the Burma Army to save their beleaguered state.[2]

We have seen how stragglers from the KMT's 8th and 26th Armies established their 'National Salvation Army for Yunnan' in Kengtung State and how, in 1959, the Shans rebelled. In the course of campaigning in the 1960 general election, Nu pledged to establish Buddhism as Burma's state religion. The pledge (later withdrawn) conclusively disillusioned the Kachins of the hopes raised at Panglong. Most senior posts in government and schools and universities and all the highest positions in the military had already gone to Burmans, and the Buddhist clergy already enjoyed privileges denied to the Kachins' pastors, priests and teachers. So, in 1961, they, too, rebelled. The rebels now included Rakhines, communists,

---

[1] Smith, 1991: 138.
[2] Nu's wife, Mya Yee, organized women to fetch food parcels to the troops on the front lines. U Thaung, 1990, 'Army's Accumulation of Economic Power in Burma (1950–1990)': 2. I am indebted to U Thaung for much of the data used in this chapter.

Karens, Karennis, Shans, Mons, Chins and Kachins. Still, the Union survived, and to the Burma Army went all the credit.

The army encouraged this view. Not only did it flatter *amour propre* and help to instil self-pride and *esprit de corps*; it also furthered their material interests. As so many soldiers risked their lives, and even died for the motherland, it was only right that they should be compensated above their normal pay—and compensated they were.

In 1951, the Defence Services Institute (DSI) opened a general store in Rangoon, catering exclusively for military personnel. The state provided the seed capital and exempted merchandise sold there from all excise taxes, customs duties and port fees. Able to offer merchandise at prices that undercut those charged by competitors, the store was hugely popular. Soldiers soon learned that they could buy more than they needed for their own use and resell the surplus at a profit. The DSI opened 18 more tax-free general stores. The Arm of Education Literature House, supplying textbooks and notebooks at first to military personnel and their families, later to the general public, was its next venture. It launched a periodical, *Myawaddy*, to 'provide balance' to a predominantly anti-government press. The most popular magazine at the time was *Shumawa*, which ran cartoons and articles by leftist authors. *Myawaddy* stole its and other writers by paying more for their articles, offered cheaper advertising and provided 'better covers with prettier girls'.[3] The DSI then established International Trading House to act as general contractor for all building work commissioned by the military. Public money spent on 'defence' rose to 40 per cent of the total national budget,[4] as senior officers looked covetously over their shoulders at their civilian counterparts and the wealth they were accumulating.[5]

Meanwhile, disenchantment steadily overtook the hopes engendered by nationalist rhetoric. Independence was not delivering the utopia nationalists had led everyone to expect. It appeared to have delivered instead a new bunch of self-vaunting politicians, not unlike the pre-war bunch, who postured and squabbled incessantly. In 1958, the League split into the 'Cleans' under Nu and a minority faction, the 'Stables', under Ba Swe and Kyaw Nyein. The Cleans formed a coalition with the National United Front (NUF), an alliance of ethnic minorities which, to the army's consternation, opposed

---

[3] Brigadier General Aung Gyi. Quoted in Callahan, 1996: 466.
[4] Between 1948 and 1951. See ibid.: 396.
[5] Ibid.: 401.

the war and pressed for peace talks. Nu conceded the principle of separate states for Rakines and Mons, and the Chins demanded a separate state. When parliament recessed, fighting erupted between the rival factions, two of Nu's ministers summoning support from PVOs and other militias.

As the people wearied of their politicians, army leaders became disenchanted with the people, in whom they discerned a 'general apathy', a susceptibility to 'skillful propaganda', and

> instincts . . . which generally are not of too high standards, viz., egoism, personal interest and continuation of existence or survival at any cost whatsoever. . . . What we dread most [concluded the speech from which these words are taken] is that unscrupulous politicians and deceitful Communist rebels and their allies may take advantage of these flaws, weaknesses, contradictions and inadequacies in the Constitution and bring about in the country gangster political movements, syndicalism, anarchism and a totalitarian regime.[6]

Having fallen hostage to Moscow's interests, claimed the generals, Nu's faction was risking 'the Union's disintegration'. Sensing trouble, Nu ordered the generals to halve the number of *pyu saw hti tat* operating in the districts and his home affairs minister to transfer UMP units from the army's command to posts near Rangoon under the government's command.[7] The effect was to reduce the power of front-line field commanders already resentful of the economic perks enjoyed by the general staff. Colonels Maung Maung and Aung Gyi persuaded Nu to abdicate on 28 October in favour of Ne Win to avert a coup.[8]

---

[6] 'Some Reflections on our Constitution', presented at an Army conference at Meiktila in 1958. Directorate of Education and Psychological Warfare, Ministry of Defence, 17 October 1958, DSHRI: CD 172; quoted in Callahan, 1996: 478–9.

[7] Ibid.: 471–2.

[8] Ne Win's relations with Nu had been tense ever since the prime minister criticized the army's lack of discipline in speeches to its commanding officers' conferences in 1955 and 1957. Nu exhorted the 1957 conference to ensure they were a 'people's *tatmadaw*' and not their generals' 'pocket army'. '[T]here may be certain elements both in the officer and private ranks . . . who swagger with revolvers dangling on their belts or with rifles in their hands, dizzy with newly-acquired power and arrogant in dealing with people.' Callahan, 1996: 459. Nu's criticism effectively confirmed an internal army report in 1950

The ensuing Caretaker Government lasted just over 15 months, and, when it ended, 134 soldiers occupied senior posts previously held by civilians in 19 government departments.[9]

Again exploiting the opportunities afforded by interest-free state capital and the advantages of tax-exempt status, the DSI established a string of new enterprises, beginning with the General Trading Company, whose subsidiary, United Coal and Coke Suppliers, took over from Heilgers & Company the business of importing 3 million tons of Indian coal supplied annually to Burma Railways and other government entities. The DSI established the blue-water Five Star Line to carry all government freight, imported Japanese busses to provide a bus service in Rangoon carrying 30,000 passengers daily, imported hundreds of one-ton lorries to enter the trucking business in competition with civilian haulage companies, and bought a bank. The move into banking opened up more opportunities for the military. The bank financed the purchase of motor tricycles fitted to carry passengers, and hundreds of these three-wheelers were imported and offered to military personnel above the rank of captain to enable them to operate taxi businesses. The officers soon learned that they could resell the scooters at a profit. The bank financed property ventures. Thousands of hut-dwellers were removed from central Rangoon to satellite towns outside the city, and the valuable sites they vacated were given to senior officers, who built on them with money lent by the bank. The houses were then rented to

---

noting that military personnel were 'in the habit of going about carrying daggers/knives' when off duty. Special War Office Council Order, No. 19/S/50, 18 July 1950, 'Discipline', in DSHRI: DR 1030; quoted in Callahan, 1996: 393. Another report, undated but probably published between 1956 and 1958, stated that some 'officers seized moveable property such as motor cars, livestock, etc. which they found in operational areas on the pretext that such property was ownerless [or] engaged on a large scale illicit trade in opium [or] abused military transport to carry commodities which they bought for the purpose of private trade [or] indulged in unwarranted inter-ference in private quarrels of civilians and in the administrative affairs of the civil authorities.' 'The Importance of Discipline', in DSHRI: DR 8117; quoted in Callahan, 1996: 392. The army recognized that its rapid expansion (from the three to four battalions that had remained loyal to the government after independence to more than 100,000 men organized in 57 infantry battalions and five regional commands by 1960) (PRO: FO 371/166395) had affected discipline (ibid.), but it is one thing for the army to criticize its own, and quite another for a civilian premier to criticize it.
[9] They were all Burmans. See Government of Burma, 1960, appendix 9: 561–7.

foreigners employed by the DSI. Another DSI enterprise, the Burma National Housing and Construction Company, which built military barracks and roads and bridges for the Public Works Department, handled the construction. According to a distinguished Burman journalist now living in exile, 'A powerful military officer could build as many rent-guaranteed houses as he wanted without investing much at all.'[10] Row & Company, once a flourishing business with 62 department stores, the largest mercantile chain in Burma, was facing failure, owing to government restrictions on import licences granted to foreign-owned firms. The DSI bought it, import licences were forthcoming, and Row & Company returned to its former glory. Other DSI entities bought during the interlude of Ne Win's *Caretaker* Government included East Asiatic Company of Burma (rice millers), John Dickenson & Company (paper distributors), Oppenheimers (produce brokers) and Steel Brothers (rice, oil, cotton and timber merchants, shipping)—all foreign-owned firms, once powerful but now crippled by taxes and restrictions, whose directors were 'more than happy to sell their assets to the inexperienced military officers with a sack of big money'.[11] Other new DSI entities included Burma International Inspection Company Limited, a joint venture with an American firm of surveyors; Burma Hotels Limited, which bought Burma's premier Strand Hotel; Rangoon Electric Works, an enterprise providing motor and assembly plants, radio and electrical equipment; and Continental Trading House, which operated fisheries, distributed fish, fish products, poultry and fuel, manufactured coke and engaged in overseas and domestic trade generally. Under the Caretaker Government, the DSI became the largest commercial institution in Burma.[12] Only the army, Ne Win decided, could save Burma from the 'economic chaos created by foreign businessmen'.[13]

The resumption of parliamentary rule in February 1960 was brief. On 2 March 1962 Ne Win mounted a *coup d'état*—to save the Union,[14] his apologists claimed; Nu was about to grant autonomy

[10] U Thaung, 1990, 'Army's Accumulation of Economic Power (1950–1990)': 5.

[11] Ibid.: 6.

[12] Smith, 1991: 179, citing Silverstein, 1977: 79.

[13] U Thaung, 1990, 'Army's Accumulation of Economic Power (1950–1990)': 4.

[14] The law establishing his BSPP was called the Law to Protect National Unity. See Mya Maung, 1998: 25.

to the Shans and other ethnic groups. But it should also be pointed out that Nu had used his brief return to office to nationalize Burma's import and export trade *at the DSI's expense.*

Having suspended the constitution, the military had no further need to concern itself with government budgets, comptrollers and auditors. Henceforth, nationalization would be by confiscation in accordance with a pseudo-religious, political and philosophical treatise called *The Burmese Way to Socialism.* The regime confiscated all private banks, domestic as well as foreign.[15] The DSI and the Burma Economic Development Corporation (BEDC), another army holding company created in 1961, and their subsidiaries were, like other private concerns, seen as obstacles to the *Burmese Way*, so the regime confiscated them as well.[16] It nationalized the private press with a printers and publishers' registration law, the first of several measures that would lead to establishing its monopoly over the written media.[17] It banned private importers (who were competing with the confiscated DSI). It promulgated a trade disputes law, allowing the government (i.e., military) to seize and suspend operations of businesses subject to labour disputes.[18] It confiscated all trading companies and cooperatives. It banned private exporters (who were competing with the confiscated DSI). It confiscated Burma Oil Company and Indo-Burma Oil Company, Anglo-Burma Mines Company, Burma Peal Syndicate, cigarette factories, Kyaukme Mines Company, Burma Corporation, Unilever Soap Factory, oil wells, 814 private schools, 17 printing firms, nine mission hospitals, 132 factories, 182 cinemas, 24 small shipping companies, ruby and jade mines, Bawsaing Mine Company, mines in Tavoy District and jade trading interests.[19] The confiscations led to the departure of between 125,000 and 300,000 Indians and Pakistanis,[20] who abandoned some 11,000 shops. The shops were handed over to military personnel, who rented or sold them.[21] The private manufacturing and commercial sector of the economy diminished from

[15] Silverstein, 1977: 156.
[16] The DSI and BEDC, like other private concerns, were seen as obstacles to the 'Burmese way'.
[17] Mya Maung, 1998: 25. See also Allott, 1994.
[18] Silverstein, 1977: 156.
[19] U Thaung, 1990, 'Army's Accumulation of Economic Power (1950–1990)': 10; Silverstein, 1977: 160.
[20] Taylor, 1987: 341; Silverstein, 1977: 160.
[21] U Thaung, 1990, 'Army's Accumulation of Economic Power (1950–1990)': 11.

493 firms employing 17,947 people in 1963 to 267 firms employing 6887 people in 1972, while, correspondingly, the state sector rose from 31.6 per cent in 1962–63 to 46.4 per cent in 1977–78.[22] Twenty-four state stores distributed merchandise formerly handled by 12,212 private stores.[23] In 1962, there were 368,301 government employees. By 1973, there were 623,529. The regime purged thousands of career civil servants, created thousands of new posts, and, in deference to its pledge to eliminate 'exploitation', filled all of them with soldiers.

The military already controlled the price and distribution of farm produce through the compulsory purchasing powers of the State Agricultural Marketing Board and its successor, the Union of Burma Agricultural Marketing Board, but the land itself was still in private hands (or, as Ne Win explained, there was still 'one unfinished business which mocks our declaration that . . . we will not permit the exploitation of man by man. . . . It concerns the continued extraction of tenancy rent by the landlords'[24]). The burning issue for nationalists in the 1930s, it will be recalled, was growing Chettiyar ownership of land. The military resumed where the Chettiyars had failed, and the *Burmese Way to Socialism* supplied the rationale.[25]

On 3 January 1974, the regime adopted a new constitution, leading some scholars to divide the 26½ years of Ne Win's rule (1962–88) into the 'Revolutionary Council Period' (while the 1947 constitution remained suspended) and the 'Constitutional Period' (which followed the adoption of the 1974 constitution). But Professor Silverstein demonstrates that the fundamental fact of military control did not change.[26] Over 10 per cent of the country's entire workforce worked in the state sector by 1985 (compared to less than 1 per cent in 1931), and only six privately owned firms (against 446 state-owned firms) employed more than 100 workers.[27] The state controlled the surviving private sector through its monopoly on raw materials and its power over foreign exchange for

[22] Ibid.: 10.
[23] Ibid.: 11.
[24] Silverstein, 1977: 157.
[25] '[T]he military government expected that [the peasant] would feel indebted to it for his new freedoms and would produce more. . . . The peasant did not respond exactly as desired.' Ibid.: 157–8.
[26] Ibid.: 120–34.
[27] Taylor, 1987: 344–5. For the continuing preponderance of large state enterprises 30 years later, see World Bank, 1995: 53.

imports of equipment and spare parts. The restrictions on economic activity in the private sector gave rise to a flourishing black economy, in which individual soldiers took bribes from the traders for grants of licences and permits and sold goods from government stocks to which they enjoyed privileged access. A popular saying during the 'Constitutional Period' was '*layhnit thahtay pyit*' (lit., 'four years rich becomes') or 'four years [on the council] equates to a rich man', or 'four years of collecting bribes guarantees wealth'.[28]

These various measures reduced Burma, once the most prosperous country in Asia, to bankruptcy. Only the black economy and increasing injections of foreign aid[29] enabled it to avoid starvation. Having been the world's largest producer of crude oil, Burma became a net importer of oil. Having rivalled Indo-China as the 'granary of the East', it was now importing rice.[30] The regime tried to supply the deficiency through coercive measures, compelling farmers to plant rice 'literally . . . at gunpoint'.[31] Desperate to alleviate interest on foreign obligations, the regime applied to the United Nations to accord it least developed country status and lifted restrictions on private trading. Traders rushed to empty their bank accounts to buy futures in the pending harvest. Then the regime recalled the three largest banknotes, thereby invalidating approximately 70 per cent of the currency.

The demonetization of 5 September 1987 was a turning point. The war on the borders had not rallied, nor was it ever likely to rally, the great mass of Burmans against the regime. Few Burmans opposed the regime's treatment of the rebels, however barbarous and cruel: the one sound thing that could be said of the regime was that it stood up for Burma. Strikes, like those of the oil workers at Chauk, the railway men at Insein and the dockers at Simalaik (1974), might be

---

[28] Mya Maung, 1992: 218.

[29] The average amount of annual foreign donor loans and grants to Burma between 1974 and 1977 was $65.5 million. Between 1978 and 1986 it was $348.5 million, and, additionally, the US contributed an annual average of $20 million for poppy eradication under the International Narcotics Control programme. Yet the IMF, World Bank and even such distinguished Burma scholars as David Steinberg continued to repose faith in Rangoon's 1972 'reforms' that, in retrospect, are seen as cosmetic gestures to attract more foreign aid. See Mya Maung, 1992: 220–1, citing Khin Maung Nyunt, 1990: 39–41; *Far Eastern Economic Review*, Ho Kwon Ping, 'The Cautious Search for Success', 18 January 1980: 36; and Steinberg, 1982: 92.

[30] Tucker, 2000: 44.

[31] Donkers and Minka Nijhuis (eds), 1996: 64.

dressed up by communist ideologues as manifestations of popular protest, but, in reality, they expressed little more than particular grievances. Students might oppose the tyrant, but their spirited clamour was mere youthful effusion. If the tyrant blew up their debating chambers, who needed debating chambers? The students' parents, for the most part, were rich, because, for the most part, they were in with the regime. If anyone was to be blamed for repression, heavy-handedness and corruption, it was the police who enforced the tyrant's edicts—not Aung San's still-admired Burma Army, which was also the employer of last resort for hundreds of thousands of Burmans, who depended on their soldier kin for rice and cooking oil, unaffordable at prices charged in the free market. But the cancellation of these banknotes went too far. For more than two decades, the regime had condoned without legitimating the black economy, and everyone who traded in the black economy (almost the entire population) had prudently kept his savings in cash. Now, with a brief announcement over the radio, most of their savings vanished—and only military and civil service personnel could redeem their cancelled banknotes.[32]

Hundreds of enraged students stormed onto the streets and began smashing and incinerating government property. Now, when the government rusticated them, the enraged folk back home saluted the students as heroes and fell into ranks behind them. The demonstrations resumed in March 1988, provoking open dissent within the army and criticism of the tyrant from one of his former cronies.[33] In July 1988, Ne Win electrified the nation by resigning. But he was succeeded by Sein Lwin, the riot police chief known for his suppression of past demonstrations as 'the butcher', then by Dr Maung Maung, the Party's intellectual and apologist, known as 'the puppet', changes seen as merely cosmetic. Mass agitation in the streets erupted again. Effigies of Ne Win, Sein Lwin and Maung Maung were ceremonially buried in coffins decorated with demonetized banknotes, and enemies of every kind, Karens and Burmans, Buddhists and Muslims, farmers and traders, rightists and leftists, old and young, suddenly found common cause in demanding democracy. Nine of the 11 surviving Thirty Comrades declared their support for the people, and soldiers and policemen began fraternizing with them ('Our military skills are not for killing

[32] Josef Silverstein, 'From a Political to an Administrative State, 1948–1988: Whatever Happened to Democracy?', in Silverstein (ed.), 1989: 16.
[33] Brigadier General Aung Gyi.

the people'). But the demonstrators also demanded the heads of the regimental commanders, and, confronted by these threats, the terrified officers did their duty. Hence the massacre of 19 September 1988 and the coup that inaugurated the era of the State Law and Order Restoration Council (SLORC).

The SLORC began life with a certain fanfare, pledging to dismantle the old state apparatus, so choking to entrepreneural initiative, and to open the market to the fresh air of free enterprise. Even foreigners were to be allowed to participate—in joint ventures, a concept that provoked wonder in officers nurtured on tales of 'foreign exploitation'. Burmans had no money to invest in joint ventures; would not Indians and Chinese soon reassert control over Burma's economy? Reputedly, Ne Win himself supplied the answer. 'My suggestion is that you run the businesses. We must not give [these] opportunities to civilians [including] Burmese civilians. . . . You just find Burmese kyats and buy the shares, and the Defence Service can sustain foreign currency from the Government account.'[34]

The SLORC, in fact, dismantled very little. It merely 'enabled individual army officers and non-commissioned officers [once more] to buy valuable land at cheap prices, receive low-interest loans to launch businesses . . . and channel privileges, contracts and resources toward private business people in exchange for substantial rewards'.[35] Hundreds of state agencies and 58 major state economic monopolies (12 owned by the Defence Ministry), operating seven state financial institutions and about 1800 factories and other enterprises, continued as before.[36] Indeed, while the SLORC's 'Second Economic Objective' was 'Proper evolution of the market-oriented economic system', its 'Fourth Economic Objective' was 'The initiative to shape the national economy must be kept in the hands of the *state* and the national people.'[37] Six months after seizing power, the SLORC reserved monopolies over teak extraction, teak trading, pearl fishing, export of pearls, jade mining, jade exports, gem mining, gem exports, ore mining, ore exports, banking, insurance, all broadcasting media, and all products 'relating to security and defence' (as defined by the SLORC),[38] and, when it

[34] U Thaung, 1998: 2.
[35] Callahan, in Pedersen, Rudland and May (eds), 2000: 47.
[36] Mya Maung, 1998: 66.
[37] Ibid.: 65. Italics added.
[38] See U Thaung, 1990 'Army's Accumulation of Economic Power (1950–1990)': 13.

announced its 'new, open-door policy' of unrestricted cross-border trade in December 1990, it simultaneously banned the export of 16 commodities, to which seven more were added in 1991 and five more in 1994. Goods and commodities proscribed for export included teak, rice, oil, gems, jewelry, gold, silver, pearls, coal, zinc, lead, bronze, tin, wolfram, rubber, arms, ammunition, antiques, pulses, beans, corn, groundnuts, cotton, coins, buffaloes, cows, elephants, rare animals, fish, shrimp, animal horns and leather.[39] In short, the SLORC lifted restrictions on everything except most things Burma produced and traded.

The effect of the SLORC's 'new economic policy' is seen most unambivalently in the Union of Myanmar Economic Holdings Company Limited (UMEHC), an entity created on 19 February 1990, when Colonel David Abel, the trade minister, signed into law notification no. 7/90 allowing the company to issue two classes of one kyat par value shares notionally worth together US $1.4 billion. The Government of Myanmar, Directorate of Defence Procurement, immediately subscribed 4 million *issued* 'A' shares, while the remaining 6 million unissued 'B' shares were reserved for military personnel, armed forces cooperatives, regimental institutes and veterans associations.[40] The state yet again was providing the seed capital for an enterprise whose benefits would accrue exclusively to soldiers as and when they chose to participate with soft loans provided by the state's banking interests.

Further Ministry of Trade notifications authorized UMEHC to issue additional capital as follows:

	million kyats	million $
1992–93	23,775	3,914
1993–94	23,247	3,690
1994–95	142,575	23,720
1995–96	11,172	1,862
1996–97	1,538,166	255,961
1997–98	1,793,014	279,185[41]

The *additional* capital of 1,793,014 million kyats authorized for UMEHC in 1997–98 compared with Burma's total budget that year of 1,036,386 million kyats.

[39] Mya Maung, 1998: 67.
[40] Ibid.: 66–7.
[41] Statistical Yearbook; quoted in U Thaung, 1998: 2.

The fanfare about opening the economy to 'free enterprise' was in part to encourage foreign grants or soft loans and in part to entice foreigners into joint ventures with the military. In the five years following the SLORC's accession to power, 28 American firms invested $287 million in Burma, 80 Thai firms, $270 million, 11 South Korean firms, $149 million, 34 Japanese firms, $101 million.[42] Texaco, Nippon Oil, Royal Dutch, Amoco, Unocal, Kirkland, Premier, BHP, Clyde, Idemitsu and Total targeted Burma's rich oil and gas deposits. Thai, Singaporean and Hong Kong Chinese boats trawled for fish and prawn in the Gulf of Martaban. Thai loggers felled trees in the Karen Hills.[43] Chinese parastatals began exploiting the rain forests of Kachin State, and in all these joint ventures the controlling partner was UMEHC. In 1994, UMEHC's subsidiary, Myanmar Oil and Gas Enterprise (MOGE), signed a memorandum of understanding to supply Thailand with natural gas from the Yadana field in the Andaman Sea. Unocal and Total then entered a joint venture with MOGE to build the pipeline. The Burma Army cleared a route through the Tenasserim and protected the pipeline against rebel attacks. Another UMEHC joint venture was Rangoon's new Hanthawaddy International Airport.[44]

By the end of 1997, only 5 per cent of firms employing more than 100 workers and 15 per cent of firms employing between 51 and 100 workers were privately owned, while no large state enterprize had been privatized[45]—hardly the dash from the command economy heralded by the SLORC. Burma's main industries, all her financial institutions, most of her external trade, much of her internal commerce, her infrastructure projects and all joint ventures with foreign interests remained under army control, still directed by soldiers and run for their benefit, the higher the rank, the greater the benefit. Continuing controls over the economy, inevitably, ensured continuing peculation.[46] Bribes spawned by the new economic policy now were of two types: *le pheye hpo* (lit., money for tea) and *mhon hpo* (lit., money for cake)—bribes in cash or kind.

[42] *Burma Alert*, vol. 5, no. 3, March 1994.
[43] Tucker, 2000: 332.
[44] Smith, 1999: 427.
[45] Mya Maung, 1998: 66.
[46] 'Service organizations connected with trade matters, such as import and export work, services sector and collection of taxes, are taking bribes according to their ranks.' Khin Nyunt, in a speech at the Ministry of Trade. *The Working People's Daily*, 22 May 1991; quoted in Mya Maung, 1998: 70.

Sometimes 'the bribe [took] the form of . . . keys to one or more expensive modern automobiles . . . as a gift at the wedding of the son or daughter of a military minister or a high-ranking government official'.[47] Golden Valley, the residential quarter of Rangoon that once was the exclusive preserve of Burma's colonial masters, was now the exclusive preserve of the generals and their colleagues in the drugs trade.[48]

[47] Ibid. I have modified the romanizations. Mya Maung's renderings are *laphet yai boe* (money for tea) and *mhon hpo mhoent boe* (money for cake). *Mhon bon* (Mya Maung, *mhoent boan*) are large biscuit tins suitable for stuffing with cash, gold or precious stones. Asked about the regime, a taxi driver replied: 'This government is really good. You get everything you want, money, jobs, girls, everything—if you're in the army!' Quoted in *Far Eastern Economic Review*, Lintner, 'Absolute Power', 18 January 1996: 25.

[48] For example, Ne Win's compound, called May Kha on May Li Kha (Jinghphaw = Nmai Hka and Mali Hka, the twin upper tributaries to the Irrawaddy) Road in Mayangone Township, comprises the nationalized mansions of Jews, Armenians and Indians. It is protected by soldiers, a large bunker, anti-aircraft guns and live electric wire encompassing even the lakefront. Ne Win lives in the main house, his wife in a smaller house opposite. Retired general Sein Lwin lives nearby in a big house formerly belonging to the Electricity Board among encamped light infantry brigades. DDIS headquarters is in the same vicinity. Retired general San Yu lives in a big house on a compound once known as Chingchaung Chan that was confiscated from its Chinese owners, divided into several plots and parcelled out to Ne Win's favourites. Shwetaung Kyar, or Golden Valley, Thanlwin or Salween (formerly Windermere) Road and the Windermere quarter of Bahan township, formerly the abode of senior civil servants, diplomats and serving cabinet ministers, are now inhabited by former Revolutionary Council members and senior military personnel or rented by them to foreigners. Correspondence with Kin Oung, 21–26 April 2000. See also Mya Maung, 1992: 221–2; Ball, 1999: 4.

9
Whither Burma?

AMONG INSURGENTS DESCRIBES a moment in January 1989 at Pajau Bum, KIA GHQ. Roosters were crowing all over the hills. Soldiers were already exercising, though it was still pitch dark. A drill sergeant shouted at them, belligerently, and they responded in unison, belligerently. A sergeant entered the room adjacent to where, until a few minutes before, I had been sleeping, lit a storm lantern and revived the fire. A dog, tied to one of the cane struts to prevent him from incinerating himself, rose slowly and, bending back like a contortionist, scratched behind his ear. I could see man and dog through the lattice of the dividing bamboo wall, hear a snapping of flames and smell the boiling resin of burning pine. I lay in my sleeping bag thinking about the Burmese Civil War:

Who and what were to blame for all this bloodletting? Burman racial arrogance and contempt for the hill peoples? The British who recruited the hill peoples to help subdue the Burmans? The Karens for siding with the British in three wars against the Burmans? The BIA for the atrocities they perpetrated on the minorities before the Japanese interceded? The Director of the Frontier Areas Administration, Henry Noel Stevenson, for failing to persuade the Kachins to continue as a British protectorate until they were able to make wise decisions about their future status? Aung San for sweet-talking them into acceding to the delusive hopes of the Panglong Agreement instead of acting on their gut distrust of the Burmans? Sama *Duwa* Sinwa Nawng for venally heeding Aung San's promise of personal preferment and persuading his people to reject Commissioner Stevenson's offer? U Saw, reputed instigator of Aung San's assassination before the 'Father of Burma's Independence' was able to honour his pledges to the hill peoples? U Nu for excluding the communists from the cabinet which carried through Independence? The Buddhist zealots who threw an incendiary bomb into the church full of Karen worshippers at Palaw on Christmas Eve 1948? The insurgents for rebelling? Successive administrations in Rangoon for insensitivity to the minorities? The greed and corruption of the drugs trade? Ne Win for twenty-six years of purblind, doctrinaire, genocidal, egomaniacal, mendacious dictatorship? The rest of the world for its myopic indifference?[1]

I have spent many hours since then pondering the Burmese Civil War. Could it have been prevented?

Britain had neither the means nor the will to protect any minority from the Burmans after quitting India in 1947, and Stevenson's 'protectorate' was never more than a mirage. The Sama *duwa*, Sinwa Nawng, was merely yielding to the inevitable in rejecting it, perhaps expecting to extract advantage from the League for the Kachins thereby. In 1948, the bitterness and distrust between Burmans and Karens were already too deep. Had there been no bomb at Palaw, there would have been another incident to trigger an inter-communal war. The communists believed themselves to be the vanguard entitled to lead the nation after independence, and nothing could have prevented them from rebelling from a League dominated by non-communists. The 'We Burmans' sense of outrage at having been robbed of their 'Golden Land' and plundered and demeaned was such that another Bandoola would have Burmanized the army had Ne Win not displaced Smith Dun. Another Anawrahta or Alaungpaya would have displaced Nu and Ne Win had they not Burmanized the army and imposed on Burma an hegemonic unitary Burman state. Aung San's ambition, inflexibility and intolerance of rivals always posited the risk of his assassination.

Would Aung San's survival have changed matters? Cady reminds us that, after independence, the 'official view was that a unity of culture existed among the peoples of the Union and that existing differences [were] only expressions of the same culture at different stages of development',[2] and this was the view Aung San espoused in negotiating his 1947 agreement with Attlee. Even so, his subsequent speeches, especially that made to the hill peoples' representatives at Panglong a fortnight after he signed the Attlee agreement,[3] evince his respect for minority rights and his acceptance

---

[1] Tucker, 2000: 73–4.

[2] Cady, 1958: 638.

[3] See 'Note by John Leyden on the Panglong Conference, 1947' (BL BOIC: M/4/2811); Tinker (ed.), 1984, vol. II, item 294: 425 ('The Burmese Government had no intention of interfering with the internal affairs of the hill peoples and was desirous that they should be allowed to rule their own territory in their own way. If, however, they desired to join with Burma then

of a federal form of government allowing regional autonomy for Burma's minorities—principles that were embodied in the 1947 constitution. But institutions succeed only if supported by those charged with implementing them. Whoever the leader, or whatever the strength of his belief in the 'Panglong spirit', violence, it seems to me, was inherent in the antagonisms between Burma's diverse communities and in intra-Burman rivalry.

The sheer inexperience of those who succeeded the colonial administrators was another destabilizing factor. What beyond demagogic platitudes and the power to prevent an orderly reconstruction of Burma's shattered institutions did the League's leaders have to offer to the people of Burma? Their 'antisocial qualities, which were their peculiar virtue in breaking up the old society, proved to be their drawback in the subsequent work of building a new one'.[4] Furnivall, one of the few Britons invited to stay on to assist the Union of Burma, describes the contrast between popular expectation and political delivery:

> When Burma gained independence, Burmans were brought for the first time into direct contact with the vital realities of the modern world in all its aspects. The modern world has a long history. . . . Yet Burmans thought to gain admission to this new world merely by pronouncing, like some 'Open sesame', the magic word of independence. The productive apparatus of the world . . . yielded a harvest of unprecedented richness. Burmans were dazzled by the wealth and thought to share in it, but they were strangers to the dynamic process which produced the wealth. . . . The magic of independence could not bridge the gap . . . But the leaders, partly fearful of disappointing the people, and still more perhaps concerned to demonstrate that Burma was a full member of the modern world, looked for short cuts to Utopia. With each new demand on their energy and invention, the machinery of government took shape under the pressure of events, and rapidly grew beyond control with the feeble means at their disposal.[5]

---

it would be necessary for them to have representatives in the Burmese Government in Rangoon for the administration of central and common subjects'). Three days prior to this speech, the Shan and Kachin representatives had defined 'common subjects' as 'Defence, Foreign Affairs, Railways, Customs, etc.' Ibid.: 424.

[4] Baw Maw, 1968: 57.

[5] Furnivall, 1960: 130–1.

We should note also that neither Aung San nor Nu enjoyed the near-universal support commanded by Jawaharlal Nehru, Mohammed Ali Jinnah, Kwame Nkruma, Julius Nyerere, Jomo Kenyatta, Hastings Banda and Kenneth Kaunda which facilitated relatively smooth transitions to self-government elsewhere. In short, there was, in my judgement, never the slightest chance of evading the cataclysm that overtook Burma after independence.

Can the antagonisms that gave rise to the Burmese Civil War be resolved? Scholars proffer various predictions, but most stress the need to find a resolution that recognizes the rights of *all* the peoples of Burma and focus their analysis on the prospects of the military devolving power to civilians as a necessary precondition of such a resolution.

Martin Smith distinguishes between former insurgents, such as the KIO, who have concluded ceasefire agreements with Rangoon, and insurgents still at war with Rangoon, notably the KNU, who now find themselves isolated almost entirely by their 'politics first' demands.[6] '[T]he ceasefire process has at last brought many protagonists together,' he notes of conditions now existing in former war-zones.[7] UN agencies and non-governmental organizations (NGOs) are allowed into border areas that previously were inaccessible to outside aid organizations, and a variety of business, infrastructure and development projects are underway.[8] The experience of peace is a dynamic of healing and reconciliation, he suggests, even bridging divisions within minorities, as between the KIO and Ting Ying's New Democratic Army (formerly CPB 101 Area).[9] Resettlement of displaced communities has started, and schools and hospitals function again, as old wounds heal and trust replaces distrust.[10] But, he reminds us, the minorities issue at the heart of Burma's troubles remains unresolved.[11] Burma has distinguished itself during the last 50 years more for 'generating rather than healing social and ethnic divisions',[12] and the bloodletting continues in the minority areas where ceasefires have not been agreed. A *sustainable* peace presup-

[6] Smith, 1999: 450–1.
[7] Smith, in Burma Center Netherlands, 1999: 49.
[8] Ibid.: 29.
[9] Ibid.: 40.
[10] Ibid., and email, Smith to author, May 2000.
[11] Indeed, a centre–minority divide has opened even between the NLD and ceasefire groups reluctant to risk disturbing their temporary accommodation with the Burma Army. Smith, 1999: 451–2.
[12] Smith, in Burma Center Netherlands, 1999: 24.

posing solutions that address the underlying causes of ethnic discontent, he believes, may depend ultimately on new leaders in Rangoon and among the minorities who are free of the historical baggage and hatreds of their predecessors.[13]

Bertil Lintner proffers no surmises regarding Burma's future. However, his observations regarding the ever-gaining dependency of Burma's economy on its drugs industry and the involvement of senior members of Burma's military in the trade augur a long continuation of the status quo.[14]

Mikael Gravers also proffers no surmises regarding Burma's future, but he states: 'Whereas the nationalism of 1947 was an anticipation of modernity including democracy, the nationalism of today signifies endless autocracy and corporate modernity in the SLORC model' simply to preserve the union as 'one unitary state'.[15] The military, he suggests, has fostered an historical 'amnesia' exemplified by a party slogan in *Nineteen Eighty-Four*—'Who controls the past, controls the future: Who controls the present controls the past'— and is redefining history to exalt itself as the primary unifying theme of 'Burmese' nationalism and custodian of 'Burmese' traditions.[16] Only 'via a prolonged social and cultural exchange with the rest of the world, as well as shared power between the [military] and civil society, can enduring and positive changes come about'.[17]

David Steinberg maintains that the military regime, though despised, is accepted as inevitable, owing to Buddhist notions of *ana*, *awza* and *cetana* which resonate with the majority population in Burma (including the military), nor is there an alternative government. *Ana*, he explains, is power vested in individuals according to their *karma* (moral merit tally of their past deeds). The military predicates its right to retain power on a duty to hold the state together, and, hence, to deny it that right is to oppose *karma*. *Awza* is a cognate notion of moral authority and influence derived from past deeds, while *cetana* denotes generosity of spirit, liberality of heart and goodwill in the gift of one who has *ana* or *awza*. When the military claims, as it always claims, to act with *cetana*, its behaviour *must* be revered, asserts Steinberg.[18] Moreover, in contrast

[13] Smith, 1999: 451–3.

[14] Lintner, in Pedersen, Rudland and May (eds), 2000: 164, esp. 184–93.

[15] Gravers, 1999: 129.

[16] See ibid., esp. 129–40.

[17] Ibid.: 135.

[18] Steinberg, in Pedersen, Rudland and May (eds), 2000: 91, 97–9.

to international norms, elections are not the sole test of legitimacy in Burma, where nationalism, Burman paramountcy, Burman religion, Burman control over the economy, and the instrument of these institutions, the Burman-dominated military, also validate the regime's claim on power.[19] Until modern times, he notes, Burmese did not even have a word for a civil society divorced from the state.[20] The *rajathat* (king's law) always controlled, and the *dhammathat* (civil rights and rule of law) has not been established.[21] While Theravada Buddhism encourages egalitarian tendencies, the military has countered these tendencies by a strong hierarchical structure based on fear. It has prevented the rise of civil society by nationalizing the press, syndicating professional bodies and instituting cooperatives and other organizations beholden to itself, such as the Union Solidarity and Development Association, whose membership may exceed one third of the adult population.[22] Steinberg agrees with Smith in suggesting that cooperation on issues of overriding shared concern, such as the HIV epidemic sweeping Burma, along with the apolitical activities of international NGOs, could help to bridge the gap between the junta and the opposition.[23] He posits the possibilities of a counter-military coup, a popular uprising or a venerable *sayadaw* in the mould of U Ottama or U Wisara rising to reconcile the contending parties, but he cautions against expecting an early change to civilian government. 'We are . . . likely to witness the gradual erosion of [military presence, though] not basic power in areas . . . [the military] regards as of national importance.'[24] A solution to the core problem, which is Burman–minority relations, not economics or franchised government, he says, seems remote.[25]

Josef Silverstein believes that the military is no longer a 'monolith'. The unity Ne Win maintained for nearly 40 years by dismissing generals who threatened his leadership and rotating regional commanders before they became too popular has 'fissured'. The intelligence chief, Lieutenant General Khin Nyunt, is not in charge, as commonly supposed. In November 1997, when the junta

[19] Ibid.: 99–103.
[20] Email, Steinberg to author, October 2000.
[21] Steinberg, in Pedersen, Rudland and May (eds), 2000: 110–11. See also, Liddell, ibid.: 54–68.
[22] Steinberg, ibid.: 112–15.
[23] Ibid.: 115.
[24] Steinberg, in Burma Center Netherlands, 1999: 1, 13.
[25] Email, Steinberg to author, October 2000.

reshuffled its members and changed its name from the SLORC to the State Peace and Development Council (SPDC), the 12 regional commanders were promoted, and these line officers, led by Burma's sole four-star general, SPDC vice-chairman and deputy commander-in-chief, General Maung Aye, now dominate the SPDC. The rivalry between the regional commanders and Khin Nyunt's SPDC faction offers some hope for change, maintains Silverstein,[26] and, tutored by the more cosmopolitan Khin Nyunt and taxed with trade boycotts, loan embargoes and investment and visa bans, the generals are no longer impervious to outside censure, as evidenced by an invitation to the International Labour Organization (ILO) to assist them in improving labour conditions in Burma.[27] '[P]art of the glue that holds the military together is the belief that the world supports them, trades with them, gives them aid and accepts them as the legitimate government of their land. That glue could give way if the reality that they serve an outlaw government which neither the people of Burma nor of the world accepts finally sinks in.'[28] The combination of tensions within the military and the generals' aroused sensitivity to international criticism, believes Silverstein, portends an eventual accommodation with Aung San Suu Kyi and her National League for Democracy (NLD). But fears of Nuremberg-style reprisals and loss of status and personal wealth deter change.[29]

While differing in detail from Silverstein, Mary Callahan supports his general perception of what she terms 'cracks in the [army's] edifice'.[30] Regional commanders have exercised a greater or lesser authority over their command areas at different times, and there has always been some measure of tension between them and the centre, but, after the 1988 coup, the junta 'delegated extraordinary authority to the more senior regional commanders, resulting in their unambiguous rise in power and status'.[31] Generation differences have opened further intra-army tensions. None of the younger officers, unlike their forebears, has had combat experience. But Callahan differs from Smith in believing the younger officers are

[26] Telephone conversation, Silverstein with author, 14 May 2000.
[27] Announced by ASEAN on 12 May 2000 in response to a June 1999 ILO resolution condemning forced labour in Burma and calling for a world embargo on trade with Burma. See http://www.ilo.org/public/english/bureau/inf/pr/1999/23.htm.
[28] Silverstein, untitled article, Burmanet #1524, 29/30 April 2000.
[29] Telephone conversation, Silverstein with author, 14 May 2000.
[30] Callahan, in Pedersen, Rudland and May (eds), 2000: 25 ff.
[31] Ibid.: 38.

even less sympathetic to the minorities or amenable to political change than their forebears.[32]

Andrew Selth stresses that Burma has vastly increased the size of its armed forces (target: 500,000 by year 2000), re-equipped them with modern weapons, armour, transport, communications systems, aircraft and ships, and expanded its intelligence apparatus. This 'gives the SPDC greater means to consolidate its political power, exercise continued control over the economy, and generally shape and manipulate Burmese society . . . to enforce its will over the country in a way never before possible',[33] and, having almost achieved its aim of bringing all Burma under Burman control, it is 'unlikely that the SPDC or any successor military regime would willingly allow large tracts of the country once again to be removed completely from its control'.[34] Another disincentive to change is the danger that 'implacable opposition . . . to Aung San Suu Kyi and the NLD' would divide the military were power devolved to the NLD.[35] Therefore, Selth sees 'no prospect of a return to democratic civilian rule in the foreseeable future'.[36] However, possible catalysts for change include Ne Win's death (precipitating 'policy differences and personal antagonisms' hitherto held in check); junior officers 'unhappy with current policies and practices' defying the command structure and thereby 'triggering a wider crisis' (a 'significant proportion of the armed forces voted for the NLD' in the 1990 elections);[37] and changes in China's foreign policy. While the military is proud of its role as defender of Burma's unity, it is also sensitive to its unpopularity and knows that its continued involvement with politics risks further alienating the people. The opposition wants a strong and united military, albeit one that acts for, and not against, the people,[38] and seeks no reprisals for past wrongs,[39] recognizing that the military's reach is so pervasive that any devolution of power would *require* an accommodation with it to avoid chaos.[40] To this extent,

[32] Ibid.: 42–3.
[33] Selth, 1999: 11. An earlier and less detailed version of this paper appears as 'The Future of the Burmese Armed Forces' in Pedersen, Rudland and May (eds), 2000: 52–90.
[34] Selth, 1999: 11.
[35] Ibid.: 16.
[36] Correspondence, Selth with author, 15 and 20 June 2000.
[37] Selth, 1999: 12.
[38] Ibid.: 13–18.
[39] Ibid.: 27.
[40] Ibid.: 20.

the interests of the military and the opposition converge, and a transition to elected government *could* be feasible without violence (the main policy difference dividing them being the extent of minority participation in power).[41] But 'the broad principles expounded by the armed forces . . . have been corrupted and distorted through years of propaganda to serve [narrow] . . . ends' and an elected government could not long survive without restaffing the military with a 'new kind of Burmese officer' recruited, educated and trained to serve the Army's 'original ideals'.[42] Burma's future thus depends on an interplay of political, economic, social, strategic and other imponderables that is unpredictable.[43]

The military's cohesion in 1988, despite admission of past failure and widespread opposition, indicates that it is unlikely to split now, believes Robert Taylor. Whatever tension may exist within its ranks, no internal pressure from groups that it perceives as 'tools of foreign masters', such as the NLD or the KNU, threatens to break its unity. Fear of losing power accounts for its huge expansion since 1988, and its leaders are resolved to 'hang together or hang separately' and will resist strongly any pressure for change, relying on their 'system of rewards/perks/corruption' to keep their officer corps in line. The military is 'overwhelmingly, the single most powerful institution in the country'. Nor is external pressure likely to shake it. Western states that proclaim their distaste for the Burman regime, while trading uncritically with other autocracies, have no strategic interest in Burma. Japan, India and the ASEAN states might share a strategic interest in containing China, but whether replacing the SPDC with a government responsive to an electorate would contain China seems doubtful; their attitude is, 'you deal with whoever is in power' to promote your 'real' interests. They are inclined to dismiss Western grandstanding over issues of 'democracy' and 'civil rights' as 'neo-imperialist sour grapes'. China is unlikely soon to develop an 'ethical foreign policy' at the expense of its interests in Burma. Taylor notes that four to five decades of intensive economic and political interaction with the West preceded 'democracy' in Thailand, Korea and Taiwan, and that change in Indonesia followed four decades of American and Japanese investment and pressures to create social and political institutions congenial to a modern economy, but, he

[41] Ibid.: 11.
[42] Ibid.: 26.
[43] Ibid.: 2.

believes, a comparable engagement with Burma is not 'politically saleable to the electorate at home'. Burma's economic backwardness is the main brake on change, and, until there is a business class to replace that destroyed by socialism, there will be no effective opposition to the generals (witness Thailand, Taiwan, Korea, the Philippines and, to some extent, Singapore, Malaysia and Indonesia). They will continue to regard elected government as a threat, not an opportunity.[44]

Morten Pedersen holds that existing strategies to influence change in Burma are of three types, coercion, persuasion and cooperation,[45] and none is likely to succeed. Like Taylor, he believes there is no significant prospect of the military splitting, that it is more firmly in control than ever.[46] Aung San Suu Kyi's convening of the Committee Representing the People's Parliament (CRPP) in November 1995 precipitated a heightened repression that galvanized the coercion strategists, but 'pro-democracy' consumer boycotts, visa bans on senior Burmese military and other officials, revocation of tariff preferences,[47] investment bans, European Parliament recognition of the CRPP,[48] suspension of government assistance and IMF, World Bank and Asian Development Bank loans, and suspension of Burma from ILO membership[49] have not induced the SPDC to yield power. Sanctions, unlike those previously applied to South Africa, are not effective, because Burma's interests are not controlled by a business class 'integrated into the global economy', and sanctions are undermined by Chinese support for Burma and ASEAN 'constructive engagement' with Burma. The 'Asian values' attitude of Burma's neighbours blunts the psychological force of external criticism.[50] Nor will persuasion induce the SPDC to yield power, owing to the military's contempt for 'legislature politics' and its self-nurtured myth imputing to itself the status of 'creators' and 'saviours' of the nation. Burma has never had a military entirely independent of politics, and the 'petty infighting among members of the contemporary pro-democratic exile movement' reinforces its contempt for civilian politicians. Nothing can overcome its aversion

[44] Email, Taylor to author, May 2000.
[45] Pedersen, in Pedersen, Rudland and May (eds), 2000: 202.
[46] Ibid.: 195, 210–11, 232–3.
[47] Ibid.: 198.
[48] Ibid.
[49] Ibid.: 201.
[50] Ibid.: 207–12.

to the NLD's declared policy of federalism, accepted by 'no military government, from the Revolutionary Council to the SPDC' and perceived by the military as undermining 'national reconsolidation . . . through a "burmanization" of the ethnic minorities'.[51] Thailand, South Korea, Hong Kong and especially Suharto's long 'New Order regime' in Indonesia, examples urged by the cooperation school for change, all enjoyed a 'high capacity for planning and implementing sound economic policies', as well as authoritarian leaders who were willing 'to limit their . . . discretionary power', were committed to economic development and had 'broad popular support'. By contrast, economic policy in Burma 'is in the hands of military leaders with little or no technical expertise, [while] widespread corruption at all levels of the state greatly increases the transaction costs and uncertainty of doing business'.[52]

Pedersen suggests a *faute de mieux* strategy for Burma's troubles. As 'we are likely to see the present deadlock continue until the military eventually succeeds in eliminating the domestic opposition and introduces some form of formal civilian rule',[53] we should not oppose the SPDC's effort to craft a new constitution reserving ultimate power for the military, he argues. We must emphasize 'common concerns rather than opposing visions of the political system', concentrate on 'increased investment in sectors such as education, health, and agriculture' that will 'raise living standards . . . facilitate the growth of civil society' and reduce the 'siege mentality' that 'hinders an objective assessment of . . . Burma's problems' by 'engaging the regime in international cooperation'.[54] Such a policy, he believes, will 'alleviate the deepening humanitarian crisis; strengthen the structural basis for effective domestic opposition to authoritarian rule; and change the outlook and mindset of current, and particularly future, military leaders'.[55] While existing arms embargoes and sanctions, economic, diplomatic and cultural, should not be lifted, they should be used as carrots for change with a declared intention of eliminating them.[56] To avoid the stigma of doing business in Burma and minimize the risk of consumer boycotts, private companies might adopt the 'Sullivan

[51] Ibid.: 218–22.
[52] Ibid.: 226.
[53] Ibid.: 233.
[54] Ibid.: 234.
[55] Ibid.: 233.
[56] Ibid.: 235–7.

principles', a code of 'guidelines for moral and constructive business behaviour' previously used in South Africa.[57] As it would be 'morally indefensible' to abandon the NLD, Pedersen proposes that '[s]ome of the smaller Western countries with little influence on the military regime, but a long tradition of supporting civil society in developing countries, could take responsibility for this aspect of the campaign for political change'.[58]

These opinions evince wide divergence. On the issue of whether an implosion within the military is likely, three views emerge: that a split is very possible, and the signs of division are apparent already (Silverstein, Callahan); that division may occur but is unlikely soon (Steinberg, Selth, Gravers, *semble* Smith, Lintner); that a split will not happen within the foreseeable future (Taylor, Pedersen). Only in respect of timing is there a measure of consensus: no change to pluralism seems imminent (Steinberg, Selth, Taylor, Gravers, Pedersen, *semble* Smith, Lintner).

I have little faith in fundamental change happening through peace as an inherent dynamic of healing and reconciliation, or trust-building by economic and social progress, as Smith envisages, or by cooperating on issues of overriding shared concern, as Smith, Steinberg and Pedersen envisage. I believe the generals' vested interest in continuing the existing system is too entrenched, their fear of reprisals too strong. Perhaps appealing to their patriotism would assist change. Save for a short period under British rule, Burma has *never* known peace or unity. Were a soldier-leader to arise who was able to unite Burma by quality of example, rather than by force, he would achieve a place in Burmese history transcending that reserved to Anawrahta and Alaungpaya, but such a development seems most unlikely. I doubt, too, that the military has succeeded in persuading the Burmese people that it is the country's saviour and protector, as Gravers implies. Most Burmans, and all minorities, see it as a praetorian guard protecting a privileged caste; to believe otherwise, it seems to me, underestimates their intelligence. Ordinary Burmese do not accept that preserving the Union requires the army to steal from them and control the minutiae of their lives, or that such is the price they must pay for bad *karma* in past lives, as Steinberg suggests. Nine years after trekking across the Kachin Hills, I went to the Burman parts of Burma. Soldiers occupied almost

[57] Ibid.: 236.
[58] Ibid.: 237.

all first-class seats on trains and flights; golf courses were their exclusive preserve. A meeting with a High Court judge had to be conducted in the presence of two colleagues, lest he be suspected of colluding with foreigners, and he stopped me from snapping a picture of the courtyard outside his office. Photography of the courtyard, he said, was forbidden. Orwellian billboards everywhere proclaimed the virtues of 'Disciplined Democracy'. 'We are very disappointed,' whispered an elderly Burman who was 20 when the British left Burma. It seems to me that a regime so intensely and comprehensively detested is *inherently* unstable and that measuring the pace of likely change by the experiences of Thailand, Korea, Taiwan and Indonesia, whose regimes enjoyed internal and external support through 40 years of Cold War, is misleading. Moreover, if we keep our sights trained on the reality that power to effect change reposes in the Burmese people, I suggest, we may be able to assist change.

Dictatorial regimes use various means of deflecting criticism from themselves. Some (such as Enver Hoja in Albania) raise spectres of imagined enemies plotting to destroy the State. Some (various African dictators) blame past exploitation of colonial powers for present hardships. Some (propagandists of the Soviet Comintern) fantasize ever-receding future utopias to relieve present hardships. Rangoon has used all these tactics to manipulate the Burmese. The politicians fostered a number of myths—that the diverse peoples of Burma were one, and Britain destroyed that unity in order to conquer and rule them; that the British deprived the 'national races' of their freedom; that British administrators regarded Burmans as their inferiors;[59] that Burma's poverty was due to British exploitation; that independence would deliver Burma from the disunity, bondage, indignity and poverty imposed on them by the British. When the Burmese wearied of the false hopes the politicians aroused, the military took over and added another myth, that the politicians ('the enemy within') were colluding with Britain and the 'neo-colonialist' Americans ('the enemy without') to keep Burma in bondage. Such myths become self-proving, tautological substitutes for the truth, and we do not help the Burmese people by pandering to them. We merely help the autocracy deceive the people.

A notorious example of pandering to such myths was the BBC's allegation that the British directed Aung San's assassination (chapter

---

[59] For a poignant example of doubtful veracity, see U Maung Maung, 1980: 2.

6), an allegation parroted by the programme's presenter in articles in the *Guardian, South China Morning News* and *Guardian Weekly*[60] and now used by the Burman military to discredit Aung San Suu Kyi (who was married to one of the *kala* who 'murdered her father').[61] The BBC is respected in Burma, its Burmese Service being one of the few uncensored sources of political news and comment. A body *independent* of the BBC should review this programme.[62]

The military argues that Burma should model its institutions on its Burman past, where the army had a place at the heart of government, and maintains that Western institutions are 'inappropriate for Burma'.[63] Its opponents counter that the right of people to

---

[60] Fergal Keane, 19 and 27 July 1997.

[61] For example: 'Myanmar's national hero General Aung San and his ministers were assassinated in July 1947 through the complicity of the colonialist government. It was the most damaging act in the history of Myanmar. It left the country almost leaderless after regaining her independence from Britain in January 1948. . . . [A]ccording to the recent release of sensitive documents to the British media, the pre-independence assassination of General Aung San and his Cabinet ministers and the [Karen] insurgency that began around 1947–48 were stage-managed by the Britain-based "Friends of Burma Hill People" with definite links to the Colonial Conservative Government of Britain.' Government of Myanmar, *c*1998: 3, 17. Rangoon media examples include: 'The view from the Embassy of Myanmar, Ottawa', *The New Light of Myanmar*, 29 July 1997, p. 5 (citing the BBC's claim of a 'conspiracy between the past colonial power and the Karen National Union'); 'Was Britain behind Aung San's death?', *The New Light of Myanmar*, 13 August 1997, p. 3 (reproducing Fergal Keane's 19 July 1997 article in the *Guardian*); 'The view from the Embassy of Myanmar, Ottawa', *The New Light of Myanmar*, 26 August 1997, p. 5 (reproducing excerpts from Fergal Keane's 27 July 1997 article in the *Guardian Weekly*; and 'Reply to Mr Cook', *The New Light of Myanmar*, 5 September 1997, p. 3 (citing Fergal Keane's article in the *Guardian* for giving 'credible substance to our belief of the hidden "British-hand" in the assassination of our national hero'). The SPDC has sponsored a book endorsing the BBC's allegations by one Ko Than, entitled *Ko twe thi gai ya thahmya - Naing-gandaw loke kyan hmu gyi*, translated, 'The national assissation [*sic*] personally known to me', and bearing an alternative English title or sub-title, 'Who Really Kill [*sic*] Aung San?', published by U Win Myint, Win Myint Aung Journals, #315, 2-Kha Suburb, Htaukkyant Extension, Mingaladon Township, Rangoon, May 1999. Email, Kin Oung to author, 13 October 2000.

[62] Almost everyone interviewed by the producer of *Who* Really *Killed Aung San* (BBC 2, 19 July 1997), most people cited in his credits, John McEnery, numerous others with knowledge of the subject and I have protested at the programme's pervasive inaccuracy. The BBC referred our correspondence to the producer and refused to acknowledge the programme's inaccuracy.

[63] Bray, 1995: vi.

choose their government is a right of international law. The relevant provisions of international law (see below) do not allude to 'democracy', and we, too, should avoid that term. Were Western states 'democracies', we would have mob rule, which, effectively, is the point the SPDC makes in its case for 'disciplined democracy'.[64] But our rulers are elected, not self-appointed, and we are governed by law, which restrains our rulers in the exercise of power and limits their tenure. By extolling 'democracy', instead of pressing for the government of elected representatives chosen by universal adult suffrage and a legal system independent of power and politics,[65] I believe we weaken the case for change.

The Burman regime's human rights abuse, and especially the ethnic cleansing occurring in Shan, Kayah and Karen states in the name of maintaining Burma's unity,[66] are an outrage to mankind, and we should intensify our condemnation of these practices. That said, campaigning for civil rights tends to divert attention from the corruption and involvement in the drugs trade that underpin the regime's hold on power. We could assist the Burmese people by more robust discussion of these other matters.

On 30 May 1990, the military regime allowed a general election in Burma, believing, apparently, that it would demonstrate popular support for its National Unity Party (NUP). To improve its chances of victory, it disqualified Aung San Suu Kyi from standing as a candidate, prevented her from campaigning (indeed, kept her under house arrest), orchestrated a media campaign vilifying her as a 'Mrs Race Destructionist',[67] accused the NLD of colluding with Burma's

[64] For example: '[I]n the United States security can never be guaranteed in most of the U.S. cities. . . . [C]an its citizen [sic] enjoy security out in the streets of most cities especially after dark? . . . [T]o keep the country perpetually stable and to have a functioning democracy Myanmar has to have a strong and everlasting constitution which will keep the country on the proper track.' Government of Myanmar, c1998 (supplied free to all visiting dignitaries): 19.

[65] Compare *Far Eastern Economic Review*, Robert S. Gelbard, 'Slorc's Drug Links', 21 November 1996: 35 ('For the past eight years, the world's attention has been focused on the struggle of Burma's people to gain a say in their future. A more fundamental problem is the collapse of the rule of law').

[66] See Heppner, 2000: 15–19.

[67] For having conceived children by a British father. The regime also calls her the 'axehandle' (used by foreign oppressor to chop up Burma), 'puppet girl' and 'puppet princess'. Callahan, in Pedersen, Rudland and May (eds), 2000: 35.

'enemies',[68] disenfranchised voters living in insurgent-controlled areas, relocated voters in widespread gerrymandering, restricted political assembly, limited political broadcasts to one pre-censored, 10-minute television statement and one pre-censored, 15-minute radio statement per party, forbade reference in campaign speeches to Ne Win, the army, the SLORC and the economy, and opened the contest to more than three dozen parties, one supporting the SLORC and all others the opposition. Nevertheless, the NLD won 392 of the 485 seats contested, against 10 for the NUP[69]—a preponderance of 40 to 1. If 83 seats won by other opposition parties are included in the tally, the preponderance of support for the opposition was 47 to 1.[70]

I submit that the resounding rejection of the regime by the people of Burma in the 1990 general election and their unequivocal choice of the NLD to rule them presents an unanswerable case for recognizing the NLD as the lawful government of Burma. The pertinent legal principles are illustrated by *Tinoco Arbitration (Great Britain* v. *Costa Rica)*, 1 RIAA 369, 379 (1923), *Great Britain* v. *Costa Rica*, AJIL, 147, 152 (1924), where Judge Taft ruled that Costa Rica was bound by the contracts of a usurper, as he 'was in actual and peaceable control without resistance or conflict or contest by any one until a few months before the time when he retired'. Burma's 1990 election results manifest a regime imposing control that *is* resisted and contested.

The right of people to choose those who govern them and the manner of their governance is enshrined in article 21 of the

---

68 Smith, 1991: 414.

69 General Aung Gyi's Union Nationalist Democracy Party won one seat.

70 After its defeat, the regime claimed that the election was to a constituent assembly for the purpose of drafting a new constitution, and not to a legislature. However, chapter II, article 3 of Pyithu Hluttaw Election Law No. 14/89, 31 May 1989, ordained that a parliament (*hluttaw*) would be formed of representatives 'elected in accordance with this Law from the *Hluttaw* constituencies', and ten days after promulgating election law no. 14/89, the regime stated, 'If [the elected representatives do] not like the two existing constitutions, they can [draft] a new constitution. Neither the Defence Forces nor the State Law and Order Restoration Council will draw up a new constitution.' 43rd News Conference organized by the Information Committee of the SLORC in Rangoon on 9 June 1989; quoted in Article 19 (Ventkateswaran), 1996: 13. Moreover, three weeks before the general election, the regime stated that 'the drafting of a constitution should be discussed and decided by elected representatives in the [emerging] assembly'. Press conference, 11 May 1990, Rangoon. Ibid.

Universal Declaration of Human Rights,[71] the UN General Assembly (UNGA) Declaration on Principles of International Law concerning friendly Relations and Co-operation among States,[72] and article I of the International Covenant on Civil and Political Rights.[73] The UN applied this principle to Spain, threatening 'measures' if 'within a reasonable time, there is not established a government which derives its authority from the consent of the governed',[74] and the Covenant's language is broad enough to impose an obligation on signatories, including the United States, Japan, Canada, Australia and all European states, to enforce the law against 'state parties' that, like Burma, are not signatories. The ILO's June 2000 directive condemning the Burman regime's use of corvée for its infrastructure projects and threatening to propose punitive action, including

[71] '1. Everyone has the right to take part in the government of his country, directly or through freely chosen representatives. . . . 3. The will of the people shall be the basis of the authority of government; this will shall be expressed in periodic and genuine elections which shall be by universal and equal suffrage and shall be held by secret vote or by equivalent free voting procedures.' Adopted and proclaimed 10 December 1948, UNGA Res. 217A [III], UN Doc. A/810, p. 71.

[72] '[A]ll peoples have the right freely to determine, without external interference, their political status and to pursue their economic, social and cultural development, and every State has the duty to respect this right in accordance with the provisions of the [UN] Charter.' UNGA Res. 2625 (XXV), 24 October 1970, adopted without a vote pursuant to the principle of equal rights enshrined in the UN Charter. *Accord*, Declaration of Independence ('We hold these truths to be self-evident. That Governments are instituted among Men, deriving their just powers from the consent of the governed. That whenever any form of Government becomes destructive of these ends, it is the Right of the People to alter or to abolish it, and to institute new Government, laying its foundation on such principles and organizing its powers in such form, as to them shall seem most likely to effect their Safety and Happiness. . . . [W]hen a long train of abuses and usurpations, pursuing invariably the same Object, evinces a design to reduce them under absolute Despotism, it is their right, it is their duty, to throw off such Government, and to provide new Guards for their future security.').

[73] '1. All peoples have the right of self-determination. By virtue of that right they freely determine their political status and freely pursue their economic, social and cultural development. 3. The States Parties to the present Covenant . . . shall promote the realization of the right of self-determination, and shall respect that right, in conformity with the provisions of the Charter of the United Nations.' Adopted 16 December 1966, UN Doc. A/6316: 999, effective date 23 March 1976.

[74] Article 19 (Ventkateswaran), 1996: 11; derived from operative paragraph 4, UNGA Resolution 39(I), adopted first session, 1945.

cessation of World Bank and IMF aid if it continues, instances this broader interpretation of core human rights norms.[75] Nor is interference in a country's internal affairs a defence when the issue of compliance with international obligations is before a competent forum.[76]

There is also a strong case for withdrawing the regime's credentials in the UNGA. The UNGA's decison as to who represents Burma is not subject to the Security Council's veto.[77] In 1974, it rejected the South African representative's credentials. Challenged on a point of order, the assembly's president upheld the decision, and the assembly sustained his ruling by a vote of 91 to 22 with 19 abstentions. Thus, there is precedent for such a measure.[78]

As Silverstein notes, the international community's recognition of the regime underpins its cohesion.[79] Withdrawing the regime's UNGA credentials and recognizing the NLD as the *de jure* government of Burma would remove that prop. It might also encourage and galvanize opposition to the regime within Burma.

Other instruments of international law can be applied to assist the Burmese people in their quest for dignity. The military's routine use of 'citizen labour for infrastructure and development projects'[80] violates article 4 of the Universal Declaration of Human Rights, article 8 of the International Covenant on Civil and Political Rights,

[75] This is the first time the ILO has instituted such a measure in its 81-year history. See http://www. ilo.org/public/english/bureau/inf/pr/2000/27.htm. For an excellent discussion of the illegality of the regime's refusal to abide by the results of the 30 May 1990 election, see Article 19 (Ventkateswaran), 1996: 10–11.

[76] See, e.g., opinion of the Permanent Court of International Justice in *Tunis and Morocco Nationality Decrees* (PCIJ, Series B, No. 4, 1923): 26.

[77] A committee appointed to examine credentials reports its findings. The UNGA then votes as a body to accept or reject the committee's report 'in the light of the purpose and principles of the Charter and the circumstances of each case'. Josef Silverstein, untitled article, Burmanet #1524, April 29/30, 2000, citing Thomas Hidgon, 'Myanmar's Regime at the UN General Assembly', a paper presented at a public meeting in Washington, DC.

[78] Silverstein, untitled article, Burmanet #1524.

[79] 'The SLORC, the Defence Services, is not bound by any constitution. The SLORC is a military government . . . recognized by countries of the world and the UN.' Decree 1/90, 27 July 1990, paragraph 6. See also Government of Myanmar, *c*1998: 18.

[80] Those able to afford the price purchase release, providing officers and NCOs with additional means of 'bleeding everyone dry'. Callahan, in Pedersen, Rudland and May (eds), 2000: 31.

articles 6 and 7 of the International Covenant on Economic, Social and Cultural Rights 1966,[81] and article 5(e)(i) of the International Convention on the Elimination of all Forms of Racial Discrimination 1966.[82] The regime's denial of religious equality to Christians and Muslims by nationalizing their schools, confiscating their hospitals, expelling foreign missionaries, forcing them to do obeisance to Buddhist monks and to assist in building Buddhist monasteries, violates articles 1 and 13 of the UN Charter, articles 2 and 18 of the Universal Declaration of Human Rights, article 18 of the International Covenant on Civil and Political Rights, and article 5(a)(viii) of the International Convention on the Elimination of all Forms of Racial Discrimination.[83] Other rights secured by these instruments and violated by the Burman regime include the right to life, personal security, thought, expression, assembly and education.[84]

I cannot agree with Robert Taylor that we have no strategic interest in a country that produces half the world's opium. There is surely a case here for a Security Council resolution demanding that Rangoon end its involvement in this trade, subject to threat of sanctions and, in the last resort, armed intervention. If, as Silverstein and Callahan indicate, division already exists in the military, there would appear to be little chance of it retaining its unity were it faced

[81] Entered into force 1976 and, by 1 January 1992, ratified by 106 states (excluding Burma). *Accord*, article 4, European Convention of Human Rights, adopted 4 November 1950 and entered into force 3 September 1953.

[82] Entered into force 1969 and, by 1 January 1992, ratified by 130 states (excluding Burma). *Accord*, article 4, European Convention of Human Rights, adopted 4 November 1950 and entered into force 3 September 1953.

[83] Although Burma is a signatory to none of the relevant covenants, it has declared its adherence to 'those provisions and principles embodied in the covenants which are taken from the Charter of the UN and the International Declaration of Human Rights or have attained the status of rules of customary international law'. Memorandum submitted by the Burmese Ambassador to the UN, U Min Wra, to the Secretary General on 2 November 1994: UN Doc. A/C. 3/49/15, 10 November 1994.

[84] Numerous reports document human rights abuses in Burma. A random selection includes Article 19 (Smith), 1994; Article 19 (Smith), 1995; Article 19 (Ventkateswaran), 1996; Article 19 (Iyer), 1999; the 1993, 1995 and 1996 reports of the Special Rapporteur of the UN Human Rights Commission, UN Documents E/CN. 4/1993/37, E/CN. 4/1995/65 and E/CN. 4/1996/65; Amnesty International, 1988, 1992, 1994 and 1996; Human Rights Watch/Asia, 1995; Smith, 1994; International Commission of Jurists, 1991; Lawyers Committee for Human Rights, 1991; Asia Watch, 1989 and 1990; and Clements, 1991. According to NGO sources, 3000 were killed for demonstrating during the summer of 1988. See Article 19 (Smith), 1991: 1.

with this threat and, hence, little likelihood of the need to implement the threat; Steinberg, Selth, Taylor, Gravers and Pedersen do not address this question. I do not underestimate the difficulties of securing agreement on such a resolution,[85] but it should be stressed that both Russia and China, permanent members of the Security Council with veto powers, have an interest here at least as great as the other members.

My final suggestion relates to the generals. Aung San Suu Kyi has stated that she neither wants nor intends to exact reprisals.[86] We should support her policy and eschew the temptation to punish the generals for 'war crimes', even offer them asylum. Compare South Korea, Chile and South Africa, where preconditions of amnesty may be viewed as critical to the peaceful transfers of power.

The military regime in Burma will not last, and, I believe, its end may come sooner than many Burma scholars expect. However, devolution of power to civilian rule will not of itself conclude Burma's troubles. Half a century of torching villages, herding people into concentration camps, using them as human mine sweepers, poisoning crops, raping women and lopping off the ears of those suspected of colluding with insurgents[87] to force Burma's minorities to submit to Burman rule has replaced what once was mere distrust with a legacy of profound and intense hatred, compounded by enduring problems of corruption, ambition, greed and mendacity. Ultimately, Burma's fate is not in man's gift. It is a matter of prayer.

---

[85] The status quo benefits both China and Thailand, and China in particular would have to be persuaded that its interests would be served better by supporting intervention. If Burma's sovereignty is overridden thus, whose might be next? China's over Tibet? Who will provide the soldiers? Who will defray the cost?

[86] Selth, 1999: 15; Aung San Suu Kyi, 'Why Burma must take steps to change', *Guardian Weekly*, London, 2 August 2000; *Far Eastern Economic Review*, Ytzen, 'Diehard Optimist', 7 May 1998: 21.

[87] See Tucker, 2000: 43, 54, 79–80, 89, 93, 95, 116, 119–20, 143, 148, 164, 181, 334–5.

Chronological Guide to the Burmese Civil War[1]

1813–26[2]   First Baptist missionaries arrive in Burma. Burmans invade Assam twice, claim part of Bengal and dispatch a large army to Arakan, igniting the First Anglo-Burmese War, which concludes with the Treaty of Yandabo ceding Arakan and Tenasserim to the British.

1830–43   Karens, hitherto enslaved by Burmans, begin converting to Christianity.

1852–53   The Second Anglo-Burmese War concludes with British annexation of Lower Burma.

1872–81   Roman Catholic and Baptist missionaries begin evangelizing the Kachins.

1875   British compel King Mindon to recognize independence of Western Karenni.

1885–1 January 1886   Third Anglo-Burmese War concludes with British annexation of Upper Burma. Burma will be administered separately as 'Burma Proper', or 'Ministerial Burma' (most of the Arakan, central Burma, Karen Hills and Tenasserim) and the 'Frontier', 'Scheduled' or 'Excluded Areas' (Karenni, Shan states and the northern hills).

1886–1915   'Pacification' campaigns oblige Shan, Kachin and Chin leaders to accept *sanad*s as Crown protectorates.

1892–1940   Burma opens to the outside world. The rural economy grows steadily more dependent on (mainly Indian) moneylenders, and increasing numbers of deracinated peasants drift into the cities. Preferment is shown to minorities in army and police recruitment, and Burmans resent non-Burmans now making most of the

---

[1] For narrative and more rounded and authoritative accounts, see especially Smith, 1999, and Lintner, 1999.
[2] The years 1813–26 are arbitrarily chosen. The ethnic and religious differences underpinning the Burmese Civil War antedated British conquest of Burma by many centuries.

important decisions affecting their lives. Alien religions are spreading among them, English is displacing Burmese as the language of the elite, and Western newspapers and books are corrupting their youth. This inversion of the 'natural' order, they sense, would not have been possible but for the treasonable collaboration of their former subjects (of whom many are Christians and Muslims) with their British masters.

1906   The YMBA is founded. Fusing Buddhist messianic notions with Western egalitarian concerns, it will play a prominent part in the nationalist movement.

1917–19   Westminster accepts self-government as ultimate aim for India, but the Montague–Chelmsford Report notes that 'the desire for elective institutions has not developed' in Burma, and that 'Burma is not India'; the Burmese are 'another race in another stage of political development'.

1918–21   U Ottama organizes nationalist societies and is arrested and imprisoned for sedition. GCBA is founded. University students protest against educational measures designed for training government administrators to serve the British and perpetuate a privileged elite, and the first student strike spreads throughout Burma Proper.

1922   Shan States Federation formed to unify administration of Shan principalities. GCBA divides on dyarchy issue. Chit Hlaing and Buddhist monks want to boycott elections to assembly. Ba Pe forms Twenty-One Party in support of participation.

1923   Burma, although remaining a province of India, gets its own governor and first elected assembly. But most powers are reserved to governor.

1925   GCBA splits into Chit Hlaing GCBA and Soe Thein GCBA.

1926   U Pu forms Home Rule Party.

1927   Soe Thein GCBA exhorts peasants to withhold payment of taxes.

1929 U Wisara dies in prison after a hunger strike reputedly lasting 166 days.

1930–32   Simon Commission recommends separating Burma from India. Saya San incites defiance with claims that tattoos and magic shirts will repel bullets. Karens are prominent in suppressing the rebellion, exacerbating Burman–Karen antagonisms.

1930–40   Indo-Burman and Sino-Burman race riots erupt. Burman nationalist organizations, such as the Dobama Asiayone (We Burmans Association), the Sinyetha (Poor Man's) Parti (founded by Ba Maw) and the Myochit (Nationalist) Parti (founded by U Saw), proliferate. The younger leaders, such as Nu and Aung San, are Rangoon University students. Dobama members address each other as *thakin* (master) as a snub to their foreign rulers.

1936–37   Nu and Aung San catapult to national fame when Rangoon University, under pressure of a strike, withdraws threats to expel them. Burma is separated from India, and Burma Proper now has a cabinet responsible to the governor and a parliament with reserved seats for specified minorities elected by popular franchise. As the governor can veto any administrative or legislative act, the more radical agitators dismiss these measures as diversionary. The minorities oppose them because 'home rule' and 'democratic' government imply a reversion to Burman hegemony and an undermining of the aristocratic basis of their rulers' authority.

1938   This is the 'year of the auspicious number revolution' (1300 in the Burmese era). Countrywide strikes include an 11-month oil fields stoppage. Ba Maw founds the Dahma Tat, U Saw the Galon Tat, 'both [private armies] . . . partaking of the character of the contemporary Black Shirts in Britain' (Donnison).

1939   Aung San and others found the CPB. Aung San is its first general secretary. Ba Maw and student nationalists form the Freedom Bloc. Aung San is its secretary.

1940   Ba Maw advises Japanese of the Freedom Bloc's readiness to organize an armed uprising. Most of its members are arrested.

1940–41   Aung San and the rest of the 'Thirty Comrades' slip out of the country and contact the Japanese, who train them and send them to Thailand to recruit other Burmans to fight for the BIA.

1942–43   Japanese occupy Burma. Fanatical nationalists, criminals and other undesirables join BIA and kill Imperial Army stragglers and civilians with suspected British sympathies, especially Karens. Ethnic war erupts. Japanese reorganize BIA and rename it BDA.

1943   Japanese grant 'independence' to Burma under *adipati* (prime minister) Ba Maw. BDA renamed BNA. Aung San is minister of defence.

1944   Communists and socialists secretly unite in what will be known as the AFPFL.

1945   BNA turns on the Japanese, now in full retreat. HMG decides to use Aung San rather than execute him for war crimes. Labour Party wins Britain's general election and adopts White Paper charting plan for Burma's independence protecting the hill peoples and honouring the Karennis' treaty rights. Aung San agrees to integrate his PBF, as it is now called, into a new Burma Army of four Burman, two Karen, two Chin and two Kachin battalions. But 3500 PBF soldiers do not enlist and form instead the PVO, a private army loyal to Aung San.

1946   Aung San incites mass rallies demanding immediate independence. HMG diminishes its control by demobilizing its forces, ordering Indian Army units　ot to intercede in Burman resistance movement activities, and merging loyal Burma Army units with PBF of doubtful loyalty. HMG abandons the White Paper (despite warnings that overriding the minorities' fears will lead to civil war). AFPFL-controlled trade unions incite police, civil servant and oilfield worker strikes. A new governor appoints Aung San as deputy chairman (prime minister) and five other AFPFL nominees to his executive council, and the strikes end. AFPFL expels communists after they accuse it of 'collaboration' and demands incorporation of Frontier Areas into Burma Proper. Westminster ignores a delegation of Karens who petition for separate independence.

27 January 1947   Attlee–Aung San Agreement effectively nullifies HMG's wartime promises to minorities; provides for FACE to determine their wishes and an elected constituent assembly to settle a future constitution; and specifies that independence is to be 'as soon as possible'.

5 February 1947   KNU is founded.

12 February 1947   Shans, Kachins and Chins sign Panglong Agreement to join Burma Proper in seeking early independence; Frontier Areas are to be subject to 'full autonomy in internal administration'.

April 1947   KNU and communists boycott election to constituent assembly; PVO intimidates voters; AFPFL wins large majority.

May 1947   FACE recommends federal union. Armed rebellion flares in Arakan. Aung San responds with vague promises of local statehood but insists on interim need to preserve unity. KNU begins organizing the militias that will become the KNDO.

19 July 1947   Martyrs Day: Burman rivals murder Aung San and six other ministers. Nu becomes AFPFL leader and prime minister.

September 1947   The constituent assembly's proposed constitution is adopted, AFPFL toadies accepting it on the Karens' and Karennis' behalf. Shans have the right to secede from the union after ten years. Karen Rifles battalions begin haemorrhaging weapons to KNDO.

4 January 1948, 0420 hours   Independence.

28 March 1948   CPB rebels and, within a year, numbers 15,000 partisans. Nu tries to stall rebels by announcing 'leftist unity' programme, while Ne Win recruits and trains *sitwundan* (Burman regional militias). UMP murder prominent Karenni nationalist, and insurrection sweeps Karenni. Ethnic units of Burma Army in Shan State defect to KNDO. KNDO, MNDO and Karen UMP units seize Thaton and Moulmein. *Sitwundan* order them to disarm and hurl grenades into Karen churches during Christmas services.

1949   Attacks on Karens continue. Karen commander-in-chief, Karen air force commander and two Karen cabinet ministers resign. Ne Win takes command of Burma Army. Karens rebel, are joined by Paos, Karennis, Mons, and a Kachin Rifles battalion under Naw Seng, and soon control most of Burma. Socialists and PVOs resign from government and press for peace negotiations. Widespread strikes further weaken the government. HMG and Delhi reinforce Burma Army, and a Burma Army Gurkha unit, a scratch force of *sitwundan*, PVOs loyal to the government and Burman irregulars repel a KNDO attack on Rangoon. The tide turns.

Constantly changing alliances and military expedients characterize the next 52 years. The most recurrent issues among the main players are:

Within the government

- Allocation of authority between centre and regions, Burmans and other ethnic groups, and protection of minority rights.
- More, versus less, central management of the economy.
- Governance by parliamentary democracy or military autocracy.
- Alliances with drug warlord private armies.
- Whether to negotiate with the rebels.
- Relations with China.

Within the CPB

- Armed struggle or the 'evolutionary path to socialism' (tactical alliances with legal opposition and front organizations such as 'peace movements' and trade unions).
- Using persuasion or intimidation to enlist popular support.
- Collectivization or land redistribution.
- Leninism (seizing cities first and expanding from there) versus 'Mao-tse Tung Thought' (seizing rural areas, thereby encircling cities).
- CPB 'vanguard' paramountcy or collaboration with opposition parties on equal terms.

Within the ethnic insurgencies

- Contesting control of territories or agreed demarcation lines and cooperation with CPB.
- Whether to submit to CPB leadership in return for arms.
- Marxist–Leninist–Stalinist–Maoist or British models in political and military organization.

Affecting all the players

- Whether to exploit, condone or prohibit the drugs trade.
- Communal rivalries.
- Personality cults.
- Personal greed, ambition, opportunism, suspicion and jealousy.

1949–61 Creeping Burmanization in minority areas under Burma Army control confirms separatists' predictions. Government, school and university posts are reserved for Burmans; Buddhist clergy receive special privileges; army is increasingly Burmanized; Aung San's Panglong promise of 'kyat for kyat' infrastructure investment parity is ignored.

1950–61　KMT remnants flee into Kengtung State and, assisted by CIA, gradually assert a monopoly over the opium trade and develop an enduring network.

1951　CPB stays operations to help Rangoon drive KMT from Burma. The DSI opens its first store.

1952–53　Combined KNU/KMT units attack government positions. KMT repatriates some troops to Taiwan after UN orders it to leave Burma.

1954　Burma Army opens major offensives against Karens, KMT and *mujahids*.

1955　Opposition parties combine in NUF and blame government for continuing the war.

1956　NUF wins 36.9 per cent of vote and 48 seats in general election.

1957　KNPP founded.

1958　Nu offers rebels 'arms for peace' amnesty. Nai Shwe Kyin rejects offer and founds NMSP. Shans found Noom Suk Harn. League splits into majority 'Cleans' under Nu, who form coalition with NUF, and 'Stables' under Ba Swe and Kyaw Nyein. NUF presses for peace talks. Government concedes principle of separate Arakan and Mon states. Chins demand their own state. Fighting erupts between rival factions. Nu averts a formal coup by transferring power to the 'Caretaker Government' (Ne Win).

1958–60　Apprehending Union's disintegration, Caretaker Government arrests and deports NUF supporters, denies Shans' right to secede, purchases *saohpas*' hereditary powers, and amends constitution to end *saohpas*' reserved seats in parliament. The DSI establishes a string of new enterprises and replaces civilian with military bosses.

1959　Karens, Karennis, Mons, Chins and communists unite in a military alliance.

1960–61　Uprisings flare across Shan State.

1960   Sao Shwe Thaike and others found Federal Movement to promote constitutional changes relegating 'Burma' to a Burman-majority state with powers not greater than other ethnic states. General election returns Nu to power on pledges to create Arakan and Mon states and to establish Buddhism as state religion.

1961   Following combined Burma Army and PLA attack, KMT evacuates nearly half its 12,000 men from Burma. Operating from bases in Thailand, it will continue dealing drugs through proxies such as Lo Hsin Han, Moh Heng and Khun Sa. KIO is founded. Rebels now include communists, Karens, Karennis, Shans, Mons, Lahus, Was, Paos, Palaungs, Chins, Nagas, Rakhines, *mujahids* and Kachins.

1962–64   Nu invites Federal Movement leaders to meet him in Rangoon to discuss concessions. Army arrests Nu, his cabinet and minorities' representatives; abrogates constitution; arrests supreme court judges; appoints soldiers to run state governments and civil service; and vests plenary executive, legislative and judicial powers in RC (Ne Win). He issues manifestos defining Buddhist, centrist, socialist and Burman principles by which he proposes to rule; creates BSPP and a pervasive body of informers; outlaws other parties; detains political leaders refusing to join the BSPP; suppresses student demonstrations; blows up RUSU building; closes Rangoon University; nationalizes banks, major commercial houses and industrial groups; seizes control of commodities trade; bans new private industry; purges civil service; closes or nationalizes newspapers and magazines and bans new ones; restricts travel abroad; rescinds powers reserved to the states under constitution; replaces missionaries with Burmans, nationalizes their schools and hospitals and expels them for alleged sympathies with insurgents; discontinues higher level English-medium schools and forms alliances with narcotics groups, arming and assisting them in their trafficking in return for their support. Growing Shan insurgency consolidates behind SSA, led by Shwe Thaike's widow. Hundreds of thousands of Indians and Chinese flee Burma, and shortages develop in staples such as rice and cooking oil.

1963–72   The economy's private sector diminishes from 493 firms employing 17,947 people to 267 firms employing 6887 people.

1963–78   The economy's state sector rises from 31.6 per cent to 46.4 per cent.

1965–69   Mao's 'Great Proletarian Cultural Revolution' sends slogan-chanting ethnic Chinese onto streets. Many are arrested, others attacked and killed. Chinese shops are looted. The Chinese Teachers' Federation building is burned down. The seal is torn from PRC's embassy. An embassy official is stabbed to death. The New China News Agency's correspondent is expelled. Peking Radio denounces Ne Win as a 'reactionary' and the BSPP as 'sham socialism'. CPB summarily executes many of its leaders. Its chairman, Than Tun (Aung San's brother-in-law), and politbureau order further purges. Bo Mya begins building the KNLA and a KNU purged of CPB sympathizers. War contesting control of opium trade breaks out between KMT and Shan warlord armies.

1968–75   Burma Army begins Four Cuts campaigns to sever rebel recruiting, intelligence, victualling and financing links to the people. Crops and villages are torched, people relocated into fortified compounds. Central Burma is cleared of rebels, but PLA regulars and Chinese Red Guards leading a force of 'national revolutionary minorities' (Was, Kokangs, Kachins, Palaungs, Shans, Lahus and Akhas) invade and occupy a large part of northern Shan State. CPB encroachment into KIO and Shan territory and the zealotry of Cultural Revolution trigger fighting between CPB, KIO and Shans. Burma Army supports KIO.

1969–70   Nu slips out of Burma, establishes 'government in exile' and forms army that builds string of bases along Thai–Burma border in alliance with KNU and NMSP.

1971   Fighting erupts between SSA and KIO.

1972–73   International criticism forces Rangoon to abandon *ka kwe yei* partnerships. Kokang, Shan and Wa warlord armies realign themselves with SSA.

1974   New constitution confirms powers already vested in Ne Win. Unlike 1947 constitution, limited autonomy is not guaranteed to ethnic states, and protection of minority languages, customs and cultures is made subject to the condition that they are not used 'to the detriment of national solidarity and socialist social order'. Riots erupt over army's attempt to bury U Thant inconspicuously. Martial law is declared. Universities and colleges are closed.

1974–88   Annual opium yield increases twentyfold.

1975   CPB agrees a defence pact with SSA. KIO's three top leaders assassinated.

1976   Karens, Karennis, Kayans, Mons, Shans, Palaungs, Paos and Rakhines, soon to be joined by Kachins, Was, Lahus and Chins, form NDF. KIO and CPB end hostilities, demarcate operational areas and agree to cooperate militarily. Brigadier Kyaw Zaw, Thirty Comrade and former Burma Army hero, broadcasts over the CPB's Voice of the People of Burma that Aung San had once considered sacking Ne Win and denounces Ne Win as 'morally depraved'.

1978   Fighting erupts within KNPP between pro- and anti-communist factions.

1980   Government announces general amnesty. More than 2000 rebels surrender.

1980–81   KIO states it will accept autonomy instead of independence. Nevertheless, peace negotiations with Rangoon fail owing to Ne Win's refusal to countenance any political concession save 'rehabilitation' and on his insistence that granting autonomy to the states would require a constitutional referendum. Rangoon and CPB also talk—but only for two days, when Rangoon demands peremptorily that CPB dissolve itself.

1981   China stops aiding CPB.

1982–83   Rangoon bans from the civil service and political office all minorities who have settled in Burma since 1824. WNO founded and joins NDF.

1984–88   Four Cuts operation in KNU areas halves excise taxes collected by KNU on cross-border trade.

1984–2000   Burmese refugees in Thailand increase from 9500 to 123,000.

1985   Khun Sa and Moh Heng's forces merge as MTA.

1986   NDF settles for autonomy and agrees to cooperate militarily with CPB, but KNU leader Bo Mya denounces pact and CPB as arrogant drug traffickers.

1986–88   US supplies 2,4-D herbicide, helicopters and aircraft to Burma and provides pilot-training to assist Burma in eradicating poppy. Burma Air Force uses herbicides to spray its enemies' poppy but exempts from spraying its allies' poppy.

5 September 1987   Rangoon invalidates 75, 35 and 25 kyat notes and replaces them with 90 and 45 kyat notes, currency units divisible by 9, because Ne Win believes 9 is auspicious. Enraged students storm onto streets and begin smashing government property.

12–18 March 1988   Tanks roar into Rangoon, and tear gas canisters disperse crowds.

June–July 1988   More demonstrations; now, however, there is open dissent within the army. Aung San Suu Kyi accuses Ne Win of destroying the country ('the country is poor while one individual is rich').

23 July 1988   Ne Win makes valedictory address ('When the army shoots, it shoots to kill') and resigns.

26–27 July 1988   Riot police commander General Sein Lwin takes over.

August 1988   10,000 demonstrators march through Rangoon and bury effigies of Ne Win and Sein Lwin in coffins decorated with demonetized banknotes. Monks report that the Buddha's image at Sula Pagoda has changed shape and that an image in the sky above the Shwedagon Pagoda is standing on its head.

8 August 1988   A general strike begins. Mass demonstrations engulf country as Burmans, ethnic minorities, Buddhists, Muslims, farmers, moneylenders, rightists, leftists, old and young find common cause in multiparty democracy. Regime responds by killing hundreds and arresting thousands. Demonstrators retaliate with Molotov cocktails, swords, spears, knives, poisoned darts and slingshot-propelled bicycle spokes.

12 August 1988   Sein Lwin resigns.

19 August 1988   Ne Win's biographer, Dr Maung Maung, takes over, lifts martial law and promises referendum on whether Burma should be a single party or multiparty state.

26 August 1988   Half a million people assemble to hear Aung San Suu Kyi.

September 1988   Nine of the surviving 11 Thirty Comrades declare support for uprising, and soldiers and policemen begin fraternizing with demonstrators. Nu proclaims a provisional government and promises a general election within a month. Maung Maung promises elections within three months and a civilian commission to prepare for them.

18–19 September 1988   Generals (SLORC) seize power, abolish 1974 constitution and counter demonstrations with a massacre. Soldiers who had mutinied rush into holy orders, and student activists join colleagues undergoing training at the borders.

22 September 1988   Aung San Suu Kyi appeals for help ('I would like every country in the world to recognize the fact that the people of Burma are being shot down for no reason at all'). SLORC replaces BSPP with NUP and (to split the opposition) lifts ban on rival parties. Of 234 parties that register, the most important is Aung San Suu Kyi's NLD, whose aim is 'to secure the highest degree of autonomy consonant with the inherent rights of the minorities and the well-being of the Union'.

October 1988   The strike collapses.

November 1988   Students training at the borders found ABSDF and unite with most of NDF and various Burman, Muslim, Buddhist and expatriate groups in DAB.

1988–1999   Burmese place names replace well-established Shan names, and junta establishes 20 museums exhibiting the military's central role throughout Burma's history.

1988–2000   Burma Army increases its numbers from 180,000–215,000 to 400,000–450,000. Schools and universities are closed for years on end to prevent student activism, while special provision is made for the education of students from military families.

1989   SLORC announces general election for May 1990. Kokangs and Was mutiny, and CPB disintegrates. SLORC controversially renames country, replacing ethnically neutral English 'Burma' with Burmese 'Myanmar'. Aung San Suu Kyi accuses Ne Win of teaching soldiers to kill their own people and exhorts army to resist 'iniquitous laws'. She and many of her supporters are arrested. Two Wa groups unite as USWA. Other ex-CPB forces are now warlord-led government militias. Heroin refineries proliferate. As the number 9 is thought to be auspicious, SLORC sets the general election for Sunday, 27 May 1990 = fourth Sunday, fifth month (4 + 5 = 9).

1989–90   SLORC relocates one million 'squatters' to improve its electoral prospects.

1989–2000   23 rebel groups, including UWSA (1989), PNO (1991), PSLP (1991), KIO (1994) and NMSP (1995), agree ceasefires on terms allowing them to keep their arms and retain control of their areas. Principal groups refusing or discontinuing ceasefires are Arakan Liberation Party, CNF, KNU, KNPP, LNO, Nationalist Socialist Council of Nagaland (NSCN), National Unity Party of Arakan (formerly NUFA), SURA and WNO.

1990   SLORC chairman General Saw Maung deplores bloodshed, estimating that the number of deaths since independence might 'reach as high as millions'. SLORC provides the seed capital to found UMEHC to facilitate joint ventures between the military and foreign companies. 3000 monks protest in Mandalay. SLORC wins only 10 of 485 seats contested and only 25 per cent of votes cast in 27 May general election. NLD wins 392 seats and 60 per cent of vote, and its ethnic allies most of the remaining seats and 15 per cent of vote. SLORC alters terms *ex post facto*, claiming that the election's purpose was to form a constituent assembly, not a parliament, and that it will not devolve power until a new constitution ensuring strong and stable government is adopted. It issues decree no. 1/90 predicating its authority on international and UN recognition and defining a sixfold procedure for transferring power: (1) a national convention to decide guidelines for a new constitution; (2) army approval of guidelines; (3) draft of new constitution prepared by a national convention; (4) revised draft prepared by an elected people's assembly; (5) army approval of revised draft; (6) approval of constitution by plebiscite. Huge crowds turn out on anniversary of '8888' massacre to offer alms to monks, signifying dispatch of mass prayers for victims' reincarnated souls. Soldiers spray them with bullets. Stories spread that left breasts of marble Buddhas swell with indignation. Most NLD leaders still at large and 40 of its MPs-elect arrested for claiming right to form a government. Monks are required to join a union after they turn down their begging bowls to soldiers. Aung San Suu Kyi's first cousin, Sein Win, and seven other MPs-elect flee to KNU GHQ and form NCGUB.

1990–2001   The regime resorts to acts of Buddhist piety, endowing monastic foundations and building new pagodas, and publishes photographs of its leaders paying respect to senior monks to curry favour with the majority population.

1991   KIO outlaws opium and heroin in areas under its control. A $400 million arms procurement does not affect Burma's reported foreign exchange reserves, indicating use of fenced drugs trade money. ASEAN ministers reject US appeal to boycott Burma and agree instead an 'Asian Way' 'constructive engagement' policy towards Burma. European Parliament brands SLORC as illegal, condemns its atrocities, demands Aung San Suu Kyi's release, and urges member countries to establish relations with NCGUB. Aung San Suu Kyi awarded Nobel Peace Prize.

1991–2000   UNGA adopts unanimously annual resolutions condemning human rights abuse in Burma and urging implementation of 1990 election choices.

1992   Scores of thousands of Karenni villagers are resettled and replaced by landless Burmans conscripted to work in the mines at Mawchi. Than Shwe replaces Saw Maung as SLORC chairman and unilaterally halts offensives against insurgencies. Josef Silverstein, doyen of living Burma scholars, calls for granting Burma's seat in UNGA to NCGUB.

1993   NCGUB's finance minister assassinated, and another member of its cabinet vanishes. SLORC offers one-on-one peace talks. NDF signals readiness to talk collectively, but KIO, in consequence of CPB's collapse (Burma Army now has 40 battalions in Kachin State) and under pressure from China, and NMSP, under pressure from Thailand, enter separate negotiations. Opium production in Burma reaches 2575 metric tonnes (an 8000 per cent increase since 1948). Desmond Tutu describes Burma as 'the South Africa of the 1990s'.

1993–2001   Junta establishes Union Solidarity and Development Association to govern country should it ever devolve power to civilians and expands it to more than eight million members.

1994   Aung San Suu Kyi calls National Convention a farce ('It makes no sense at all, because if people are . . . just there to nod their heads, there's nothing'). Eight ethnic groups in ceasefire mode form Peace and Democratic Front and demand release of Aung San Suu Kyi and swifter progress towards NLD government. 300 Buddhists defect from KNLA and name themselves the Democratic Karen Buddhist Army (DKBA), enabling Burma Army to seize positions vital to defence of KNLA GHQ at Manerplaw. MOGE signs a memorandum of understanding to supply Thailand with natural gas from the Yadana field in the Andaman Sea, and the army begins clearing a route through the Tenasserim to protect the pipeline against rebel attacks.

1995   Burma Army takes Manerplaw.

1996   Khun Sa surrenders TRC/MTA HQ at Homöng and moves to luxurious quarters in Bangkok. His children take over management of his business interests, and the Burma Army assumes responsibility for protecting his heroin factories. 50,000 Shan villagers are moved to SLORC-controlled areas. Army arrests more than 250 NLD supporters and several NLD MPs-elect, relocates 20,000 Karennis and masses troops along Thai border for new offensive against KNLA. SLORC mob attacks cars carrying Aung San Suu Kyi and her colleagues. HIV epidemic estimated at half a million carriers. Student protests trigger closing of all universities once more.

1997   KNU and 13 other groups attending 'Ethnic Nationalities Seminar' at Mae Tha Raw village reject national convention as a ruse to perpetuate autocracy and pledge to 'dismantle military dictatorship' and 'join hands with pro-democracy forces' working for genuine federal union. Burma Army opens offensive against KNLA. KNLA's 16th Battalion defects, delivering much of its Sixth Brigade to the Burma Army. Fourth Brigade resists strongly. 15,000 Karens flee to Thailand (joining 90,000 Karen refugees already there). Burma Army and DKBA attack refugee camps. Relocation of tens of thousands of Shan State villagers after SURA attacks Burma Army. Khin Nyunt brands foreign journalists, NGOs, and NLD supporters as 'terrorists'. Burma joins ASEAN. 'Friendship Bridge' spanning Moei River between Mae Sot and Myawadi opened.

1 July 1997   ASEAN ministers agree to urge SLORC to open discussions with Aung San Suu Kyi.

September 1997   NLD announces it will convene parliament; then appoints committee to exercise the mandate of the 251 MPs-elect remaining from the 485 elected. Shwe Thaike's son repeats Silverstein's suggestion that the most effective pressure on SPDC would be to withdraw its UNGA credentials.

15 November 1997   SLORC arrests three of its ministers for corruption, retires 11 others, and changes its name to SPDC.

10 December 1997   Fiftieth anniversary of Human Rights Day. Aung San Suu Kyi states: 'If [the NLD] don't have the support of the Burmese people, why is it necessary to put our people in jail?' SSA leader Yod Suk blames Rangoon's unrelenting oppression of ethnic nationalities for continued opium cultivation. NLD files suit in Burma High Court, alleging unlawful arrest and false imprisonment of its members.

4 January 1998   Golden Jubilee of Independence. SPDC chairman Than Shwe declares: 'We must be vigilant against various wily schemes of some neo-colonialists . . . [and] build the three strengths of the Union—political power, economic power and national defence power.'

March 1998   Further Burma Army/DKBA attacks on Karen refugee camps in Thailand.

7 April 1998   KNU forestry minister decamps to Rangoon with millions of bahts from KNU's treasury.

May 1998   *Far Eastern Economic Review* quotes a 'senior official' in Washington as stating that 'everything indicates that the [Burmese] government is deeply involved in the drug trade.' NLD demands convening of the parliament elected in 1990 within 60 days.

June–August 1998   All ceasefire groups reject NLD's demand for convening 'people's parliament'. ILO Commission of Inquiry report condemns Burma for 'widespread and systematic recourse to forced labour as part of a disturbing pattern of human rights abuses [noting] in particular [that] the military treat the civilian population . . . as an unlimited pool of labourers and servants to build and maintain . . . roads and railways . . . military camps, logging camps, hotels and other infrastructure . . . amount[ing] to a saga of untold misery and suffering, oppression and exploitation of large sections of the population. . . . [T]he depredations and human rights abuses suffered by the population since 1988 are such that most people find no escape, except fleeing the country. No segment of the population, including women, children and elderly persons, are exempt from the forced labour requirements, which are almost never remunerated or compensated.' First gas pumped from the Yadana field to Thailand.

August–December 1998   1000 NLD supporters, including 200 NLD MPs-elect, are detained and 43 NLD offices are closed, as NLD forms ten-member Committee Representing the People's Parliament and begins repealing the regime's edicts and issuing new laws. Small groups of students protest in flash street manifestations.

10 September 1998   UN special rapporteur for UN's Economic and Social Council's Human Rights Commission (HRC), Rajsoomer Lallah, cites Burma's failure to implement UNGA's and HRC's resolutions and its refusal to allow him entry.

9 November 1998   UNGA's human rights committee deplores Burma's continuing extrajudicial and arbitrary executions, rape, torture, inhuman treatment, mass arrests, slave labour and forced resettlement.

1999   KNU leader Bo Mya claims Burma Army is conducting a campaign of systematic terror and predicts a further flood of refugees to Thailand. Reports of growing dissent within army's ranks, desertions and sacking of four regional commanders in Rangoon area. ILO again condemns forced labour in Burma and threatens to call for a world embargo on trade with Burma.

January 2000   NSCN leader Thuingaleng Muivah arrested in Bangkok.

February 2000   San Ba Thin succeeds Bo Mya as KNU general secretary.

April 2000   Former ABSDF chairman arrested in Bangkok. Tan Sri Razali Ismail appointed UN Special Envoy to Burma.

May 2000   Thailand accuses Rangoon of colluding with drug traffickers in flooding Thailand with methamphetamines.

July 2000   Peking blames drugs production in Burma, Thailand and Laos for rise in number of addicts from 148,000 in 1991 to 681,000.

22 August 2000   Rajsoomer Lallah reports continuing extortion, rape, torture, forced labour, forced portering, forced relocation, and arbitrary arrests, imprisonment and executions of especially Shans, Karens, Karennis and Rohingyas.

September 2000   Rumours of purges of senior Burma Navy officers. NLD announces plan to draw up a new constitution. Aung San Suu Kyi and eight other NLD leaders are placed under house arrest.

Reports that 5000 villagers are fleeing Burma for Thailand every month.

October 2000   SPDC, reputedly responding to a Razali initiative and influenced by Malaysian Prime Minister Datuk Seri Dr Mahathir Mohamad, opens a dialogue with Aung San Suu Kyi.

November 2000   Lallah issues another damning report and resigns. ILO asks its 174 member states to impose sanctions on Burma, an action unprecedented in its history.

December 2000   KNU liaison officers meet with SPDC.

January 2001   Burma Army intensifies scorched earth policies against the Karens. US Secretary of State Albright welcomes the talks between the NLD and the SPDC but warns that 'Burma needs a new beginning, not another false dawn'. NLD chairman Tin Oo and 84 other NLD members are released from custody. Aung San Suu Kyi voices 'cautious' optimism, expressing the hope that her talks with the SPDC will lead to something 'more substantive'.

January–March 2001   SSA and KNLA execute a succession of hit-and-run attacks on demoralized Burma Army units occupying Shan State and Karen hill country.

February 2001   Burma Army seizes a hill in a disputed area north of Chiang Rai to attack the SSA, killing two Thai villagers and wounding nine Thai soldiers. Thai forces expel the invaders. Rangoon accuses Thailand of aiding the SSA; the commander of the 3rd Thai Army accuses Rangoon of invading Thai territory and collaborating with the UWSA to flood Thailand with narcotics. Another Burma Army incursion and detention of 19 Thai soldiers exacerbates tension. Anti-Muslim riots at Akyab sponsored by the *junta* to encourage the exodus of Rohingyas spread to other parts of Arakan. Aung San Suu Kyi reports that talks with the SPDC continue, that the SPDC had relieved most of the pressure on the NLD and that more confidence-building measures were needed to manifest the regime's seriousness about seeking a peaceful resolution of Burma's problems. Paulo Sergio Pinheiro appointed to succeed Lallah as the HRC's special rapporteur. Lieutenant General Tin Oo, Burma Army chief of staff and fourth highest ranking member of the SPDC, Major-General Sit Maung and another member of the *junta*, all reputedly aligned with Maung Aye's 'hardline' faction, die in a helicopter crash. There are speculations based on three prior attempts on Tin Oo that the crash was organized by rivals. KIA, dismayed by the inaccessibility of their leaders, constraints on their soldiers, stagnation in political negotiations with Rangoon, the size of the Burma Army garrison in Kachin State (40 battalions), growing Chinese immigration, seizure of their jade mines and devastation of Kachin State's forests, replaces KIO chairman and KIA chief of staff Zau Mai with General Tu Jai and dismisses vice-chief of staff Colonel Zau Hpang and Brigadier Zau Ing.

March 2001   State Department's annual review allows that Rangoon's drug eradication efforts have contributed to a decline in production but repeats previous years' claims that 'officials' are involved in the trade. Burma Army murders nine KIA soldiers and two Kachin civilians supervising crop-substitution projects in the KIA's 4 Brigade Area southeast of Musé and tries to conceal the murders by burning and burying the corpses.

April 2001   Burma Army reinforces its troops along the Thai border by two brigades. Pinheiro is allowed to visit Burma (the first HRC special rapporteur allowed there in five years) and meets both Aung San Suu Kyi and the SPDC.

Annotated Bibliography

Books

Adas, Michael (1974) *The Burma Delta: Economic Development and Social Change on an Asian Rice Frontier* (Madison, WI: University of Wisconsin Press). A well-researched, detailed, concisely and lucidly presented picture of the impoverishment of Burman cultivators wrought by new technology, Indian immigration and the change from subsistence to market economy agriculture in Lower Burma following British conquest.

Allen, Louis (1984) *Burma: The Longest War* (London/Melbourne: J.M. Dent). A lucidly unfolding account of the Japanese invasion and Allied reconquest of Burma, well-researched and drawing on Japanese as well as Allied sources.

Allott, Anna Joan (1994) *Inked over, Ripped out: Burmese Storytellers and the Censors* (Chiangmai: Silkworm).

Anslinger, Harry Jacob (1961) *The Murderers* (New York: Farrar, Strauss and Cudahy).

Aung San (1946) *Burma's Challenge* (Rangoon: The New Light of Burma Press) 3rd edn 1974 (Rangoon: Aung Gyi); reprinted in Silverstein, 1993.

Aung San Suu Kyi (1984) *Aung San of Burma: A Biographical Portrait by his Daughter* (St Lucia: University of Queensland Press); 2nd edn 1991 (Edinburgh: Kiscadale). A commendably detached, short biography of Aung San by his daughter.

Aung San Suu Kyi (1995) *Freedom from Fear* (London: Penguin, revised edn).

Aung-Thwin, Michael Arthur (1998) *Myth & History in the Historiography of Early Burma* (Singapore: Institute of Southeast Asian Studies). A carefully researched analysis disputing previously held views about the kingdom of Pagan.

Aye Kyaw (1993) *The Voice of Young Burma* (Ithaca, NY: Cornell University Southeast Asia Program). A useful, if somewhat eccentric, contribution to the story of student participation in the nationalist movement. The author believes that scholarship has ruled Burma more often than arms.

Ba Maw (1968) *Breakthrough in Burma: Memoirs of a Revolution, 1939–1946* (New Haven, CT: Yale University Press). An ably

237

argued justification for Burma's wartime alliance with the Japanese by the leader of the Japanese puppet state.

Ba U (1959) *My Burma* (New York: Taplinger).

Ball, Desmond (1998) *Burma's Military Secrets: Signals Intelligence (SIGINT) from the Second World War to Civil War and Cyber Warfare* (Bangkok: White Lotus).

Běcka, Jan (1983) *The National Liberation Movement in Burma during the Japanese Occupation Period (1941–1945)* (Prague: Czechoslovak Academy of Sciences, Oriental Institute). An account of the BIA and wartime Burma drawn entirely from Burman nationalist sources, painstaking but ideologically driven.

Belanger, Francis W. (1989) *Drugs, the U.S., and Khun Sa* (Bangkok: Editions Duang Kamol).

Boucaud, André and Louis (1985) *Birmanie—Sur la piste des Seigneurs de la Guerre* (Paris: L'Harmattan); trans. Diana-Lee Simon sub tit. *Burma's Golden Triangle: On the trail of the Opium Warlords* (Bangkok: Asia Books).

Burma Center Netherlands (1999) *Strengthening Civil Society in Burma: Possibilities and Dilemmas for International NGOs* (Chiangmai: Silkworm). A collection of interesting essays discussing the difficulties of reinstating civil institutions after four decades of military rule.

Cady, John Frank (1958) *A History of Modern Burma* (Ithaca, NY: Cornell University Press). A scholarly, informative, political history of Burma from the late eighteenth century to 1956 drawn mainly from Western sources but attempting to balance British and nationalist perspectives; somewhat marred by a bias once common to American scholars inclined to treat work by British scholars as partisan.

Callahan, Mary Patricia (1996) 'The Origins of Military Rule in Burma', PhD dissertation, Cornell University (microfilm 9628415, UMI Dissertation Services, 300 North Zeeb Road, PO Box 1346, Ann Arbor, MI 48106–1346, USA; 1–800 521–0600, http://www.bellhowell.inforlearning.com). An original contribution that links many of Burma's past troubles and its future prospects to individual soldiers' political and material ambitions and tensions within the military. The author is fluent in Burmese and draws on archival material in Burma's Defence Services Institute and other military sources rarely accessed by outside scholars.

Calvert, Michael and Chinnery, Philip Dennis (1996) *Fighting Mad* (Shrewsbury: Airlife).

Carey, Bertram Sausmarez and Tuck, Henry Newman (1896) *The Chin Hills: A History of the People, our Dealings with them, their Customs and Manners, and a Gazetteer of their Country* (Rangoon: Superintendent, Government Printing and Stationery Office); reprint 1983 (Delhi: Cultural Publishing House). A compendious, pioneering study of the beliefs and customs of the Chin tribes at the turn of the twentieth century.

Carey, Peter (ed.) (1997) *Burma: The Challenge of Change in a Divided Society* (London: Macmillan).

Carrapiett, William James Sherlock (1929) *The Kachin Tribes of Burma* (Rangoon: Superintendent, Government Printing and Stationery Office). A good, brief survey of Kachin mythology, beliefs, moral code, physical and social attributes, customs, crafts and way of life written as a guide for officers of the Burma Frontier Service by a member of the BFS.

Chinnery, Philip Dennis (1997) *March or Die: The Story of Wingate's Chindits* (Shrewsbury: Airlife).

Clements, Alan (1991) *Burma: The Next Killing Fields* (Berkeley, CA: Odonian Press).

Cochrane, Wilbur Willis (1915) *The Shans* (Rangoon: Superintendent, Government Printing and Stationery Office).

Coèdes, George (1962) *Les Peuples de la Peninsule Indochinoise* (Paris: Dunod); (1966) trans. H.M Wright sub tit. *The Making of South East Asia* (London: Routledge & Kegan Paul).

Collis, Maurice (1938) *Trials in Burma* (London: Faber & Faber).

Collis, Maurice (1956) *Last and First in Burma* (London: Macmillan). A well-written discussion of Britain's engagement with Burma, particularly the events leading to independence, critical of some aspects of British rule and somewhat sympathetic to nationalist views.

Crosthwaite, Charles Haukes Todd (1912) *The Pacification of Burma* (London, Frank Cass); reprint 1968 (London: Frank Cass). An authoritative, candid account of the extension of British administration over the Shans, Kachins and Chins following the annexation of Upper Burma. The author, who was Commissioner for Burma at the time of the events he describes, believed that the benefits of imposing British administrative order on Burma outweighed the cost.

Davies, Henry Rodolph (1909) *Yün-nan: The Link between India and the Yangtze* (Cambridge: Cambridge University Press). Concerned mainly with Yunnan, this book also describes tribes living on the

Burmese side of the border at the turn of the century. A pioneering work that supplements Shway Yoe (1882) and Scott and Hardiman (1900–1).

Donkers, Jan and Nijhuis, Minka (eds) trans. P.J. van de Paverd (1996) *Burma behind the Mask* (Amsterdam: Burma Centrum Nederland).

Donnison, Frank Siegfried Vernon (1956) *British Military Administration in the Far East, 1943–46* (London: HMSO). Two useful sections on Burma drawn from the author's military and civilian administrative experience and written with his characteristic clarity and concision.

Donnison, Frank Siegfried Vernon (1970) *Burma* (London: Ernest Benn/New York: Praeger). A clear, concise, authoritative account of Burma's history stressing the events leading to independence. The author served as chief secretary to the last three British governors of Burma.

Dun, Smith (1980) *Memoirs of the Four-Foot Colonel* (Ithaca, NY: Cornell University Southeast Asia Program). An informative study of the Karens and their perspective on the transfer of power to Burmans drawn from previous studies and the author's experience as commander-in-chief of the Burmese Armed Forces and written with an admirable lack of rancour.

Enriquez, Colin Metcalf Dallas (1933) *The Races of Burma* (New Delhi: Government of India, Manager of Publications, 2nd edn). A very good, brief, though somewhat dated, survey of Burma's diverse ethnic communities compiled as a recruitment guide for the Burma Military Police, Frontier Force and Army. Draws on and augments Lowis (1919) and Carrapiett (1929).

Falla, Jonathan (1991) *True Love and Bartholomew: Rebels on the Burmese Border* (Cambridge: Cambridge University Press). Difficult to read owing to a somewhat mannered interweaving of personal stories with social commentary, but contains a usefully individual perspective on the hill Karens, among whom the author worked as a nurse.

Fellowes-Gordon, Ian (1957) *Amiable Assassins* (London: Robert Hale). A lively account of the Northern Kachin Levies by the commander of an NKL company.

Fellowes-Gordon, Ian (1971) *The Battle for Naw Seng's Kingdom* (London: Leo Cooper); reprint 1972 sub tit. *The Magic War* (New York: Scribners). A survey of the war in the Kachin Hills and its strategic importance.

Fergusson, Bernard (1945) *Beyond the Chindwin* (London: Collins). An account of the first Chindit expedition by the commander of a Chindit column.

Fergusson, Bernard (1956) *The Wild Green Earth* (London: Collins).

Fink, Christina (2001) *Living Silence: Burma under Military Rule* (London and New York: Zed/Dhaka: University Press/Bangkok: White Lotus). A detailed and intelligent description of the pervasive social effects of four decades of police state rule.

Fischer, Edward (1980) *Mission in Burma: The Columban Fathers' Forty-three years in Kachin Country* (New York: Seabury Press). A thin but useful account of Roman Catholic missions in Kachinland.

Fletcher, James Solly (1997) *Secret War in Burma* (published by the author, 169 Wilhelmia Drive, Austell, GA 30001–6903, USA). A personal account of service with the Kachin Rangers.

Fürer-Haimendorf, Christoph von (1939) *The Naked Nagas* (London: Methuen).

Furnivall, John Sydenham (1948) *Colonial Policy and Practice: A Comparative Study of Burma and Netherlands India* (Cambridge: Cambridge University Press); 2nd edn 1960 (New York: New York University Press). A pragmatic, nuts and bolts analysis of the problems of administering Burma.

Furnivall, John Sydenham (1960) *The Governance of Modern Burma* (New York: International Secretariat, Institute of Pacific Relations, 2nd edn). Contains a useful retrospection of the failure of Burma's parliamentary government. The author was one of the few British civil servants retained to assist the post-independence administration.

Geary, Grattan (1886) *Burma after the Conquest* (London: Sampson, Low). A lively, but journalistic account of the annexation of Upper Burma and an assessment of the arguments for and against the imposition of British rule there.

Ghosh, Parimal (2001) *Brave Men of the Hills* (London: Hurst). A rewording of Crosthwaite (1912), Cady (1958), Woodman (1962), Herbert (1982), Ni Ni Myint (1983) and others which argues that warlord-led local gangs, dacoity, millenarian expectations, economic grievances and British incomprehension and mismanagement fuelled Burman nationalism and the violence attending the pacification and Saya San Rebellion more than Burman resentment at the loss of their king.

Gilhoedes, Charles (1922) *The Kachins: Religion and Customs* (Calcutta: Catholic Orphan Press/London: Kegan Paul); reprints

1961 and 1995 (New Delhi: Mittal) and 1996 (Bangkok: White Lotus). A study of the shamanism, social customs, oral history and traditions of the Kachins before their conversion to Christianity; a useful corollary to Hanson (1913).

Government of Burma (1960) *Is Trust Vindicated?* (Rangoon: Director of Information).

Government of the Union of Burma (1953) *Kuomintang Aggression Against Burma* (Rangoon: Ministry of Information).

Grant, Ian Lyall and Tamayama, Kazuo (2000) *Burma 1942: The Japanese Invasion* (Chichester: Zampi Press, 6 St Martin's Square, Chichester PO19 1NT). A masterful study of the Japanese conquest drawn from both Allied and Japanese sources. Grant, who was a major in the Bengal Sappers, imputes blame for Japanese successes in Malaya and Burma to Churchill's Eurocentric strategy.

Gravers, Mikael (1999) *Nationalism as Political Paranoia in Burma* (London: Curzon, 2nd edn). A broad, theoretical, interesting and provocative analysis of the history and effect of the interaction of British colonial attitudes, Burman-Buddhist nationalism and minority response. Supports Aung San Suu Kyi's thesis that fear spawns more fear.

Guyot, Dorothy Hess (1966) 'The Political Impact of the Japanese Occupation of Burma', PhD dissertation, Yale University (microfilm 67–71, UMI Dissertation Services, 300 North Zeeb Road, PO Box 1346, Ann Arbor, MI 48106–1346, USA; 1–800 521–0600, http://www.bellhowell.inforlearning.com). A fascinating discussion of the effect of pre-war politics, the Japanese occupation, the BIA/BDA/BNA, and the war on Burma's post-war politics drawing on personal interviews with many of the participants, on Japanese, Indian, British, American, Burmese primary and secondary sources, and on material at the Burma Defence Services Historical Research Institute.

Hall, Daniel George Edward (ed.) (1955) *Michael Symes: Journal of his Second Embassy to the Court of Ava in 1802* (London: Allen & Unwin). An edited and annotated selection of Symes's diaries and correspondence pertaining to his visit to the Burman court in 1802–3.

Hall, Daniel George Edward (1960) *Burma* (London: Hutchinson, 3rd edn). The most readable short history of Burma.

Halliday, Robert (1917) *The Talaings* (Rangoon: Superintendent, Government Printing and Stationery Office); reprint 2000 (Bangkok: White Lotus).

Hanson, Ola (1913) *The Kachins: Their Customs and Traditions* (Rangoon: American Baptist Mission Press). An authoritative distillation of more than 20 years of close study of the mythology, oral history, religious beliefs, social customs and traditions of the Kachins before their conversion to Christianity.

Harvey, Godfrey Eric (1946) *British Rule in Burma 1824–1942* (London: Longmans). A concise study of British administrative institutions in Burma.

Harvey, Godfrey Eric (1957) *The Wa People of the Burma–China Border: St. Anthony's Papers No. II, Far Eastern Affairs, No. One* (London: Chatto & Windus).

Harvey, Godfrey Eric (1967) *History of Burma: From the Earliest Times to 10 March 1824, The Beginning of the English Conquest* (London: Frank Cass); first published 1925 (London: Longmans, Green). A difficult but scholarly survey of Burma's pre-colonial history drawing on both indigenous and Western sources.

Herbert, Patricia Mary (1991) *Burma* (Oxford: Clio, World Bibliographical Series). The most comprehensive and authoritative bibliography on Burma, with fully annotated listings of over 1500 entries grouped under 30 subject headings and easily located by title, author and subject indices. The author was the curator of the Southeast Asia collection of the British Library for many years.

Hilsman, Roger (1990) *American Guerrilla* (McClean, VA: Brassey's).

Hodson, Thomas Callan (1911) *The Naga Tribes of Manipur* (London: Macmillan).

Houtman, Gustaf (1999) *Mental Culture in Burmese Crisis Politics: Aung San Suu Kyi and the National League for Democracy* (Tokyo: Tokyo University Institute for the Study of Languages and Cultures of Asia and Africa).

Hutton, John Henry (1921) *The Angami Nagas* (London: Macmillan).

Khin Maung Nyunt (1990) *Foreign Loans and Aid in the Economic Development of Burma 1974–75 to 1985–86* (Bangkok: Institute of Asian Studies, Chulalongkorn University).

Khin Yi (1988) *The Dobama Movement in Burma (1930–1938)* (Ithaca, NY: Cornell Southeast Asia Program). A study of the most important of pre-war nationalist movements drawn mainly from accounts of the movement's participants. Confused in presentation but containing much valuable material.

Kin Oung (1996) *Who Killed Aung San?* (Bangkok: White Lotus, 2nd edn). A commendably detached, well-written study examining the official version of Aung San's murder drawing on the judgment reprinted in the appendix of Dr Maung Maung's study and on personal, British and other sources.

Lamour, Catherine (1975) *Enquête sur une Armée Secrète* (Paris: Éditions du Seuil).

Leach, Edmund Ronald (1954) *Political Systems of Highland Burma* (London: G. Bell); reprint 1986 (London: Athlone). An anthropological treatise describing adjacent societies' influence on Kachin values which argues that studies assuming that tribal beliefs, values and customs remain fixed are flawed. Difficult to read, and the self-evident central thesis has little interest for the general reader, who, however, can glean from the work interesting details of individual Kachin communities.

Lintner, Bertil (1989) *Outrage: Burma's Struggle for Democracy* (Hong Kong: Review Publishing). A brief, lively survey of Burma's political history preceding the 1988 street protests, the protests themselves and their immediate aftermath.

Lintner, Bertil (1990a) *The Rise and Fall of the Communist Party of Burma (CPB)* (Ithaca, NY: Cornell University Southeast Asia Program). The most authoritative account by a Western author of the communist movement in Burma. Draws on interviews with many of the leading participants.

Lintner, Bertil (1990b) *Land of Jade* (Whiting Bay, Isle of Aran: Kiscadale/Bangkok: White Lotus). The story of an enterprising trek across the Naga, Kachin, Kokang and Wa hills and a sojourn at CPB general headquarters in 1986. Contains a wealth of primary material on the northern insurgents and many useful observations.

Lintner, Bertil (1990c) *Aung San Suu Kyi and Burma's Unfinished Renaissance* (Clayton, Vic.: Monash University Centre of Southeast Asian Studies/Whiting Bay, Isle of Aran: Kiscadale).

Lintner, Bertil (1994) *Burma in Revolt: Opium and Insurgency since 1948* (Boulder, CO: Westview Press); 2nd enlarged edn 1999 (Chiangmai: Silkworm). An excellent broad study of the ideological, ethnic, commercial and political complexities of the Burmese Civil War; especially valuable for its examination of the drugs trade as a sustaining cause of conflict.

Lintner, Bertil (1999) *The Kachin: Lords of Burma's Northern Frontier* (Chiangmai: Teak House).

Lowis, Cecil Champain (1919) *The Tribes of Burma* (Rangoon: Superintendent, Government Printing and Stationery Office). A pioneering assay on prehistoric migrations seeking to explain the disposition of Burma's diverse ethnic communities, and a brief, though dated, description of these communities by a superintendent of the Ethnographical Survey of India.

Lunt, James (1986) *The Retreat from Burma* (London: Collins). A very readable account of British Burma's unpreparedness to meet the Japanese invasion and the military debacle that followed, interspersed with the author's experiences soldering with 2nd Burma Rifles.

Marrat, Jabez (1890) *The Apostle of Burma: A Memoir of Adoniram Judson, D.D.* (London: Charles Kelly).

Marshall, Harry Ignatius (1922) *The Karen People of Burma: A Study in Anthropology and Ethnology* (Columbus, OH: Ohio State University Press); reprint 1997 (Bangkok: White Lotus). A detailed description of Sgaw Karen life in the Irrawaddy Delta by a missionary who spent many years with them.

Maung Maung, Dr (1956) *Burma in the Family of Nations* (Amsterdam: Djambatan).

Maung Maung, Dr (1959) *Burma's Constitution* (The Hague: Martinus Nijhoff).

Maung Maung, Dr (1962) *A Trial in Burma: The Assassination of Aung San* (The Hague: Martinus Nijhoff). Describes broadly the police investigation and trial of U Saw and others for the murder of Aung San and six of his executive council colleagues. Characteristically well-written and concise. An appendix reproduces the Special Tribunal's judgment. As scholars are not allowed access to the police record, the transcript of the trial or even contemporary local media reports of the case, this book is our main source for the facts, but it accepts the official version of Saw's guilt uncritically and appears to have been written as an apology for the official version. The author shared Ne Win's contempt for 'legislature politics', Ne Win appointed him Chief Justice of Burma, and he wrote an adulatory biography of Ne Win.

Maung Maung, Dr (ed.) (1962) *Aung San of Burma* (The Hague: Martinus Nijhoff for Yale University Press Southeast Asia Studies). A collection of Aung San's speeches and writings and eulogistic essays by his friends and colleagues. Seriously flawed by selective editing.

Maung Maung, Dr (1969) *Burma and Ne Win* (Rangoon: Religious Affairs Department Press/London: Asia Publishing House). A sycophantic eulogy of Ne Win set against the political developments in Burma from the turn of the century to the mid-1960s.

Published under Ne Win's Revolutionary Council's censorship laws.

Maung Maung, Dr (1974) *To a Soldier Son* (Rangoon: Sarpay Beikman Press). A nostalgic reflection on Japanese military training and a grossly exaggerated vaunting of the BNA's role in expelling the Japanese. Published under Ne Win's censorship laws.

Maung Maung, Dr (1999) *The 1988 Uprising in Burma* (New Haven, CT: Yale University Southeast Asia Studies). After Ne Win ostensibly relinquished power to Sein Lwin in 1988, the author became head of state. Having failed to end the street demonstrations, he argues that Burma would have been spared another military autocracy had the people trusted him to implement his promised reforms.

Maung Maung, U (1980) *From Sangha to Laity: Nationalist Movements of Burma 1920–1940* (New Delhi: Manohar, for Australian National University); reprint 1996 (Bangkok: White Lotus). A somewhat disjointed and badly edited account of the nationalist movement in pre-war Burma by a former brigadier of the Burma Army; influenced by Cady but adds material drawn from Burman sources.

Maung Maung, U (1989) *Burmese Nationalist Movements 1940–1948* (Edinburgh: Kiscadale/Honolulu: University of Hawaii Press). A well-researched study of pre-independence nationalist politics from a Burman nationalist perspective drawing on both British and Burman sources.

Maung Maung Pye (1951) *Burma in the Crucible* (Rangoon: Khittaya/Madras: Diocesan Press).

McCoy, Alfred William (1972) *The Politics of Heroin in Southeast Asia* (New York: Harper & Row). The definitive study of the symbiotic relationship between the drugs trade and politics in Vietnam, Cambodia, Laos and Burma.

McCoy, Alfred William (1991) *The Politics of Heroin: CIA Complicity in the Global Drug Trade* (New York: Lawrence Hill). A reworking of the author's first title incorporating more recent material.

McCoy, Alfred William and Block, Alan A. (eds) (1992) *War on Drugs: Studies in the Failure of US Narcotics Policy* (Boulder, CO: Westview Press).

McEnery, John (1990) *Epilogue in Burma 1945–48: The Military Dimension of British Withdrawal* (Tunbridge Wells: Spellmount); reprint 2000 (Bangkok: White Lotus). A clear, authoritative and critically important analysis of the effect of reducing British ground forces while negotiating the terms of Burma's independence. The author served in Burma Command, whose responsibility covered all army units in Burma until independence.

McLeish, Alexander (1928) *Christian Progress in Burma* (Rangoon: American Baptist Mission Press); reprint 1929 (London: World Dominion Press).

McLeish, Alexander (1942) *Burma: Christian Progress to the Invasion* (London: World Dominion Press).

McMahon, Alexander Ruxton (1876) *The Karens of the Golden Chersonese* (London: Harrison). The first general study of the Karens; draws on the author's experience as a government administrator in Toungoo and the Tenasserim.

Mills, James Philip (1922) *The Lhota Nagas* (London: Macmillan).

Mills, James Philip (1926) *The Ao Nagas* (London: Macmillan).

Mills, James Philip (1937) *The Rengma Nagas* (London: Macmillan).

Mirante, Edith (1993) *Burmese Looking Glass: A Human Rights Adventure and a Jungle Revolution* (New York: Grove Press). A vigorously written, interesting and informative adventure narrative of travels in the Mon, Karen, Karenni and Shan areas of Burma bordering Thailand and interviews with insurgents.

Morrison, Ian (1947) *Grandfather Longlegs: The Life and Gallant Death of Major H.P. Seagrim, G.C., D.S.O., M.B.E.* (London: Faber & Faber). A well-researched and moving account of the Karens and their history, the Japanese invasion, the Karen resistance, Burman atrocities perpetrated on the Karens, Hugh Paul Seagrim's work as an undercover agent, the loyalty and devotion he inspired, and his voluntary surrender and death to spare the Karens further reprisals.

Morse, Hosea Ballou (1913) *The Trade and Administration of China* (London: Longmans Green).

Moscotti, Albert D. (1974) *British Policy and the Nationalist Movement in Burma, 1917–1937* (Honolulu: University of Hawaii Press). 'A careful study of the complex political development relating to Burma in the period 1917 to 1937 and of the impact of colonialism on Burma' (Herbert).

Mouhot, Henri (1864) *Travels in Indo-China* (London: John Murray).

Mya Maung (1991) *The Burma Road to Poverty* (Westport, CT: Praeger). This and the two following titles chart the growth in military ownership of Burma's economy and Burma's corresponding impoverishment.

Mya Maung (1992) *Totalitarianism in Burma: Prospects for Economic Development* (New York: Paragon House).

Mya Maung (1998) *The Burma Road to Capitalism: Economic Growth versus Democracy* (Westport, CT: Praeger).

Neill, Stephen (1964) *A History of Christian Missions* (London: Penguin Books).

Ni Ni Myint (1983) *Burma's Struggle Against British Imperialism 1885–1895* (Rangoon: The Universities Press). A nationalist account of resistance to the extension of British power to Upper Burma, the Shan States, the Kachin Hills and the Chin Hills.

Nu, U (1954) trans. J.S. Furnivall, *Burma under the Japanese* (London: Macmillan).

Nu, U (1975) trans. Law Yone, *Saturday's Son* (New Haven, CT: Yale University Press).

O'Brien, Harriet (1991) *Forgotten Land: A Rediscovery of Burma* (London: Michael Joseph).

O'Brien, Terence (1987) *The Moonlight War: The Story of Clandestine Operations in South-East Asia, 1944–5* (London: Collins).

Orwell, George (1949) *Burmese Days* (London: Secker & Warburg); reprint 1967 (London: Penguin Books).

Owen, David Edward (1934) *British Opium Policy in India and China* (New Haven, CT: Yale University Press).

Owen, Frank (1946) *The Campaign in Burma* (London: Central Office of Information, prepared for South-East Asia Command). A concise survey of the war against the Japanese in Burma.

Pe Kin (1994) *Pinlon: An Inside Story* (Rangoon: Guardian Press). A partisan account of the Panglong Conference. Published under the SLORC's censorship laws.

Pedersen, Morten B., Rudland, Emily and May, Ronald J. (eds) (2000) *Burma Myanmar: Strong Regime Weak State?* (London: C. Hurst/Adelaide, South Australia: Crawford House). A collection of thoughtful, stimulating essays assessing the prospects of the Burma military devolving power to civilian rule.

Pe Maung Tin and Luce, Gordon Hannington (1923) *The Glass Palace Chronicle of the Kings of Burma* (London: Oxford University Press).

Perrett, Bryan (1978) *Tank Tracks to Rangoon: The Story of British Armour in Burma* (London: Robert Hale); reprint 1992 (London: Robert Hale).

Phayre, Arthur Purves (1883) *History of Burma, including Burma Proper, Pegu, Taungu, Tenasserim and Arakan: from the earliest Time to the End of the First War with British India* (London: Trübner); reprint

1969 (New York: Augustus M. Kelley). The first history of Burma by a Western author. It draws on Burmese sources and fixes the historiography and nomenclature conventions used by most interim historians.

Pye, Lucian Wilmot (1962) *Politics, Personality and Nation Building: Burma's Search for Identity* (New Haven, CT/London: Yale University Press). A social scientist's evaluation of Burma's prospects of political order predicated on notional character and personality attributes.

Renard, Ronald Duane (1996) *The Burmese Connection: Illegal Drugs and the Making of the Golden Triangle* (Boulder, CO/London: Lynne Rienner).

Rong Syamananda (1977) *A History of Thailand* (Bangkok: Chulalongkorn University).

Rotberg, Robert (ed.) (1998) *Burma: Prospects for a Democratic Future* (Washington, DC: Brookings Institution Press/Cambridge, MA: The World Peace Foundation and Harvard Institute for International Development). A collection of essays ranging widely over Burma's political past and assessing Burma's future.

Saimong Mangrai (1965) *The Shan States and the British Annexation* (Ithaca, NY: Cornell University Southeast Asia Program). A study of the Shan, Karenni and Wa states, the historical value of their dynastic chronicles, and their relations with first the Burmans, then the British.

San Crombie Po (1928) *Burma and the Karens* (London: Elliot Stock). Describes communal tensions between Karens and Burmans past and present and certain Karen attributes giving rise to mutual misunderstanding and argues the case for a separate Karenland. Draws on both British and indigenous sources.

Scott, James George, assisted by Hardiman, John Percival (1900–1) *Gazetteer of Upper Burma and the Shan States* (Rangoon: Superintendent, Government Printing and Stationery Office). A compendious, detailed, pioneering, five-volume study of the history, ethnography, languages, religions, superstitions, customs, temples, geology, agriculture, forestry, trade and industry of Upper Burma, the Shans and northern hill peoples, and an annotated catalogue of towns and villages in Upper Burma and the Shan states at the turn of the century.

Scott, James George (1912) *Burma: A Handbook of Practical Information* (London: O'Connor).

Scott, James George (1924) *Burma: From the Earliest Times to the Present Day* (New York: Knopf).

Shakespear, Leslie Waterfield (1914) *History of Upper Assam, Upper Burma, and Northeastern Frontier* (London: Macmillan).

Shway Yoe (James George Scott) (1882) *The Burman: His Life and Notions* (London: Macmillan); reprint 1963 (New York: Norton) and 1989 (Edinburgh: Kiscadale). A guide to values and traditions governing Burman behaviour 'which still has relevance today' (Herbert).

Silverstein, Josef (1977) *Burma: Military Rule and the Politics of Stagnation* (Ithaca, NY/London: Cornell University Press). A characteristically well-written, incisive analysis of the effect of British rule on pre-colonial Burman institutions, society and economy and the suffocating effects of military rule on post-colonial Burma.

Silverstein, Josef (1980) *Burmese Politics: The Dilemma of National Unity* (New Brunswick, NJ: Rutgers University Press). A stimulating identification of the core issue of Burmese politics, the governance of diverse, often antagonistic communities, as one nation. Originally a DPhil dissertation arguing that prior histories of Burma are without a minorities dimension and, hence, are incomplete, this book is 'the only account of politics in Burma which attempts to penetrate the prejudices and stereotyping of the non-Burman segment of the polity' (Chao Tsang Yawnghwe).

Silverstein, Josef (ed.) (1989) *Independent Burma at Forty Years: Six Assessments* (Ithaca, NY: Cornell University Southeast Asia Program). Six stimulating essays by Burma scholars surveying the period from 1948 to 1988.

Silverstein, Josef (ed.) (1993) *The Political Legacy of Aung San* (Ithaca, NY: Cornell University Southeast Asia Program, revised edn). A short, discursive study of the development of Aung San's political ideas, and an anthology of his published speeches and writings.

Slim, William Joseph (1956) *Defeat into Victory* (London: Cassell). The definitive story of the war in Burma told with sensitivity and respect for the common fighting man by the commander of Allied forces.

Smeaton, Donald MacKenzie (1887) *The Loyal Karens of Burma* (London: Kegan Paul). An interesting, early study of Karen beliefs, traditions and customs.

Smith, Donald Eugene (1965) *Religion and Politics in Burma* (Princeton, NJ: Princeton University Press).

Smith, Martin (1991) *Burma: Insurgency and the Politics of Ethnicity* (London: Zed); 2nd enlarged edn 1999 (London and New York: Zed/Dhaka: The University Press/Bangkok: White Lotus). An awesomely authoritative and detailed study of the complexities of the Burmese Civil War drawn from years of research of the London archives and interviews with many of the leading participants.

Smith, Martin (1994) *Ethnic Groups in Burma: Development, Democracy and Human Rights* (London: Anti-Slavery International).

Stargardt, Janice (1990) *The Ancient Pyu of Burma: Volume I, Early Pyu Cities in a man-made Landscape* (Cambridge: Cambridge University Press, Publications on Ancient Civilizations in Southeast Asia).

Steinberg, David Isaac (1981) *Burma's Road toward Development: Growth and Ideology under Military Rule* (Boulder, CO: Westview Press).

Steinberg, David Isaac (1982) *Burma: A Socialist Nation of Southeast Asia* (Boulder, CO: Westview Press). A brief survey of Burma's political history with provocatively interesting material and argument on the Buddhist influence on Burman political perspective.

Steinberg, David Isaac (1990) *The Future of Burma: Crisis and Choice in Myanmar* (Lanham, MD/New York/London: University Press of America/The Asia Society). An account of SLORC rule from its seizure of power in 1988 to 1990. Lists the members of the SLORC.

Steinberg, David Isaac (2000) *Burma: The State of Myanmar* (Washington, DC: Georgetown University Press).

Stevenson, Henry Noel Cochrane (1944) *The Hill Peoples of Burma* (London/Rangoon: Longmans Green).

Symes, Lieutenant Colonel Michael (1795) *An Account of an Embassy to the Kingdom of Ava in the Year 1795* (Edinburgh: Constable); abridged edn prepared by D.G.E. Hall, 1955 (London: Allen & Unwin). A period piece vividly reflecting British concerns in the late eighteenth century.

Tatsuro, Izumiya (1981) *The Minami Organ* (Rangoon: Translation and Publications Department, English edn). Colonel Suzuki, the Minami Organ, the 'Thirty Comrades', the embryonic BIA, the disaffection of the BIA after the 'Moulmein incident', measures taken in the interest of public order, the choice of Ba Maw as head of state, and the reasons for the failure of Japan's Burma Expeditionary Force of 300,000 to secure Burma are examined in this short, but authoritative, memoir by a member of the Minami

Organ, commander of the camp where the 'Thirty Comrades' received their training and adviser to the Northern Expedition.

Taylor, Robert (1987) *The State in Burma* (London: C. Hurst/Honolulu: University of Hawaii Press). A study of the manner and effects of the exercise of state power in Burma from the restoration of the Toungoo dynasty in 1587 to Ne Win's military 'stewardship'; Taylor argues that the essential functions and attributes of central control of society, including the elimination of rivals, have remained constant.

Taylor, Robert (ed.) (2001) *Burma: Political Economy under Military Rule* (London: Hurst).

Tegenfeldt, Herman Gustaf (1974) *A Century of Growth: The Kachin Baptist Church of Burma* (South Pasadena, CA: William Carey). A careful, well-documented account of the introduction and growth of Christianity in Kachinland.

Thant Myint-U (2001) *The Making of Modern Burma* (Cambridge: Cambridge University Press). The author, who is U Thant's nephew, argues that modern Burma, territorially, socially, psychologically and economically, is not a state modelled on pre-colonial Burma, but the product of a mix of circumstances, events and conditions contemporaneous with British conquest and the ensuing pacification. Elegantly written but based mainly on secondary sources.

Tinker, Hugh (1959) *The Union of Burma: A Study of the First Years of Independence* (London: Oxford University Press, 2nd edn). A vivid account of political developments in Burma from the end of colonial rule to the mid-1950s, well-supported and readable, but narrated entirely from the conspectus of Burma Proper.

Tinker, Hugh (ed.) (1984) *Burma: The Struggle for Independence 1944–1948* (London: HMSO). An annotated selection of many of the most important, uncensored, official, archival documents tracking Burma's transition to independence.

Trager, Frank Newton (1966) *Burma: From Kingdom to Republic: A Historical and Political Analysis* (New York: Praeger/London: Pall Mall). A general account of the transition from British to AFPFL rule which relies mainly on secondary sources, is written with a doctrinaire, anti-colonial, pro-nationalist, pro-Burman bias, and is factually unreliable.

Trager, Frank Newton (ed.) (1971) *Burma: Japanese Military Administration, Selected Documents, 1941–1945* (Philadelphia: University of

Pennsylvania Press). A collection of important documents pertaining to the Japanese occupation preceded by an introduction defending the nationalist alliance with Japan as a tactical step towards achieving Burma's independence.

Tucker, Shelby (2000) *Among Insurgents: Walking Through Burma* (London: Radcliffe Press/New Delhi: Penguin Books/Bangkok: White Lotus/London: 2001 HarperCollins). The story of a trek through the Kachin Hills with a KIA column in 1989. Includes brief surveys of the conflicts between Burmans and non-Burman minorities, the Burmese Civil War, the history of the KIA and the evangelization of the Kachins, and material on Kachin beliefs and customs.

U Thaung (1990) *Ne Win and his Hang Men* (Rego Park, NY: International Network for Democracy in Burma).

U Thaung (1995) *A Journalist, a General and an Army in Burma* (Bangkok: White Lotus). An authoritative, contemporary account of the power struggle between Nu and Ne Win and Ne Win's *coup d'état* and his takeover of the Burmese press.

Waley, Arthur (1958) *The Opium War Through Chinese Eyes* (London: George Allen and Unwin).

Woodman, Dorothy (1962) *The Making of Burma* (London: Cresset). A history of the British conquest of Burma and settlement of various frontier issues. Extensively researched but reflecting the anti-colonial bias of the author, who was an intimate of Kingsley Martin, editor of the *New Statesman*, and an official guest at the AFPFL's Independence celebrations.

Yawnghwe, Chao Tzang (1987) *The Shan of Burma: Memoirs of a Shan Exile* (Singapore: Institute of Southeast Asian Studies). A personal and somewhat disjointed but valuable account of the history of Shan–Burman relations, the misunderstandings that led to the Panglong Agreement, the Shan rebellion, and the opium factor in modern Shan politics. The author is the eldest son of the late Sao Shwe Thaike, the Yawnghwe *saohpa*, who was head of the Supreme Council of the United Hill Peoples and the first president of the Union of Burma.

Yang Li (Jackie Yang) (1997) *The House of Yang: Guardians of an Unknown Frontier* (Sydney: Bookpress). A short, but authoritative, history of Kokang and the Yang dynasty by a member of the Yang family.

Papers and Articles

Allott, Anna Joan (1984) entry of Thakin Ko-daw Hmaing, *Encyclopedia of World Literature in the 20th Century*, vol. 4: 429 (New York: Frederick Ungar).

Amnesty International (1988) 'Burma–Extrajudicial Execution and Torture of Members of Ethnic Minorities' (London).

Amnesty International (1992) 'Myanmar: "No law at all": Human rights violations under military rule' (London).

Amnesty International (1994) 'Myanmar: Human Rights Still Denied' (London).

Amnesty International (1996) 'Myanmar: Renewed Repression' (London).

Anonymous (1986) 'Who really killed Aung San?', *Karen National Union Bulletin* (Manerplaw).

Article 19 (Smith, Martin) (1991) *State of Fear: Censorship in Burma* (London: International Centre against Censorship).

Article 19 (Smith, Martin) (1994) *Paradise Lost? The Suppression of Environmental Rights and Freedom of Expression in Burma* (London: International Centre against Censorship).

Article 19 (Smith, Martin) (1995) *Censorship Prevails: Political Deadlock and Economic Transition in Burma* (London: International Centre against Censorship).

Article 19 (Ventkateswaran, Koduvayur Subramanian) (1996) *Burma beyond the Law* (London: International Centre against Censorship).

Article 19 (Iyer, Venkat) (1999) *Acts of Oppression: Censorship and the law in Burma* (London: International Centre against Censorship).

Asia Watch (1989) 'Killing its Own People: Asia Watch Condemns Burma's Death March of Prisoners and Crackdown Against Opposition' (New York).

Asia Watch (1990) 'Human Rights in Burma' (New York).

Asian Survey (a monthly periodical published by the University of California Press, Berkeley, CA; the February issue contains a summary of the main political developments in Burma for the previous year).

Ball, Desmond (1999) *Burma and Drugs: The Regime's Complicity in the Global Drug Trade* (Canberra: Australian National University, Strategic and Defence Studies Centre).

Bray, John (1992) 'Ethnic minorities and the future of Burma', *The World Today*, vol. 48, nos 8–9 (London: The Royal Institute of International Affairs).

Bray, John (1995) 'Burma: The politics of constructive engagement' (London: The Royal Institute of International Affairs).

Brooke, Micool (1998) 'The Armed Forces of Myanmar', *Asian Defence Journal* (London).

Bulletin of the Burma Studies Group (periodical published twice annually in March and September by Southeast Asia Collection, Northern Illinois University Libraries, DeKalb, IL 60115–2854; rcooler@niu.edu; http://www.niu.edu/acad/burma/index. html).

Bureau for International Narcotics and Law Enforcement Affairs, US Department of State (1998) 'International Narcotics Control Strategy Report, 1998', http://www.state.gov/www/global/narcotics_law/1998_narc_ report/seasi98.html.

Bureau for International Narcotics and Law Enforcement Affairs, US Department of State (1999) 'International Narcotics Control Strategy Report, 1999', http://www.state.gov/www/global/narcotics_law/1999_narc_report/seasi99. html.

Burma Alert (monthly periodical published until May 1997 by Associates to Develop Democratic Burma, c/o Harn Yawnghwe, R.R.4, Shawville, Quebec J0X 2Y0, Canada).

Burma Debate (periodical published intermittently by the Burma Project of the Open Society Institute, PO Box 19126, Washington, DC 20036; http://www.soros.org/ burma.html).

Burma Newsletter (published once annually from 1979 to 1981 by Maureen Aung-Thwin, Hong Kong, from 1987 to 1988 by the Burma Studies Group of the Asia Society, New York, and from 1988 to 1995 by The Center for Burma Studies, Northern Illinois University, DeKalb, IL 60115–2854).

Burma Review (periodical published until July 1995 by International Network for Democracy in Burma, PO Box 7726, Rego Park, NY 11374).

'Burma: Statement of Policy by his Majesty's Government, 1945', Cmd. 6635 (London: HMSO).

Burma Socialist Programme Party (1962) *The Burmese Way to Socialism* (Rangoon: Government Printing Press).

Burma Socialist Programme Party (1963) *The System of Correlation of Man and his Environment* (Rangoon: Government Printing Press).

Clinton, William Jefferson (1999) 'Report to Congress on Conditions in Burma and US Policy toward Burma for the period March 28, 1999–September 28, 1999' (Washington, DC).

Davis, Anthony and Hawke, Bruce (1998) 'Burma: The Country that won't kick the Habit', *Jane's Intelligence Review*, vol. 10, no. 3 (London).

Dawn News Bulletin (bi-weekly periodical published by the All Burma Students' Democratic Front, PO Box 1352, Bangkok 10500).

Far Eastern Economic Review, Ho Kwon Ping (1980, 18 January) 'The cautious search for success' (Hong Kong): 36–43.

Far Eastern Economic Review, Lintner, Bertil (1989, 1 June) 'Left in disarray': 26–7.

Far Eastern Economic Review, Lintner (1990, 28 June) 'The phoney war': 20–1.

Far Eastern Economic Review, Lintner (1990, 28 June) 'A fix in the making': 20–3.

Far Eastern Economic Review, Lintner (1990, 28 June) 'The new dealer': 22–3.

Far Eastern Economic Review, Lintner (1990, 28 June) 'Head on a plate': 26.

Far Eastern Economic Review, Lintner (1991, 28 March) 'Triangular ties': 22–6.

Far Eastern Economic Review, Lintner (1991, 28 March) 'The new dealers': 26.

Far Eastern Economic Review, Lintner (1991, 28 March) 'Pushing at the door': 28.

Far Eastern Economic Review, Lintner (1991, 23 May) 'Spiking the guns': 12–13.

Far Eastern Economic Review, Lintner (1991, 23 May) 'Army of occupation': 13.

Far Eastern Economic Review, Lintner (1991, 6 June) 'Hidden reserves': 12–13.

Far Eastern Economic Review, Lintner (1992, 20 February) 'Fields of dreams': 23–4.

Far Eastern Economic Review, Lintner (1992, 20 February) 'Chasing the dragon': 24–5.

Far Eastern Economic Review, Lintner (1992, 5 November) 'Smack in the face': 24, 26.

Far Eastern Economic Review, Lintner (1993, 18 March) 'Tracing New Tracks': 25.

Far Eastern Economic Review, Lintner (1993, 3 June) 'A Fatal Overdose': 26–7.

Far Eastern Economic Review, Lintner (1994, 20 January) 'Khun Sa: Asia's Drug King on the Run': 22–6.

Far Eastern Economic Review, Lintner (1994, 21 July) 'Plague Without Borders': 26.

Far Eastern Economic Review, Lintner (1996, 18 January) 'Absolute Power': 25.

Far Eastern Economic Review, Lintner (1996, 25 January) 'Drug Triangle Handshake': 15–16.

Far Eastern Economic Review, Lintner (1996, 7 November) 'Drug Buddies': 36, 38.

Far Eastern Economic Review, Gelbard, Robert S. (1996, 21 November) 'Slorc's Drug Links': 35.

Far Eastern Economic Review, Lintner (1997, 27 March) 'Heroin Haven': 24–5.

Far Eastern Economic Review, Lintner (1997, 10 April) 'Ethnic Scapegoat': 18–19.

Far Eastern Economic Review, Lintner (1997, 8 May) 'Speed Demons': 28.

Far Eastern Economic Review, Lintner (1997, 14 August) 'Safe at Home': 18–19.

Far Eastern Economic Review, Lintner (1998, 16 April) 'The Dream Merchants': 26–7.

Far Eastern Economic Review, Lintner (1998, 7 May) 'Velvet Glove': 18–20.

Far Eastern Economic Review, Lutterbeck, Deborah (1998, 7 May) 'Dollar Diplomacy': 20–1.

Far Eastern Economic Review, Ytzen, Flemming (1998, 7 May) 'Diehard Optimist': 21–2.

Far Eastern Economic Review, Crispin, Shawn W. (1998, 13 August) 'Internal Matter': 24, 26.

Far Eastern Economic Review, Crispin (1998, 27 August) 'Heading for a Fall': 56, 58.

Far Eastern Economic Review, Lintner (1999, 2 September) 'The Army Digs in': 23–4.

Far Eastern Economic Review, Lintner (1999, 9 September) 'Drug Tide Strains Ties': 24, 26–7.

Far Eastern Economic Review, Lintner (1999, 18 November) 'Cultural Revolution': 24.

Far Eastern Economic Review, Crispin (2000, 7 September) 'Going Nowhere': 21.

Fletcher, James Solly (1984) 'Jingpaw Rangers', *Military History Review*, vol. 1, no. 5 (Sacramento, CA).

Fletcher, James Solly (1985) 'The Capture of Myitkyina—Part I', *Military*, vol. 2, no. 1 (Sacramento, CA).

Fletcher, James Solly (1985) 'The Capture of Myitkyina—Part II', *Military*, vol. 2, no. 2 (Sacramento, CA).

Fowells, Gavin (2000) *From the Dogs of War to a Brave New World and Back Again—Burma '47* (published by the author, 5 Sunley House, Gunthorpe Street, London E1 7RW).

Frontier Areas Committee of Enquiry (1947) *Report*, Cmd. 7138 (London: HMSO/Rangoon: Superintendent of Government Printing & Stationery Office).

George, Edward Claudius Scotney (1892) 'Memorandum on the Kachins on our Frontier', *Census of India, 1891*, vol. IX, Burma, Appendix A: x–xxxviii (Rangoon: Superintendent of Government Printing & Stationery Office).

Guyot, Dorothy Hess (1978) 'Communal Conflict in the Burma Delta', in McVey, Ruth T. (ed.), *Southeast Asian Transitions: Approaches through Social History*: 191–234 (New Haven, CT/London: Yale University Press).

Heppner, Kevin (2000) 'A Village on Fire: The Destruction of Rural Village Life in Southeastern Burma', *Cultural Survival Quarterly*, vol. 24, no. 3 (Cambridge, MA).

Herbert, Patricia (1982) *The Hsaya San Rebellion (1930–1932) Reappraised* (Melbourne: Monash University Centre for Southeast Asian Studies).

Human Rights Watch/Asia (1995) '"Burma": Entrenchment or Reform? Human Rights Developments and the Need for Continued Pressure' (New York).

International Commission of Jurists (1991) 'The Burmese Way: To Where? Report of a Mission to Burma' (Geneva).

International Labor Organization (1998) 'Forced Labour in Myanmar (Burma)' (Geneva).

Journal of Burma Studies (periodical published intermittently by The Center for Burma Studies, Northern Illinois University, DeKalb, IL 60115–2854; rcooler@niu.edu; http://www.niu.edu/acad/burma/index.html).

Journal of the Burma Research Society (published biannually from 1911 to 1977 by The Burma Research Society, Rangoon; indexed, Than Aung (1978) *Index to the Journal of the Burma Research Society (1911–1977)* (Rangoon: Department of Library Studies).

Lawyers Committee for Human Rights (1991) 'Summary Injustice—Military Tribunals in Burma' (New York).

Lewis, Elaine T. (1957) 'The Hill Peoples of Kengtung State', *Practical Anthropology*, vol. 4, no. 5 (New Canaan, CT).

Leyden, John (1947) 'Note by John Leyden on the Panglong Conference, 1947' (BL OIOC: M/4/2811); reproduced in Tinker, Hugh (ed.), *Burma: The Struggle for Independence 1944–1948*, vol. II, item 294: 423–30.

Lintner, Bertil (1984) 'The Shans and the Shan States of Burma', *Contemporary Southeast Asia*, vol. 5, no. 4 (Singapore: Singapore University Press for the Institute of Southeast Asian Studies).

Lintner, Bertil (1991) 'Cross-border Drug Trade in the Golden Triangle' (Durham: Boundaries Research Press for University of Durham Department of Geography).

MacGregor, Charles Reginald (1887) 'Journey of the Expedition under Colonel Woodthorpe, R.E., from Upper Assam to the Irawadi, and return over the Patkoi Range' (London: Proceedings of the Royal Geographical Society, vol. 9).

Matthews, Bruce (1994) 'Religious Minorities in Myanmar—Hints of the Shadow', discussion paper submitted to Burma Studies Group (DeKalb, IL: Northern Illinois University).

Maung Aung Myoe (1998) 'Building the Tatmadaw: The Organisational Development of the Armed Forces in Myanmar, 1948–98' (Canberra: Australian National University, Strategic and Defence Studies Centre).

Maung Aung Myoe (1999) 'Military Doctrine and Strategy in Myanmar: A Historical Perspective' (Canberra: Australian National University, Strategic and Defence Studies Centre).

Maung Aung Myoe (1999) 'The Tatmadaw in Myanmar since 1988: An Interim Assessment' (Canberra: Australian National University, Strategic and Defence Studies Centre).

Mirante, Edith (1987) 'Destroying Humanity: Report of a Survey on Human Rights Abuse in Frontier Areas of Burma, 1986–1987', *Project Maje* (0104 S.W. Lane Street, Portland, OR 97201).

Mirante, Edith (ed.) (1989) 'Burma in Search of Peace', *Cultural Survival Quarterly*, vol. 13, no. 4 (Cambridge, MA).

Morse, Stephen (1988) 'US Policy and Narcotics Eradication Strategy in Burma', mimeograph (Chiang Mai).

Government of Myanmar (c1998) *Political Situation of Myanmar and its Role in the Region* (Rangoon: Government Printing Press).

OGD (1998) 'Report, III. South East Asia, Far East and Pacific Ocean, Burma' (L'Observatoire Géopolitique des Drogues, BP 190, 75463 Paris Cedex 10, France; www.ogd.org).

Overholt, William H., 'The Wrong Enemy', *Foreign Affairs*, no. 77, winter 1989–90 (New York).

Pritchard, B.E.A. (1914) 'A Journey from Myitkyina to Sadiya viâ the N'Mai Hka and Hkamti Long', *Geographical Journal*, vol. 43 (London).

Sandeman, J.E. (1887) 'The River Irawady and its Sources' (London: Proceedings of the Royal Geographical Society, vol. 4).

Selth, Andrew (1996) 'Transforming the Tatmadaw: The Burmese Armed Forces since 1988' (Canberra: Australian National University, Strategic and Defence Studies Centre).

Selth, Andrew (1997) 'Burma's Intelligence Aparatus' (Canberra: Australian National University, Strategic and Defence Studies Centre).

Selth, Andrew (1997) 'Burma's Defence Expenditure and Arms Industries' (Canberra: Australian National University, Strategic and Defence Studies Centre).

Selth, Andrew (1997) 'The Burma Navy' (Canberra: Australian National University, Strategic and Defence Studies Centre).

Selth, Andrew (1997) 'The Burma Air Force' (Canberra: Australian National University, Strategic and Defence Studies Centre).

Selth, Andrew (1998) 'The Myanmar Air Force since 1988: Expansion and Modernization', *Contemporary Southeast Asia*, vol. 19, no. 4 (Singapore: Singapore University Press for the Institute of Southeast Asian Studies).

Selth, Andrew (1999) 'The Burmese Armed Forces Next Century: Continuity or Change?' (Canberra: Strategic and Defence Studies Centre, Australian National University).

Silverstein, Josef, untitled, Burmanet #1524, 29/30 April 2000, http://www.burma.net.

Sladen, Edward Bosc (1871) 'Expedition from Burma, viâ the Irrawaddy and Bhamo, to Southwestern China' (London: Proceedings of the Royal Geographical Society, vol. 41).

Taylor, Robert (1973) 'The Foreign and Domestic Consequences of the KMT Intervention in Burma' (Ithaca, NY: Cornell University Southeast Asia Program).

Taylor, Robert (1978, April) 'Politics in Late Colonial Burma: The Case of U Saw', *Modern Asian Studies*, vol. 10, no. 2 (London: Cambridge University Press).

Taylor, Robert (1981, March) 'Party, Class and Power in British Burma' *Journal of Commonwealth and Comparative Politics*, vol. xix, no. 1 (London, Frank Cass).

Taylor, Robert (1983) 'An Undeveloped State: The Study of Modern Burma's Politics' (London: University of London School of Oriental and African Studies).

UN Human Rights Commission (1993) Report of the Special Rapporteur, UN Document E/CN. 4/1993/37.

UN Human Rights Commission (1995) Report of the Special Rapporteur, UN Document E/CN. 4/1995/65.

UN Human Rights Commission (1996) Report of the Special Rapporteur, UN Document E/CN. 4/1996/65.

US Committee for Refugees (1990) 'The War is Growing Worse and Worse: Refugees and Displaced Persons on the Thai-Burmese Border' (Washington, DC: US Government Printing Office).

US General Accounting Office (1989) 'Drug Control: Enforcement Efforts in Burma are not Effective' (Washington, DC: GAO/NSIAD-89–197, US Government Printing Office).

U Thaung (1990) 'Army's Accumulation of Economic Power in Burma (1950–1990)', published by the author, 1976 SW 67th Terrace, Pompano Beach, FL 33068; reprinted in U Thaung (1990) *Ne Win and his Hang Men*.

U Thaung (1998) 'A Report on the Burmese Economy', published by the author, 1976 SW 67th Terrace, Pompano Beach, FL 33068.

Walker, James Thomas (1892) 'Expeditions among the Kachin Tribes of the North East Frontier of Upper Burma compiled by General J.J. Walker from the reports of Lieut. Eliot, Assistant Commissioner' (London: Proceedings of the Royal Geographical Society, vol. 14).

World Bank (1995) 'Myanmar, Policies for Sustaining Reform' (Washington, DC).

Index

Compiled by Auriol Griffith-Jones

Note: Page numbers in bold refer to illustrations. For acronyms and abbreviations *see* pages xiii–xv.

BM